ANCIENT
RHETORIC AND POETIC

THE MACMILLAN COMPANY
NEW YORK · BOSTON · CHICAGO · DALLAS
ATLANTA · SAN FRANCISCO

MACMILLAN & CO., LIMITED
LONDON · BOMBAY · CALCUTTA
MELBOURNE

THE MACMILLAN CO. OF CANADA, LTD.
TORONTO

ANCIENT
RHETORIC AND POETIC

INTERPRETED FROM REPRESENTATIVE WORKS

BY

CHARLES SEARS BALDWIN

PROFESSOR OF RHETORIC IN COLUMBIA UNIVERSITY

ΤΟ ΜΕΝ ΔΗ ΠΟΙΗΤΙΚΟΝ ΦΥΛΟΝ ΕΛΕΥΘΕΡΟΝ

Lucian

New York
THE MACMILLAN COMPANY
1924

NELSON GLENN McCREA
ARTIS VTRIVSQVE
LITTERATE PERITO
HVNC LIBRVM
COLLEGA AMICVS
D. D. D.

PREFACE

To interpret ancient rhetoric and poetic afresh from typical theory and practise is the first step toward interpreting those traditions of criticism which were most influential in the middle age. Medieval rhetoric and poetic in turn, besides illuminating medieval literature, prepare for clearer comprehension of the Renaissance renewal of allegiance to antiquity. Thus the historical survey needed to focus many important detached studies itself needs a preliminary volume of exposition. The influences of ancient oratory, drama, and story cannot be measured surely without more specific knowledge of ancient precept and practise, firmer grasp of ancient conceptions, than has been offered by any synthesis in English. Even in other languages the available compends are generally rather digests, or dictionaries of terms, than interpretations of leading ideas. Instead of risking once more the inadequacy and the forced emphasis that beset such a method, I have tried to make the most representative ancients speak for themselves.

Though the very choice of spokesmen interposes the chooser, scholars generally, I hope, will accept Aristotle for the theory of rhetoric as the energizing of knowledge, Cicero for its scope and skill in practise, Quintilian for its teaching, and so on through a list chosen for representative significances. Nor does the plan of spokesmen preclude sufficient indications of general theory and practise. It shows in Cicero the influence not only of Aristotle, but of Isocrates. In poetic, ancient epic art is revealed most definitely and most largely in the *Æneid* because Vergil, besides being one of the greatest of poets, was so studious a craftsman as to choose from all the ancient experience the most vital ways of narrative. Historically the New Comedy seems more significant than the Old; and the same consideration has included not only Ovid, but even Seneca. These analyses of ancient achievement are made complementary to ancient theory by being strictly limited to composition.

All the authors chosen have been already expounded and translated, some of them again and again, but rather as philosophers, or as orators, or as men of letters, or simply as Greeks or Romans, than as writers on composition. Yet composition was not only one of the greatest ancient achievements; it was a constant preoccupation and a consistent technic. No other body of technic is more thorough and comprehensive than ancient rhetoric; and few have been so generally recognized. Every writer had it in mind; and since commentators have often had in mind something else, I have felt myself bound always to explore the technical connotations of the originals, and usually to retranslate. Verification is facilitated by exact citation, and comparative study by the indexes. What may thus serve incidentally as a book of reference is primarily, however, a progressive exposition from ideas through principles to details. The Greek philosophy of rhetoric is confirmed and applied in the great period of Rome by the most influential orator of history. Aristotle's theory and Cicero's vindication put us in the best position to comprehend the method and the detail of Quintilian. This in turn guides appreciation of that abundant study of style which is exemplified typically in Dionysius of Halicarnassus and illuminated by the genius who wrote the *De sublimitate*. Through such spokesmen, with complementary technical analysis of ancient achievement, the way seems surest toward recovering inductively the ancient artistic experience.

This experience has remained too long in abeyance for speakers, writers, and teachers of English. In the United States, though composition has been studied during the past fifty years more generally, perhaps, than in any other country except France, neither our theory nor our pedagogy has applied very widely the ancient lore. Jesuit schools, indeed, have maintained the tradition of rhetoric, as have some others teaching composition consecutively through Latin; but in general the multitude of modern text-books of English composition shows little use of ancient experience. Thus it has been possible to propose as new, and even to try, methods exploded in Rome two thousand years ago. There is no question of reviving an equally exploded archaism. Nor need we fall again into the Ciceronianism of the Renaissance. Ancient deviation, as I have tried to show, is no less instructive than ancient progress. The point is so to comprehend what the ancients learned in singularly fortunate conditions as to guide our own theory away from vain repetition toward progressive realization of our own opportunities.

Metric, except where it bears incidentally on prose rhythms, has been deliberately excluded. In the present divergence of critical interpretation an entire volume would hardly suffice for a really contributory synthesis. The larger movements of poetic, dramaturgy and the development of verse narrative, show a consistency that warrants a synthesis of ancient poetic; and there is even greater consistency in ancient rhetoric. But we may not lightly speak of ancient metric, as if it were continuous from Greek through Latin. Nor is the metric of either Greek or Latin, significant as it is incidentally, necessary to the comprehension of ancient rhetoric or poetic.

The innovation of expounding rhetoric and poetic side by side was suggested by the demands of that historical treatment which is proposed for a later volume. But though it was designed for this larger purpose, it has meantime facilitated the immediate task. Actually the experience of the ancients seems to be best approached from their conception of composition as twofold. Logical composition and imaginative composition are, indeed, distinct; but each technic, defined within its own scope, helps to define the other by contrast. Making each more distinct, the contrast further exhibits interrelations and confusions highly significant for the history of both pedagogy and criticism. Not merely as archæology, then, ancient rhetoric and poetic demand reconsideration, but as the theory of widely suggestive experiences in the progressive art of words.

The bibliographies at the head of each chapter or section, and the notes, are strictly selective. Enumeration of what I have read myself could only embarrass the guidance of readers who wish to proceed from this book to further study. Omitting, therefore, all mere acknowledgment of my long and manifold indebtedness, omitting also the obvious books of reference, whether histories or topical digests, the apparatus directs immediately to interpretations either of the authors themselves or of those principles and habits of ancient art which seem most significant for the study, the practise, and the teaching of composition. For example, the references are not to Volkmann and Christ-Schmid, but to Heinze, Rhys Roberts, Hendrickson, Hubbell, to Sandys the editor rather than to Sandys the historian; and preference has been given to works in English.

Personal indebtedness begins with a scholar who was professor of Greek before he became professor of English. The late Thomas R. Price revealed the study of composition as embracing all ordered expression from a periodic sentence to a tragedy. The working out of that integrating conception has been furthered by so many colleagues that specific acknowledgment must perforce be limited to those interested immediately in this volume. Professor LaRue VanHook read my translation of Dio Chrysostom's *Oratio LII;* Professor Nelson Glenn McCrea, the entire manuscript and the proof. For criticism of the manuscript I am no less deeply indebted to Professors Brander Matthews and Ashley H. Thorndike; for valuable suggestions on the proofs, to Professors Edward D. Perry, Frank G. Moore, and Donald L. Clark, and to the Rev. Professor Francis P. Donnelly, S. J. In 1920 Professor Rhys Roberts, after sharing his acute and sympathetic scholarship in conversation on the plan of both volumes, did me the honor to read in manuscript the first draft of Chapter II. High appreciation of all this generosity and a grateful sense of this fellowship of letters at once acquit these scholars of all responsibility for my interpretations and encourage my hope of contributing toward a more fruitful criticism of ancient composition.

C. S. B.

BARNARD COLLEGE
  MAY, 1924

CONTENTS

ANCIENT
RHETORIC AND POETIC

ANCIENT RHETORIC AND POETIC

CHAPTER I

RHETORIC AND POETIC

The two great works of Aristotle on composition, the *Rhetoric* and the *Poetic*, presuppose an ancient division. That a philosopher should have written either is itself significant; that he should have written both implies his ratification of the ancient idea that the art of speaking and writing is not throughout its various phases single and constant, but distinctly twofold. On the one hand, the ancients discerned and developed an art of daily communication, especially of public address, τέχνη ῥητορική, *ars oratoria*, rhetoric; on the other hand, an art of imaginative appeal, τέχνη ποιητική, *ars poetica*, poetic.

A distinction between the two in diction, the idea that the language of poetic is more freely imaginative, is both commonplace and superficial. The ancients, of course, were aware of it, and frequently thus contrasted poetry with oratory [1] or with history. But the distinction between the diction of public address and the diction of drama or epic, between prose style and poetic style, was not in ancient thought fundamental. Rather the ancients saw here common ground. Their discussions of

---

[1] Quintilian, for instance, appreciates Lucan as "ardens et concitatus et sententiis clarissimus, et, ut dicam quod sentio, magis oratoribus quam poetis imitandus." *Inst. Or.* X. i. 90.

prose style freely draw examples from poetry; for their
rhetoric, more explicitly than most modern rhetoric, realized that the appeal of public address, in so far as it is an
appeal of style, is largely imaginative and rhythmical.[2]
Polybius, indeed, reproaches Phylarchus for his eagerness
to be pathetic and his habit of visualizing the terrible,
"as do the writers of tragedies"[3]; but as a restriction on
style in history this is quite exceptional and would involve disparaging Thucydides.   The common view of
history is summed up playfully by Lucian: "Let the
[historian's] thought, in so far as it too is high-sounding
and uplifted, appropriate and seize something of poetic,
especially when it is involved in arrays and battles by land
or sea; for then there will be need of a poetic wind to fill
the sails and bear the tall ship over the waves."[4]   In oratory the ancients specifically inculcated imaginative visu-
alization, and taught it from the poets. Their general distinction of style between prose and verse was in the habit
of rhythms. No, the ancient distinction between rhetoric
and poetic is far more than a differentiation of style.

The difference that Aristotle saw between history and
poetry is far deeper; and perhaps this was in the mind of
Polybius when he went on to say,[5] "the end of history is
not the same as that of tragedy, but the opposite," and
complained that Phylarchus was too fond of working
up crises ($\pi\epsilon\rho\iota\pi\acute{\epsilon}\tau\epsilon\iota\alpha\iota$). Even the flippant Lucian may
have meant to imply, though he does not carry out, a
deeper difference when he said:[6] "the undertakings of the

[2] Typical of this habit of thought is: "Exigitur enim iam ab oratore
etiam poeticus decor . . . ex Horatii et Vergilii et Lucani sacrario
prolatus." Tacitus, *Dialogus, 20.*

[3] Polybius, II. 56.   [4] Lucian, *Quomodo historia,* 45.
[5] Polybius, II. 56.   [6] Lucian, *Quomodo historia,* 8.

poetic art [in general] and of poems [in particular], and the appropriate rules, are one thing; those of history, quite another." At any rate, the Aristotelian distinction of history from poetry, repeated by Polybius in the second century B. C. and by Lucian in the second century A. D., is not merely in diction, not in prose or verse, but in composition.

So, even more evidently and pervasively, is the broader distinction between oratory and poetry. Rhetoric and poetic connoted two fields of composition, two habits of conceiving and ordering, two typical movements. The movement of the one the ancients saw as primarily intellectual, a progress from idea to idea determined logically; that of the other, as primarily imaginative, a progress from image to image determined emotionally. This distinction is more fundamental than that of so-called literary forms. The ancients were well aware that a particular composition might shift from one movement to the other, a play of Euripides lean toward oratory, an oration of Isocrates move for a while in the mode of poetry. What they contemplated in their division was not primarily a composition, but composition as a general habit, the predominant and determining way of composing, the difference between the habitual movement of a Demosthenes and that of a Sophocles. Finding these to be distinct essentially, as typical processes of conceiving, ordering, and uttering, Aristotle treated them separately as two distinct technics, rhetoric and poetic.[7]

That the distinction between the habitual composition, or movement, of rhetoric and that of poetic is not oftener made explicitly by ancient critics need cause little surprise.

[7] The terms *rhetoric* and *poetic* are contrasted in Lucian, *Demosthenis encomium*, 5–8, 17–18; Strabo, I. ii. 6 (C. 17, end).

The distinction may have been familiar enough to be
tacitly assumed. It is, in fact, often assumed; it was
quite clear in the mind of whoever wrote the *De sublimitate;*
but it is sharply defined and fully carried out only by
Aristotle. We must remember that ancient criticism had
no second Aristotle, that it was preoccupied with rhetoric,
and that it usually discussed speaking and writing, as
modern criticism does no less usually, in terms of style.
The long history of criticism shows few outstanding works
on composition in the large. None the less for the meager-
ness of criticism, the active presence of the distinction is
seen in the greatest works of antiquity.

Nor is the distinction unknown to modern criticism.
It is misinterpreted, for instance, at the beginning of
Blair's Lecture XXXVIII, confirmed by De Quincey's
distinction [8] between literature of knowledge and literature of power, and revived in the division, cited by Renard [9] from H. Balzac, into "*écrivains d'idées* and *écrivains
d'images.*" But in spite of significant occurrences and
recurrences, it seems not to have controlled any consecutive movement of modern criticism.

Again, the four "forms of discourse" widely accepted
by American textbooks naturally combine into exposition
and argument under rhetoric on the one hand and, on the
other, description and narrative under poetic. But
obvious as this seems, the older, simpler, more fundamental
division does not widely control modern pedagogy. None
the less its pedagogical aspect, in either ancient or modern
times, is more important than that of many more current
critical distinctions. For learning to write, the distinction
between rhetoric and poetic is more directive than the

[8] Essay on Pope.
[9] G. Renard, *La méthode scientifique de l'histoire littéraire,* page 385.

distinction, for instance, of literary forms. It is also more supported and interpreted by psychology; for it divides not merely what is composed, but the typical habits of composing.

Thus the experience of the ancients with composition, an experience so prolonged and so progressive as to constitute a full and distinct chapter in the history of art, may be approached first by dividing as they divided. Each technic, defined within its own scope, helps to define the other by contrast. Making each more distinct, the contrast further exhibits interrelations and confusions highly significant for the history of both pedagogy and criticism.

Rhetoric in the philosophy of Aristotle is essentially the art of giving effectiveness to truth. Accepting this theory, Cicero nevertheless feels rather the tradition of rhetoric as the art of giving effectiveness to the speaker. The constructive review of a great orator exploring his art is thus complementary to the analysis of the philosopher. Even after Aristotle and Cicero there was room for a third survey. Quintilian showed how rhetoric pervaded and largely directed ancient education. For that ancient art which was at once useful and fine, an education and a career, had great spokesmen. We shall begin best, and go on most surely, by letting them speak: Aristotle for the function and scope of rhetoric, Cicero for its pursuit and achievements, Quintilian for its method.

CHAPTER II

THE *RHETORIC* OF ARISTOTLE

The only art of composition that concerns the mass of mankind, and is therefore universal in both educational practise and critical theory, is the art of effective communication by speaking and writing. This is what the ancients and most moderns call rhetoric. More ample and exact definition, though unnecessary for elementary practise, is demanded for fruitful theory; and the theory of rhetoric has always concerned so many more people than the theory of any other art as to be part of every pedagogy. Here the practise of education not only may be guided by philosophy; it must be. For any coherence in its teaching, rhetoric must be comprehended not only in its immediate functions, but in its pervasive relations to other studies. It is at once the constant in educational schemes and the art among sciences. How we are in a given time and place to learn or teach rhetoric depends on how we understand its function and scope in specific relations.

The importance of a theory of rhetoric in this aspect was discerned by the greatest philosopher of antiquity. In Aristotle's comprehensive survey of thought and action rhetoric is not merely included; it has substantive place. Aristotle's *Rhetoric*,[1] though professedly

[1] *Text*, edited with notes, commentary, and index, COPE, E. M., and SANDYS, J. E., 3 volumes, Cambridge, 1877.

Translations (the best recent ones in English), WELLDON, J. E. C., with analysis and critical notes, London, 1886; JEBB, R. C., edited with intro-

more analytical than constructive, has a consecutive development. Neither his ethics nor his politics receives more scrutiny or shows more penetration and grasp. As if he dared not slight it, he shows in this work, comparatively brief though it is, the full reach of his intelligence. In detail it has been questioned; but in conception and plan, in direction of thought and order of presentation, it has remained fruitful.

Book I

Book I *surveys by definition and division the opportunity of the public speaker.* (i) Rhetoric is the complement of logic (dialectic). It is the art of persuasion formulated by investigating the methods of successful address; and its object is to promote a habit of discerning what in any given case is essentially persuasive. Proof as contemplated by rhetoric proceeds by such means as may be used in public address. Instead of the syllogism, which is proper to abstract logic, rhetoric typically uses the enthymeme, that approximate syllogism which is proper and necessary to the actual concrete discussion of public questions. Thus rhetoric serves as a general public means (1) of maintaining truth and justice against falsehood and wrong, (2) of advancing public discussion where absolute proof is impossible, (3) of cultivating the habit of seeing both sides and of exposing sophistries and fallacies, and (4) of self-defense. (ii) The means of persuasion outside of rhetoric

duction and supplementary notes by SANDYS, J. E., Cambridge, 1909. Welldon's tabular view is valuable. Jebb's rendering of technical terms is generally more discerning.

Criticism. Aristotle having engaged the attention of nearly every important writer on rhetoric—and of many quite unimportant—for over two thousand years, a list of the commentaries and criticisms would be endless and bewildering. Nor would any addition here to the bibliographies already available be especially suggestive. The history of Aristotle's *Rhetoric* will emerge incidentally throughout this work. The best single exegesis in English, especially of the relations of the *Rhetoric* to the Aristotelian philosophy, remains E. M. Cope's *Introduction to Aristotle's Rhetoric*, London, 1867.

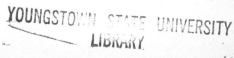

(πίστεις ἄτεχνοι) are witnesses, documents, and other evidence; the means within the art of rhetoric (ἔντεχνοι) are the moral force of the speaker, his adaptation to the disposition of the audience, and his arguments. (iii) The three fields of rhetoric are: (1) deliberative address to a popular assembly, discussing the expediency of a proposal for the future; (2) forensic address to a court, discussing the justice of a deed in the past; and (3) panegyric, commemorating the significance of a present occasion. The eleven remaining chapters of this book analyze each of these fields in its main aspects, or fundamental topics, e. g., wealth, happiness, government, crime, virtue, etc.[2]

The bare digest will show that Aristotle's *Rhetoric* is hardly a manual. In fact, it is rather less a manual than is his *Poetic*. It is a philosophical survey. The scope of rhetoric is measured not by any scheme of education, but by the relations of knowledge to conduct and affairs. To be comprehended, this great work should be read consecutively, for it is not merely systematic; in spite of parts undeveloped, it is progressive, and its chief significance, perhaps, is from its total development. The following discussion presupposes a fresh and consecutive reading.

About rhetoric Aristotle would first of all have right thinking, conceptions large enough to be suggestive and distinct enough to be true. So the definition in his first chapter is slowly inductive. First we are to distinguish rhetoric from logic.[3] As modes of thought the two are alike general, both applicable universally, neither having its own subject-matter. As modes of utterance they differ typically in that while logic is abstract, rhetoric is concrete; while the one is analytic, the other is synthetic; while the one is a method of study, the other is a method of communication.

[2] Quoted from the author's article on Aristotle in the *Cyclopedia of Education*.   [3] 1354 a.

Rhetoric, no less than logic, has subject-matter in every given case. Only its perverters teach it as merely an art of dealing with persons, of reaching an audience. No less than logic, it is a means of bringing out truth, of making people see what is true and fitting. But rhetoric contemplates having truth embraced. It is the application of proof to people. Its distinction from logic is here, in the typical mode of proof. The type in logic is the syllogism; the type in rhetoric Aristotle calls the enthymeme.[4] By this he means concrete proof, proof applicable to human affairs, such argument as is actually available in current discussion. The enthymeme is not inferior to the syllogism; it is merely different. Actually, public address on current public questions cannot be carried on by syllogisms or by final inductions. That by which it can be carried on, the strongest proof possible to actual discussion, Aristotle calls enthymeme.

From this typical mode of rhetoric Aristotle gathers its fourfold function: first and foremost, to make truth prevail by presenting it effectively in the conditions of actual communication, to move; second, to advance inquiry by such methods as are open to men generally, to teach; third, to cultivate the habit of seeing both sides and of analyzing sophistries and fallacies, to debate; and finally to defend oneself and one's cause. That truth does not always prevail shows the need of effective presentation. The first function, then, of rhetoric is to make truth prevail among men as they are. Truth cannot be learned by the mass of men through scientific investigation; for that demands special training. A second direction, then, of rhetoric is to make the results of investigation generally available, to teach truth in general human terms. Debate,

[4] 1355 a.

Aristotle's third item, which is one whole field of rhetoric, may indeed be mere logical fence, using terms and propositions as mere counters; but real skill in debate, the habit of seeing both sides and of analyzing sophistries and fallacies, tends to make truth emerge from current discussion. The fourth use of rhetoric, for self-defense, seems added merely for completeness and to rebut the common objection that rhetoric is abused. That, says Aristotle, is no argument against it.[5]

The definition implied and sketched in Chapter I and formulated in Chapter II, may be summed up in the word persuasion, if we are careful to speak of persuasion not as achievement, but as method. Just as we ask of medicine, not that it shall infallibly heal—a degree of achievement impossible in human affairs—but that it shall discern and use all the means of healing available in the given case, so the true end of rhetoric is to induce such habitual skill as shall *discern in any given case the available means of persuasion.*[6]

As means of persuasion we must include both those that are extrinsic and those that are intrinsic,[7] those that lie outside the art of rhetoric in the domains of subject-

[5] 1355 b.

[6] 1355 b τὸ ἐνδεχόμενον πιθανόν, or, as the preceding context puts it, τὰ ὑπάρχοντα πιθανά.

[7] αἱ μὲν ἄτεχνοί εἰσιν αἱ δ᾽ ἔντεχνοι. Cope, *Introduction*, page 150, translates "unscientific and scientific"; Welldon, "inartistic or artistic"; Jebb, "inartificial or artificial." None of these translations is satisfactory in connotation. *Scientific*, or *artistic*, or *artificial* suggests associations not borne out by the context and ultimately misleading. Aristotle says simply "means that lie outside of the art and means that lie within it." The means that lie within are hardly, in fact or in his intention, *scientific.* They are *artistic* in the broadest sense of being attainable by art, not in the narrower sense of belonging to fine art, nor in the colloquial sense of being pretty. *Artificial* they are not at all, except when they are misapplied.

matter and those that lie within, the facts of the case and
the technic of making them tell. For rhetoric has to
include subject-matter, the forces of knowledge. Though
this is extrinsic in the sense of lying outside the art of
rhetoric, it is essential. Rhetoric is an art, as Aristotle is
careful to show; but it differs from other arts in the degree
of importance it must always attach to its subject-matter.
The division here into extrinsic means and intrinsic
means as both necessary to persuasion is not merely the
obvious one into matter and manner, substance and
style; it is a division of the springs of composition, the
sources of effectiveness, into those that lie outside and
those that lie inside of utterance, or presentation. It
frankly accepts rhetoric as more than artistic, as never
self-sufficient and absolute, as always relating presentation to investigation.

Equally philosophical is the following division [8] of the
intrinsic means of persuasion into: (1) those inherent in
the character or moral potentiality ($\mathring{\eta}\theta os$) of the speaker,
(2) those inherent in his actual moving of the audience,
and (3) those inherent in the form and phrase of the
speech itself. That the three are not mutually exclusive
is evident and must have been deliberate. Aristotle is
telling us that rhetoric as an art is to be approached from
these three directions and in this order. The division is
comprehensive not only as being satisfying psychologically,
but as constituting an outline for the whole work, the
headings of the development in three books: first, the
speaker himself; secondly, the audience; and finally, in the
light of these two, and as the bringing of the one to bear
on the other, the speech. Book I deals with the speaker as
himself the prime means of persuasion. Rhetoric, Aristotle

[8] 1356 a.

implies, is necessarily ethical in that everything consecutively imparted or communicated, as distinct from the
abstractions of geometry or logic, is subjective. Moreover, in making the speaker the point of departure Aristotle admits that other trend of classical pedagogy which
made rhetoric a cultivation of personality. Book II,
proceeding to the second item of the division above, deals
with the audience, with knowledge of human nature, especially of typical habits of mind; for rhetoric in this aspect too is ethical. It deals with the interaction of moral
forces in speaker and audience, and also with the direct
arousing of emotion. The speech itself, the final utterance,
which is the subject of Book III, has thus been approached
as the art of adjusting the subject-matter of a given case
through the intelligence and emotion of the speaker to the
intelligence and emotion of the audience. This is the only
book of very specific technic; and it comes last psychologically.

Aristotle's division and its order are the division and the
order not merely of analysis, but of much the same synthesis as underlies the actual processes of composition. I
begin with myself; for the subject-matter else is dead, remaining abstract. It begins to live, to become persuasive,
when it becomes my message. Then only have I really a
subject for presentation. A subject, for purposes of address as distinct from purposes of investigation, must include the speaker. It is mine if it arouses me. I consider
next the audience, not for concession or compromise, but
for adaptation. What is mine must become theirs. Therefore I must know them, their ἦθος and their πάθος. My
address becomes concrete through my effort to bring it
home. The truth must prevail—through what? Against
what? Not only through or against reasoning, but through

or against complexes of general moral habit and the
emotions of the occasion. I must establish sympathy,
win openness of mind, instruct in such wise as to please
and awaken, rouse to action. My speech is for these
people now. Only thus am I ready to consider composition; for only thus can I know what arguments are available, or what order will be effective, or what style will
tell.

This is the philosophy of presentation. What is its
practise? Rhetoric ranges for subject-matter most often
in the fields of social ethics and politics, tempting its
professors, Aristotle adds acutely, to assume the mask
of politics.[9] It deals with "the ordinary and recognized
subjects of deliberation," [10] with matters still in dispute
and doubt. Thus dealing with social and political conduct, it can neither proceed, as logic does, by absolute
propositions nor arrive at logical demonstration. Its
premises are not universals, but generally accepted
probabilities. That is, to resume his previous distinction,
the mode of rhetoric is not the syllogism or induction
proper to logical formulation, but the enthymeme or
instances proper to actual presentation. The mode of
scientific induction emerges to-day in the "gas laws" or
the formula of the velocity of light; the mode of rhetoric
emerges in Huxley's "Piece of Chalk." Abstract deduction is summed up in the syllogism; [11] concrete deduction,
in the enthymeme. By enthymeme, as Aristotle has now
made fully clear, is meant a "rhetorical syllogism" in the
sense of a deduction available concretely for presentation,
as distinct from a deduction formulated abstractly for
analysis. His enthymeme is deductive method used constructively. It is not mere popular reasoning, logic

[9] 1356 a.   [10] 1357 a.   [11] 1356 a.

modified for popular consumption, but public reasoning, such reasoning as is available with the public for building up public opinion and policy.

Therefore the headings, or "topics," of rhetoric are not peculiar to a particular field of investigation, but general or "common topics" such as justice or expediency, which express common human relations. To deviate from these into the method peculiar to a given subject-matter, physics for example, is to pass [12] from rhetorical method for presentation over to scientific method for analysis; and this, of course, the speaker must do to the extent of mastering his subject-matter before he presents it. Though he must not forget that his ultimate task is to present to an audience and therefore concretely, neither can he forget that what is to be presented must be acquired. In so far as he investigates he will follow scientific method, the analysis proper to the field, the "special topics." Thus for his education he needs some study of the "special topics" of those sciences that furnish most of his subject-matter, the "special topics" of ethics and politics. Of these he must have, as part of his equipment, a practical or working knowledge, the orator's equipment for considering each case within its own field as well as in its general relations to human nature. Aristotle's distinction here between general and special "topics" coincides with his earlier division (page 10) of the means of persuasion into intrinsic and extrinsic. The extrinsic means are knowledge, to be got by the methods of getting; the intrinsic means are utterance, to be given by the methods of giving.

At this point, the opening of Chapter iii,[13] Aristotle makes his scientific division of rhetoric by its fields. The three fields of rhetoric are: (1) the *deliberative*, persuasion

[12] 1358 a.   [13] 1358 b.

in public assemblies as to matters of current discussion, looking to the future, urging expediency; (2) the *forensic*, accusation and defense in courts, looking to the past, urging justice; and (3) the *occasional*,[14] praise or blame, looking to the present, urging honor. The underlying, general, or "final topics" of rhetoric, as distinct from the special topics that it uses from other studies, are thus seen to be expediency (including practicability), justice, honor, and their opposites; and the special topics drawn by rhetoric from philosophy, ethics, and politics may be grouped in a speaker's compend of these studies according as they apply to the deliberative, the forensic, or the occasional field.

In deliberative oratory [15] the speaker deals with good and bad, not in the abstract as the philosopher contemplates virtue or happiness, but in concrete matters of doubt and dispute. So his topic of possibility is not abstract, as in mathematics, but concrete, in relation to human will. So in general Aristotle disclaims for his classification of the ordinary subjects of deliberative oratory any attempt at scientific division or scientific method of investigation. Those he follows in his other works; here the analysis that he provides is avowedly practical. Since in politics,[16] for example, the public speaker needs to know something of finance, war, commerce, legislation, Aristotle gives him a suggestive sum-

---

[14] Of the various translations of Aristotle's ἐπιδεικτικός, "demonstrative" is flatly a mistranslation, "oratory of display" is quite too narrow a translation, and "epideictic" is not a translation at all. The nearest word in current use is "*panegyric*," which is right as far as it goes. But English use, though it lacks a single equivalent word, is none the less familiar with the thing. The kind of oratory that Aristotle means is the oratory of the Gettysburg Address, of most other commemorative addresses, and of many sermons. The French equivalent is *discours de circonstance*.

[15] Chapter iv. 1359 a.   [16] 1359 b–1360 a.

mary of what he should learn. In our modern educational systems such a summary has far less importance; but the correlation remains vital. Pedagogically as well as philosophically, deliberative oratory must be correlated with its natural subject-matter. So to-day college courses in rhetoric demand correlation with college courses in history, sociology, economics, and politics. The professors of these subjects train for investigation, teaching the scientific method proper to each; the professor of rhetoric trains for presentation, teaching general methods, Aristotle's general or "final topics," for handling all such material. But unless each method of training can make use of the other, both will suffer. Rhetoric must lean upon such real knowledge of a given subject-matter as is furnished by the studies dealing with that subject-matter scientifically, i. e., by its "special topics." Meantime Aristotle's summary is intended not to explore these special topics, but to show what they are.

Similarly the student of deliberative oratory needs such a survey of philosophy [17] as will acquaint him with current ideas concerning happiness, whether of rank, offspring, wealth, honor, health, beauty, or strength, and concerning a good old age, friendship, fortune, and virtue. Therefore Aristotle, summarizing these conceptions, supplies [18] a cursory examination of good in general and of goods, or good things, in particular, proceeding [19] both by definition and by comparison, and not limiting his discussion to the deliberative field. To the latter, and to politics, he reverts in the concluding chapter [20] of this section by enumerating briefly the common forms of polity: democracy, oligarchy, aristocracy, and monarchy.

[17] 1360 b–1361 b.
[18] Chapter vi. 1362 a–1363 b.
[19] Chapter vii. 1363 b.
[20] Chapter viii. 1366 a.

Since occasional oratory [21] demands an equipment primarily ethical, Aristotle provides a summary of moral nobility [22] by definition and comparison. This is applied more specifically than the preceding section to rhetorical method, in this case to the method of enhancing or heightening and to the method of comparison.

For forensic oratory [23] Aristotle provides as a speaker's compend of philosophy a survey of the objects and conditions of crime. He makes no specific mention of what we now call criminal tendencies; and his division of "extrinsic proofs," i. e., of legal evidence (laws, witnesses, contracts, tortures, the oath) is for the modern lawyer neither scientific nor significant.

Book II

As Book I is the book of the speaker, Book II is the book of the audience. The audience is not merely discussed; it furnishes the point of view. As Book I considers the necessities and opportunities of the speaker, so Book II considers the attitude of the audience. Book I is rhetoric as conceived; Book II is rhetoric as received.

Since rhetoric is for judgment—for even deliberative speeches are judged, and forensic is [concerned entirely with] judgment —we must see to it not only that the speech shall be convincing and persuasive, but also that the judge shall be in the right frame of mind. For it makes a great difference to persuasion, especially in deliberative speeches, but also in forensic, how the speaker strikes the audience—both how the hearers think he regards them, and in addition how they are disposed toward him. How the speaker strikes the audience is of more

[21] Chapter ix. 1366 a–1368 a.
[22] τὸ καλόν, treated again in Book II from the point of view of the audience.
[23] Chapters x–xv. 1368 b–1377 b.

practical concern for deliberative speeches; how the hearer is
disposed, for forensic. The effect is not the same on a friendly
audience as on a hostile one, on the angry as on the tranquil,
but either different altogether or different in degree. . . .
Three [impressions] constitute persuasiveness—three, that is,
outside of the arguments used: wisdom, virtue, and good will
[i. e., a speaker's persuasiveness, in the sense of his personal
effect on his hearers, depends on their believing him to be wise,
upright, and interested in them]. . . . . From what sources
[in moral habits, ἦθος], then, the speaker may strike his
hearers as wise and earnest we must gather from the analysis
of the virtues, whether his immediate purpose be to make his
audience feel thus and so or to appear thus and so himself; but
good will and affection we must discuss now under the head of
the emotions (πάθη). By emotions I mean any changes,
attended by pain or pleasure, that make a difference to men's
judgment [of a speech]; e. g., anger, pity, fear, etc., and their
opposites. The consideration of each emotion—anger, for
instance—must have a threefold division: (1) how people are
angry, (2) what they are angry at, and (3) why; for if we should
know only one or two of these, not all three, it would be impossible to excite anger, and so with the other emotions.[24]

In this way Aristotle proceeds to analyze, in Chapters ii–xi, the common emotions: anger, love, fear, shame,
benevolence, pity, envy, emulation, and their opposites.
The relation of these to the formation of character leads
to six chapters on character in youth, in age, in the prime
of life, and on the typical dominant traits of character
seen respectively in persons of social rank, of wealth, of
power, and of good fortune.[25] The classification here will

[24] Chapter i. 1377 b. "In regard to πάθη and ἦθη, which move
juries, the most important part is to know how these emotions are
aroused and allayed. This alone, judging that it is none of their business,
the rhetors have not borrowed from Aristotle, though they have borrowed everything else." Philodemus, *Rhetorica*, trans. Hubbell, Trans-
actions of the Connecticut Academy, vol. 23 (September, 1920), page 338.
[25] "The import of these 'characters,' as of the ἦθη τῶν πολιτειῶν in

be more satisfying as psychology if we remember that it
analyzes the common types of character and emotion in a
crowd.   Aristotle is attempting neither an analysis of
mental operations nor a science of human nature, but such
a practical classification as may inculcate the habit of
adaptation to the feelings of an audience.

The psychological analysis of the audience concluded
with Chapter xvii, Aristotle returns to rhetoric in our
ordinary sense at Chapter xviii with a recapitulation.[26]
"The use of persuasive discourse," he says, resuming the
language of the opening of this book, "is for judgment," or
decision; i. e., persuasion connotes an audience to be
persuaded.   After showing that this is true in all cases,
and summarizing briefly the main aspects of Books I and
II, he concludes his transition by saying: "it remains for

I. 8. 6, and the use to which they are to be applied, may be thus expressed
in other words.   Certain ages and conditions of men are marked by different and peculiar characteristics.   A speaker is always liable to be con-
fronted with an audience in which one or other of these classes forms the
preponderating element.   In order to make a favorable impression upon
them, he must necessarily adapt his tone and language [Aristotle means
rather his method and arguments] to the sentiments and habits of
thought prevailing amongst them, and the feelings and motives by which
they are usually influenced.   And for this purpose he must study their
characters, and make himself acquainted with their ordinary motives
and feelings and opinions.   And the following analysis will supply him
with topics for this purpose." Cope, *Introduction*, foot-note to page
248.

[26] Certain difficulties here in the text, with the principal emendations
proposed, are discussed by Cope in his *Introduction*, and more largely in
the Cope and Sandys edition.   Vahlen was so convinced of an error in
transmission that he proposed to restore what he considered the original
order by transposing bodily Chapters xviii–end and Chapters i–xvii.
But in spite of difficulties of detail, the present order shows sufficiently
clear progress if we remember that these latter chapters (xviii–end) are
written, as all the rest of the book is written, from the point of view of
the audience.   So viewed, what has seemed repetition and expansion of
Book I is seen to be distinct, and not merely additional, but progressive.

us to go on with the common topics." [27]   With these he
actually goes on, not merely extending the treatment of
them in Book I (see page 14), but considering them now
as to their availability, their effect upon hearers.   More
explicit statement, however, of this distinction might well
have made the bearing of these latter chapters clearer.
The topic of possibility [28] implies the range of the argument from antecedent probability (a priori).   Example [29]
includes analogy, both from history [30] and from fiction,
with specific mention of fables.   In this wide sense, including mere illustration, it means little more than vividness of presentation through the concrete and specific; but
that its persuasive value far exceeds its logical cogency
no one doubts who knows audiences.   This is the angle,
too, from which Aristotle discusses maxims.[31]   "They
have great service for speeches because audiences are
commonplace.   People are pleased when a speaker hits
on a wide general statement of opinions that they hold in
some partial or fragmentary form." [32]   The same point of
view controls the further discussion of enthymemes,[33]
which includes a hint of something like Mill's Canon of
Concomitant Variations,[34] directions for logical exclusion,
for analysis demanding particulars, for dilemma, and for
reductio ad absurdum.   Remarking the popularity of the re-
futative, or destructive enthymeme over the constructive,
and touching the fallacies of petitio principii and post hoc,
the book concludes [35] with methods of refutation (λύσις).

[27] 1391 b.   [28] τὸ δυνατόν.   Chapter xix.
[29] παράδειγμα.   Chapter xx.   [30] πράγματα προγεγενημένα.
[31] γνῶμαι.   Chapter xxi.   [32] 1395 b.   [33] Chapters xxii–xxiv.
[34] Opening of Chapter xxiii.   [35] Chapters xxv–xxvi.

Book III

Book III studies the speech itself. Book I having presented rhetoric from the view of the speaker, and Book II from the view of the audience, Book III now applies it directly to the speech.[36]

Since rhetoric must treat systematically three things: (1) what the means of persuasion are to be, (2) the diction, [37] (3) how to arrange [38] the parts of the speech, . . . [the first has been discussed]. We have next to speak of the diction. For it is not enough to know what we ought to say; we must also know how we ought to say it, and this contributes much to the effect of the speech. The first subject of our inquiry [(1) above] was naturally that which comes first by nature, the facts themselves—in what aspects they are persuasive. The second is the expression of these in the diction. The third [*not* (3) above], which is of very great importance, is the delivery.

The threefold division sketched here seems at first sight to coincide, so far as it goes, with the one that afterward became traditional. Classical rhetoric as a whole assumes a fivefold division: (1) εὕρεσις, *inventio*, the gathering and analysis of the material; (2) τάξις, *dispositio*, *collocatio*, the arrangement, sequence, or movement in the large; (3) λέξις, *elocutio*, the diction, or the choice of words and their combination in phrases, clauses, and sentences, the movement in detail; (4) ὑπόκρισις, *pronuntiatio*, delivery, or "elocution"; (5) μνήμη, *memoria*, memory. But

[36] 1403 b.

[37] λέξις. It should be observed that Aristotle is not here divorcing "manner" from "matter." Book III opens a third approach, which presupposes the preceding approaches. This seems to be insufficiently considered by H. P. Breitenbach (The *De compositione of Dionysius of Halicarnassus considered with reference to the Rhetoric of Aristotle*), who regards Book III as a deviation from the philosophic position of the preceding books.

[38] τάξαι.

Aristotle's division neither corresponds to this nor is consistent with itself. The first item is the same in both. Aristotle's second item is clearly the same as the later third, and has the same name (λέξις, diction). The third item of his opening sentence seems equivalent to the traditional second (τάξις), and uses the corresponding verb (τάξαι); but below he makes his third item instead delivery (ὑπόκρισις), which is the fourth item of the traditional division, and then proceeds in the same chapter to include delivery, by implication, under diction.[39] In a word, the opening division of Book III is baffling. But the actual development of the book is quite clear: chapters i–xii on λέξις, diction, or, in the widest sense, style; chapters xiii–xix, on τάξις, or arrangement.

Delivery, after declaring it to have the greatest force (δύναμιν . . μεγίστην), he dismisses in a few sentences. Tantalizing in its brevity, this passage is nevertheless suggestive; for it sketches an analytic division of delivery into voice-placing and volume, pitch, and rhythm; it points to the value for public speaking of the arts of dramatic recital; and, most important of all, it relates delivery to the whole idea of style as concrete presentation *versus* abstract formulation.

In thus uniting delivery and diction as alike means of effective utterance Aristotle has seemed to some readers to disparage both. He has seemed to express, as in a similar passage of Book I,[40] a philosophic contempt for style. But this impression is not confirmed by scrutiny. Not only can he hardly be thought to despise that to which he devotes himself cordially throughout a large part of his treatise, but his words here hardly yield the inference that

[39] The fifth traditional item, memory, he omits altogether.
[40] Chapter i, 1354.

has been drawn from prejudicial translation. They may be rendered more precisely as follows:

An art [of delivery] is not yet settled; for even that of diction emerged but late and seems a bore when regarded ideally. But [41] since the whole practise of rhetoric is gauged to actual effect upon hearers (πρὸς δόξαν), we must give delivery our care, not of [abstract] right, but of necessity. [Abstract] justice, indeed, demands of our speech nothing more than that it should neither offend nor propitiate. For [abstractly] just [method] is so to make one's plea with the facts that everything beyond exposition is superfluous. Nevertheless [delivery] is of great importance, as I have said, because of the human frailty of the hearer. Indeed, the consideration of the hearer is in a degree necessary in all teaching; for even in explanation it makes some difference whether we speak thus or thus—not so much, however [as in active persuasion], all these things [i. e., of diction and delivery] being means of suggesting images [42] and gauged to the hearer. Therefore no one thus teaches geometry.

That art, then [of delivery], when it comes, will produce the same effects as acting; and some authors, as Thrasymachus on the pathetic, have made a slight attempt at it. Acting is both a natural gift and less reducible to art; but diction has its technic. That is why those who have mastered it take prizes regularly, as do the histrionic orators; [43] for written speeches prevail more by diction than by thought.

"No one thus teaches geometry" cannot be taken as a slur on style. It simply reminds us, by applying to diction a distinction made with great fulness in the first two chap-

[41] 1404 a.   [42] φαντασία.

[43] Welldon's translation "rhetorical actors" can hardly stand. The phrase τοῖς κατὰ τὴν ὑπόκρισιν ῥήτορσιν means rather *acting orators*, or, more exactly, orators who practise the art of the actor, who are skilled in delivery. Their advantage appears in their winning prizes for written speeches, which can be memorized and declaimed and which are sometimes *tours de force*, showing more style than thought. Such speeches—I think Aristotle cites them as an extreme case—show the separable value of style, including delivery.

ters of Book I, that rhetoric is not geometry. Formulation, as in geometry, is colorless because it is abstract; but any actual presentation, even mere information (ἐν πάσῃ διδασκαλίᾳ), demands style, whether concreteness or the arts of delivery, for mere lucidity (πρὸς τὸ δηλῶσαι), much more for any sort of appeal. For any sort of presentation, Aristotle is saying, we must study style; and we must include the study of delivery except in those written addresses which depend on style even more than on thought.

The appeal of style, Aristotle says in this same first chapter,[44] was first discerned by the poets. The method of suggestion, in other words, belongs to poetic. This is more than a critical distinction; it has an application directly pedagogical. The teaching of style, always delicate and difficult, may well begin through poetry, which in descriptive heightening and in harmony of sound with sense, especially of pace with mood, most plainly exhibits style as adaptation. The connection of this with delivery, both with reading aloud and with dramatic recital, though obvious, is often neglected. Elocution in our modern sense may, if rightly related, be one of the gateways to appreciation of style.[45]

Chapter ii,[46] after glancing at the fundamental virtue of lucidity, considers the choice of words for appropriateness and for suggestiveness, i. e., for their connotation, and especially for the descriptive vividness of the concrete, as in metaphors. Chapter iii [47] deals with the inappro-

[44] 1404 a.

[45] At the close of this first chapter Welldon's translation "rhetorical style" is misleading. Aristotle says, as Jebb correctly translates, "that style of which we are speaking," i. e., prose style, the style of public address. "The other style," he adds, "has been treated in the *Poetic*."

[46] 1404 b.   [47] 1406 a.

priateness arising from bad taste; [48] Chapter iv,[49] with
the extension of metaphor into simile. Chapter v [50] passes
from single words and phrases to their combination in
clauses and sentences. The distinction is important, and
is kept throughout the classical rhetoric from Aristotle
down. The choice of words is ἐκλογή (*electio*); the shaping
of clauses and sentences is σύνθεσις (*compositio*). Frequent translation of the latter by our English word *composition*, which has a meaning so much wider as to be quite
different, misses the specific point of technic, and often
makes the ancient writers say what they did not mean.[51]

As the primary virtue in the choice of words is precision,
so the first consideration in their combination, says Aristotle, is purity, idiom, conformity to usage. This assured,
the next considerations of movement in detail are dignity,[52]
which he presents as mainly amplification, and appropriateness.[53] Appropriateness here is not merely of the
single word, as in Chapters ii and iii, but of the movement,
or pace. It is gauged both to the moral habit (ἦθos) of the
audience and to the emotion (πάθos) of the occasion.

From this general idea of appropriate movement Aristotle passes [54] to specific consideration of rhythm with his
oft-quoted dictum:

> The order [55] of the diction must be neither metrical nor un-
> rhythmical. The former, by seeming artificial, is unpersua-

---

[48] τὰ ψυχρά.   [49] 1406 b.   [50] 1407 a.

[51] Style (λέξις, *elocutio*) consists of:

    (1) choice of the right word (ἐκλογή, *electio*);

    (2) the movement, rhythm, or pace of sentences and clauses (σύνθεσις,
compositio). Chapters v–xii deal with (2).

[52] ὄγκος. Chapter vi, 1407 b.   [53] Chapter vii, 1408 a.

[54] Chapter viii, 1408 b.

[55] The Greek word σχῆμα is quite general, applicable to any sort of
guiding principle, outline, system, or plan. Our English words *outline*,
plan, etc., though otherwise fairly equivalent, have visual, graphic,

sive and at the same time distracting. For it makes us think
of recurrences and wait for them to come, as children anticipate
the answer to the heralds' "Whom does the freedman choose
as his attorney? Cleon." On the other hand, the unrhythmical is immeasurable, and a measure we must have, though not
by metrical recurrence; for the boundless can be grasped
neither by the ear nor by the mind. Now measure in the most
general sense is number; [56] and number as applied to the order
of the diction is rhythm, of which meters are sections. Rhythm,
therefore, the speech must have, but not meter, or it will be
a poem—rhythm not too nice, that is, not carried too far.

Of the three rhythms the heroic is solemn and lacking in
prose harmony.[57] The iambic is the very diction of the crowd;
i. e., it is heard oftener than any other measure in speech, and
it lacks capacity to lift and startle. The trochaic [58] is too suggestive of comic dancing, as is evident in trochaic tetrameters,
which are a skipping rhythm. There remains the pæan.

Having laid down the principle that prose movement
should be rhythmical, but not metrical, why does Aristotle
proceed immediately to discuss it in terms of meters?
Simply, perhaps, because these terms are familiar and
definite. How else, indeed, shall we speak of a particular
movement specifically? Perhaps also because the consideration of the larger, freer rhythms of prose is best
opened through the fixed rhythms of verse, i. e., because

static associations quite foreign to the context. Aristotle's images for
style are drawn not from architecture or painting, but from music and
other modes of movement. By *the* diction he means—indeed, he says
later—prose diction.

[56] Literally, "all things are measured by number."

[57] λεκτικῆς ἁρμονίας. Cope and Welldon translate "conversational
harmony." The literal sense of the phrase is "speech harmony," "harmony of diction, or of style"; but since Aristotle can hardly mean to
say that the heroic measure lacks harmony of diction *in verse*, and since
he is talking of prose, I translate "prose harmony." Ἁρμονία may be
taken either in the general or in the particular (musical) sense of harmony; but in the latter sense its application is restricted to melody.

[58] 1409 a.

meter is the gateway to appreciation of rhythm, as poetry in a wider sense (see page 24) is the gateway to style in a wider sense. For us moderns it is the more significant that the classical doctrine of clauses and sentences deals so largely with rhythm, since our doctrine throws the emphasis on logic. That the σύνθεσις, or *compositio*, should be idiomatic, dignified, appropriate, Aristotle has urged briefly; that it should be rhythmical he proceeds to set forth in detail, consecutively showing how.[59]

Thus that the diction should be rhythmical, not unrhythmical, what rhythms make it rhythmical, and in what modes, has been set forth.

Now diction [60] [in its sentence-movement] is connected either loosely and only by conjunctions, as the preludes in the dithyrambs, or compactly, as the antistrophes of the old poets. The former movement is the old one, as in Herodotus; for, though once universal, it is now exceptional. By calling it loose I mean that it has no end in itself except as its subject-matter runs out. It is unsatisfying to the ear by its indefiniteness, since we all wish to glimpse the end. That [natural desire] is why [runners] lose wind and heart only at the goal. They do not give out before because they are looking ahead to the finish.

The loose movement, then, of diction is this; the compact, on the other hand, is the one by periods [or definite units]. By *period* I mean a diction having a beginning and an end in itself and a length to be grasped as a whole. Such sentence-movement is both satisfying to the ear and easily followed by the mind; [61] *satisfying* as being the opposite of endless and as

---

[59] For a modern scientific discussion of prose rhythm see W. M. Patterson, *The Rhythm of Prose*, New York, Columbia University Press, 1916. See also Morris W. Croll, *The cadence of English oratorical prose.* Studies in Philology, 16:1, University of North Carolina, January, 1919.

[60] Chapter ix, 1409 a.

[61] 1409 b; ἡδεῖα δ᾽ ἡ τοιαύτη καὶ εὐμαθής. The translation of Cope and of Welldon, "easily learnt" is amiss; and Welldon's foot-note thereon about learning speeches by heart is still more misleading. The

giving the hearer the sense of always having hold of something,
because something has always been ended by itself, whereas
the unsatisfying is neither to see ahead nor to get through;
easily followed, as being easily held in mind, and that because
periodic diction has number, which is the chief aid to memory. That is why verses are more easily remembered than
loose prose, because verse has number to measure it. The
period should also be completed with the sense, not broken
off. . . .

A period [62] is either in members or simple. Composed in
members, it is such a diction as makes a rounded whole and
yet is distinct in its parts, and such as the breath will carry
easily, not by [arbitrary] division, but as a whole. A member
is one of its parts; and by simple period I mean a period of one
member. Both members and periods should be neither curt [63]
nor long. For short [members] often make the hearer stumble,
since while he is still surging ahead, if he is pulled up by the
stopping of the measure that he carries in his head as a guide,
he must stumble as in a collision. Long [members] on the other
hand make the hearer feel himself left behind, as by walking

εὐσύνοπτον (end of 1409 a), "easily grasped as a whole," of the preceding
sentence does not imply writing and reading; and there is no other word in
the context even to suggest this except the reference to memory, which
in the classical rhetoric is rarely applied to memorizing. The translation
"easily learnt" is precluded both by the general trend of the passage and
by the specific figures of walking, running, and breathing. Here, as
throughout the *Rhetoric* and the *Poetic*, Aristotle avoids speaking of style
in the visual terms common to modern generations of writers and readers.
His terms, whether literal or figurative, are generally auditory and motor.
When he uses others, it is to distinguish something special, as in Chapter xii (below) the exceptional, literary opportunity of such compositions
as those of Isocrates. Not only does his *Rhetoric* deal primarily and generally with oral composition, but in particular this section on σύνθεσις
(*compositio*) deals with movement almost exclusively. Not until he has
explained the period rhythmically does he add our modern definition
that it should *also* be concluded with the sense, i. e., with the syntax.
Meantime he finds the period superior to the loose sentence—for oratory
—first because it satisfies the ear by being heard as a definite rhythm,
and secondly because it satisfies the mind by being intended and appre-
hended as a definite unit of thought.

[62] 1409 b.   [63] The admirable rendering of Jebb.

companions making the turn beyond the usual stretch. . . .
Over-use of short members, since it precludes the periodic form,
drags the hearer headlong.

In other words, the period is a sentence movement
forecast and fulfilled by the speaker, divined and held by
the hearer, as a definite rhythmical and logical unit. Its
characteristic is that conclusiveness which satisfies at
once ear and mind. In sound and in syntax it is the
opposite of formless aggregation, of the addition of clause
to clause as by afterthoughts. Forethought, indeed, is
its very note. Thus its typical advantages are rather for
oratory than for narrative. Oratory moves by grouping
around ideas; narrative, by adding image to image. The
style of Herodotus is in this sense aggregative. Its aim
being to proceed not from idea to idea in thought, but from
fact to fact in time, it is "loosely joined," "running on,"
without other rhythmical value than fluency. That
Aristotle means to disparage Herodotus when he calls
this movement old and unsatisfying need hardly be
inferred. Old it is typically, the movement of all early
prose, of Herodotus no more than of Froissart and Villani.
Unsatisfying, unpleasing to the ear (ἀηδές) it is not—in
its place; but its place is not in oratory, which demands
definite measures to mark definite stages of thought.
Otherwise the audience is frustrated and loses the way.

What Aristotle means by his comparison of the two
movements is that the former is unsatisfying, not absolutely, but for the purposes of the latter, i. e., for oratory.
This interpretation is confirmed by what he adds concerning the length of members, or clauses. That staccato
habit of short statements which in oratory "drags the
hearer headlong," [64] unsatisfied and uncomprehending,

[64] 1409 b (toward end).

may in narrative be actually superior. To drag the hearer
headlong is sometimes precisely what a story-teller desires. Examples abound, for instance, in Victor Hugo, for
whom this movement became a mannerism. Neither of
the two sentence movements, which from the point of
view of Aristotle's time we may call the historical and
the oratorical, has remained through the long development
of prose quite the same. Narrative has developed in
modern times a movement more and more consciously
poetic, while history in our special modern sense has
turned more and more to the conscious group-movement
which he associated with oratory. To-day we see much
the same difference between our prose fiction and our
expository history that he saw between Herodotus and
Demosthenes. But the change is in application, not in the
movements themselves. It remains true, and important,
that there is on the one hand a prose movement rhythmically and intellectually loose, indefinite, and current, and
on the other hand a prose movement compact, conscious,
concluded point by point. The latter, the periodic, remains
the typical movement of public address; for the audience,
in order to follow, in order "to have hold of something [65]
and to get something done," demands definite measures.[66]

Having laid down as fundamental the distinction

[65] 1409 b.

[66] For the contrast between the two movements in modern prose, see
my *College Composition*, pages 184–188; for the effect of a passage
of short sentences *vs.* that of a passage of long sentences, pages 69–
71. Though the sentence unit, in our modern logical sense, is not
always clear from the punctuation of even modern editions of ancient
texts, it will usually be clear from the conclusion of the rhythm. In the
earlier stages of modern prose, on the other hand, it is sometimes so
dubious as to suggest that it was not always felt distinctly. The artistic
development of modern prose, in other words, is partly the progressive
distinction of periods.

between the two typical prose movements, Aristotle proceeds to details: the balance of member against member,[67] and the heightening of the individual member [68] by visualizing metaphor. His recurrence here to metaphor is unexpected, since he has discussed this already in Chapter ii [69] under the choice of words; but here something is added. The connotation of figurative language is explored further as a means to make a whole statement telling. Aristotle is inquiring how such pithy sayings as he has just exemplified in balance and antithesis are made forcible [70] by other means; and he implies that the process is essentially poetic, as being imaginative first in realization and secondly [71] in movement.

Imaginative realization in metaphor and simile is considered here as intellectual suggestion. As enthymemes, so metaphors and similes must steer between the obvious and the subtle. The best images, like the best enthymemes, stimulate the hearer to coöperate, to see the relation for himself.

As to sense such are the popular enthymemes; as to style [they are popular] if the order, or movement [72] is antithetical. . . So for the terms; if metaphorical, they must be neither far-fetched, for then they are hard to grasp, nor trite, for then they stir no emotion; and besides [as to movement] they must put [the thing] before our eyes; for we must see it in action rather than in intention (happening rather than about to happen, present rather than future). The essential elements, then, are three: metaphor, antithesis, actuality.[73]

Numerous examples follow [74] of ἀστεῖα, or pithy sayings, and Chapter xi [75] expands

---

[67] Chapter ix, 1410 a.   [68] Chapter x, 1410 b.   [69] 1404 b.
[70] τὰ ἀστεῖα καὶ τὰ εὐδοκιμοῦντα, lively and pleasing, smart and popular.
[71] Chapter xi, below.   [72] σχῆμα.
[73] ἐνέργεια.   [74] 1411 a.   [75] 1411 b.

what is meant by " before our eyes " and how this is to be done.
I mean that those passages put the thing before our eyes which
show it in action.[76] For instance, to say that a good man is
" square " is metaphor . . but it does not show him in action,
whereas " in flowering vigor " does, and so does " at large."
And in " Straightway the Greeks with bounding feet" the
" bounding " is at once actuality and metaphor. . . . In all
these [instances from Homer] by being alive (living, organic)
[the subject] seems to be in action. . . . They all make the
subject moving and living; and actuality is movement.[77]

Aristotle's recurrence, then, to metaphor in the midst
of his doctrine of sentence movement is because metaphor
has the wider implication. It may be more than a single
vivid word; it should extend to a whole habit of realizing
a thing in action; and this involves expression in a sentence
movement that shall heighten the suggestion by its pace.

In like manner the recurrence to aptness, or adaptation,
is not repetition. Chapters ii [78] and iii [79] deal with aptness
of single words; chapter xii,[80] with aptness of sentence
movement. From the general definition [81] of apt movement as adaptation both to the moral habit of the audience
($\tilde{\eta}\theta os$) and to the emotion of the occasion ($\pi\acute{a}\theta os$) Chapter xii now proceeds to the typical adaptations offered
by the several fields of oratory: the deliberative, the
forensic, and the occasional.[82]

It must not be forgotten that one style is appropriate to one
kind [of oratory], another style to another. Style for writing is
not the same as style for debate, nor style for public debate the
same as style for legal pleading. Both [style for writing and
style for debate] have to be known: the latter, as command of

[76] $\acute{e}\nu\epsilon\rho\gamma o\hat{u}\nu\tau a$. Here, perhaps, is the suggestion for Lessing's famous
doctrine in the Laokoön as to Homeric description.   [77] 1412 a.
    [78] 1404 b.   [79] 1406 a.   [80] 1413 b.   [81] Chapter vii, 1408 a.
  [82] For this division see Book I, Chapter iii, 1358 b.

correct (or idiomatic) utterance; the former, as deliverance
from the necessity of keeping silence when one wishes to com-
municate— [an inhibition] which those suffer who do not know
how to write. Style for writing is the most precise; style for
debate, the most histrionic (the best adapted to delivery).
The latter is [adaptation] of two sorts: expression of character,
and expression of emotion. This is why actors also seek such
plays, and dramatists such personæ [as give expression to
character and emotion].

The distinction here between style for writing (to be
read aloud) and style for speaking (for immediate utterance) is general, as appears in the following reference to
asyndeton and in the comparison of public speaking to
the broad brush work of fresco; but it is also particular.
It distinguishes occasional, or panegyric oratory as demanding a style more literary. "Style for writing,"
above, must from its context refer to panegyric; and below
Aristotle adds: "The style of occasional oratory is best
suited to writing; for its function is to be read." [83]

The final section [84] of Book III deals with the larger
parts of a speech: exordium, statement of facts, proof,
peroration. This discussion of τάξις (dispositio) is both
meager and perfunctory, hardly more than a rehearsal of

[83] ἡ μὲν οὖν ἐπιδεικτικὴ λέξις γραφικωτάτη · τὸ γὰρ ἔργον αὐτῆς ἀνάγνωσις
(1414 a). The intervening reference to Chæremon, a poet said to have
been better to read than to hear, as "precise as a professional speech-
writer," should not deviate us here into consideration of speeches written
out to be memorized. For a full discussion of the professional speech-
writer (λογογράφος) see Cope and Sandys on Book II. xi. 7. Here Aristotle is discussing something different, the adaptation of occasional
oratory as nicer and more literary in sentence movement. Perhaps he
implies too that such speeches had better be composed, as well as elaborated, in writing. Certainly this kind of oratory, from Isocrates down,
regularly included many compositions which we should call essays and
which were not even intended to be spoken.

[84] Chapters xiii–xix.

those definitions and counsels which were already familiar
in teaching and apparently in manuals,[85] and which were
to be handed on by later tradition. Its importance is
therefore primarily historical. It has little other significance, little of the Aristotelian discernment and suggestiveness. What the modern teacher of rhetoric misses,
both here and throughout the later classical discussions
of *dispositio*, is some definite inculcation of consecutiveness.
That consecutiveness was achieved in the best practise
there can be no doubt; how it was taught we are left to
guess. As to movement in this larger sense, what we
commonly mean by composition, Aristotle's *Poetic* is
more definite and more suggestive than his *Rhetoric*.

He begins [86] by saying that the only essential parts of a
speech are proposition and proof. It is presently apparent that by "parts" here he means components, or
elements, of any and every sort of speech. The statement
of facts, for instance, is not a part in the sense of a distinct
division except in forensic; and Aristotle rightly objects [87]
to subdivisions by "parts" which are neither distinct nor
applicable generally. Even refutation, as he shows later,[88]
is not a distinct part, either in function or in method or in
place. The most that can be allowed are four: proposition and proof as essential, exordium and peroration as
usual.

With the same common sense he shows that the first
function of the exordium [89] is to put the hearers in a position to understand; its second, to win their sympathy.[90]
Chapter xvi [91] passes to the recital of facts (διήγησις).
The common rendering of this term by *narrative* has been

---

[85] τέχναι. See Cope, *Introduction*, page 331.
[86] Chapter xiii, 1414 a.   [87] 1414 b.   [88] 1418 b.
[89] Chapter xiv, 1415 a.   [90] 1415 b–1416 b.   [91] 1416 b.

widely misleading.   True, the corresponding Latin term
is *narratio*, and the thing is narrative in the sense of being
sometimes, though not always, chronological; but *narrative* in our modern use, and especially in our modern text-
books, is associated with objects and methods which
Aristotle is not here considering at all, and which he rightly
relegated to poetic. The Greek term διήγησις and the
corresponding Latin *narratio* mean exactly what is called
in a modern lawyer's brief the "statement of facts," as
distinct from the following "argument."   It therefore
belongs properly, as a distinct part having a distinct
place, to forensic.   When used in occasional oratory,[92] it
should on the contrary be broken up, not as in forensic
continuous.   In deliberative oratory[93] it has least scope,
i. e., it hardly appears as a separable part.

But the recital of facts, though it corresponds to the
"statement" of a brief in substance, need not be so limited
in style.   A speech is not a brief; and the pleader, ancient
or modern, must make his facts live.[94]

Speak also from the emotions, reciting what goes with them
(i. e., their physical expression), both what is familiar and what
is characteristic of yourself or your opponent: "He left me
with a scowl"; or, as Æschines said of Cratylus, "hissing and
shaking his fists."   [Such descriptive suggestions are really]
elements of persuasion; for the familiar images become tokens
of what you are trying to impress.   Many such expressions are
to be had from Homer: "So she spoke, and the old woman
covered her face with her hands," as we commonly put our
hands to our eyes when we begin to weep.

[92] Chapter xvi, 1416 b.   The counsel is too often forgotten by pane-
gyrists in Congress, perhaps because they are lawyers.
[93] 1417 b.
[94] See above on style in general (1404 a), on the vividness of the concrete
(1404 b), on visualizing metaphor (1410 b), and on describing in action
(1411 b).

As to persuasion by argument [95] Aristotle begins with a
mere hint of that determination of the main issue and
character of the case which was afterward elaborated into
the classified doctrine of the στάσις (*status*).

> Examples [παραδείγματα, he goes on] are more suited to de-
> liberative oratory; enthymemes, to forensic.[96] . . . Do not
> speak in enthymemes seriatim, but mix them in [with other
> means of persuasion]; or they will impair one another. There
> is a quantitative limit. . . . Do not seek an enthymeme for
> everything; or you will write like some philosophers; . . .
> and do not speak in enthymeme when your immediate aim
> is emotional . . . or ethical.
> The peroration [97] consists: (1) of disposing the hearer well
> toward oneself and ill toward one's adversary; (2) of enhancing
> and disparaging; (3) of stirring the hearer to emotion; (4) and
> of recapitulation. . . [For this last function] the primary idea
> is that what was promised has been given in full, so that we
> must tell both what [we have said] and why. This is told
> by comparison [of our own case] with our opponent's. . . .
> Asyndeton [98] befits the final words, that they may be perora-
> tion, not oration: "I have spoken; you have heard; you have
> it; judge."

With no less abruptness Aristotle's *Rhetoric* stops. It
can hardly be said to conclude; and certainly it has no
peroration.

[95] Chapter xvii, 1417 b.   For the place of Chapters xvii and xviii in relation to the whole work see foot-note 5 to page 197 of Jebb's translation.

[96] 1418 a.   [97] ἐπίλογος.   Chapter xix, 1419 b.   [98] 1420 a.

CHAPTER III

RHETORIC IN THE *DE ORATORE* AND *ORATOR* OF CICERO [1]

/ Cicero remains after two thousand years the typical orator writing on oratory. The most eminent orator of Roman civilization, he wrote more than any other orator has ever written on rhetoric; and historically he has been more than any other an ideal and model. Conscious of

[1] Besides many incidental references, Cicero left seven works dealing mainly or entirely with rhetoric: *De inventione* (about 86 B. C.), *De oratore* (55 B. C.), *Partitiones oratoriæ* (about 54 B. C.), *Brutus* (46 B. C.), *Orator* (46 B. C.), *De optimo genere oratorum* (about 46 B. C.), *Topica* (44 B. C.). Of these the most explicit and suggestive are *De oratore* and *Orator*, which are used as the basis of the following chapter.

The most convenient bibliographical guide to Cicero's rhetorical doctrine is Laurand, L., *De M. Tulli Ciceronis studiis rhetoricis* (University of Paris thesis, 1907), which also summarizes lucidly its derivation and progress.

The best editions in English are: Wilkins, A. S., *M. Tulli Ciceronis De Oratore*, Oxford, 1893 (3d ed.), 3 volumes (introduction, including a sketch of the history of rhetoric and a tabular analysis of the treatise *Ad Herennium* formerly ascribed to Cicero; analyses, notes, index); Sandys, J. E., *M. Tulli Ciceronis Orator . . .* Cambridge, 1885 (introduction, including a sketch of the history of rhetoric, a brief analysis of Cicero's rhetorical works, a study and an abstract of *Orator*, and a list of editions, commentaries, and translations; notes, indices).

English translations of *De oratore:* Guthrie, W., London, 1808 & 1840; Watson, J. S., London (Bohn), 1855 & 1896; Calvert, F. B., Edinburgh, 1870; Moor, E. N. P., (Book I only), London, 1904. Of *Orator* Sandys (page xcvii) cites three English translations, of which only Yonge's seems to be available in this country. The French translation by Colin (*Traduction du traité de l'orateur de Cicéron, avec des notes, par M. l'Abbé Colin,* Paris, 1737), though somewhat paraphrastic, is accurate so far as I have used it. Another accompanies Bornecque's edition, Paris, 1921.

Among recent critical studies the following will be found suggestive in

37

his own range and of the narrowness and low esteem that seem from the beginning to have cursed teachers and especially manuals of rhetoric, he is anxious in his greater works, *De oratore* and *Orator*, to appear not as a rhetorician, but as a philosopher. Though no treatment could well be more different from Aristotle's, he is at pains to urge the Academic theory that rhetoric is a branch of philosophy, and to avoid the technical terms of the art while keeping its traditional categories. In this attitude he is but the more typically the artist discussing his own art. He writes as the man of letters in any age writes on literary composition. We may be annoyed at a certain condescension toward teachers—as if they might think themselves able to impart anything like his skill! We may be baffled in trying to reduce some of his elaborations to specific terms. But rather we should be grateful to find rhetoric presented, for once at least, pleasantly as well as suggestively, and still more to find the orator insisting that it must have the same large scope as is claimed for it by the philosopher. Where Aristotle and Cicero agree, we may feel sure.

Cicero has been disparaged as a maker of phrases. That he is certainly. "They write Latin," says Newman [2]

their several directions: Hendrickson, G. L., *The Peripatetic mean of style and the three stylistic characters*, Amer. Jo. Philol. xxv. 125 (1904); *Ancient characters of style*, Amer. Jo. Philol. xxvi. 249 (1905); *Cicero's Brutus and the technique of citation in dialogue*, Amer. Jo. Philol. xxvii, 184 (1906); Hubbell, H. M., *The influence of Isocrates on Cicero, Dionysius and Aristides* (Yale thesis, 1914); Nassal, F., *Æsthetisch-rhetorische Beziehungen zwischen Dionysius von Halikarnass und Cicero* (Tübingen thesis, 1910). For study of rhetorical terms see Causeret, C., *Étude sur la langue de la rhétorique et de la critique dans Cicéron*, Paris, 1886, which is classified by the five-fold division, *inventio, collocatio*, etc. The influence of Cicero in the middle age and the Renaissance will be discussed in a later volume.

[2] *Literature*, the second lecture on *University Subjects* in the *Idea of a University*.

of other great authors; "Cicero writes Roman." His own style is the final answer to his detractors. He is evidently, indeed, a very conscious man of letters, and filed his speeches for publication; but can we deny vigor of thought to the maker of such vigorous phrase without lapsing into the separation of style from substance? Mere style is incredible—unless, as no one pretends of Cicero, the style is bad. So much *a priori;* and in fact his works will bear analysis. But he is not creative. He clarifies the thoughts of others and brings them to bear. His habit and skill are not at all scientific. His achievement is of style to the extent that it is an achievement of presentation. What he says of rhetoric, for instance, others have said before him; he says it better, more clearly, more vividly. He says it so much better, indeed, that his phrase has a certain finality. It witnesses not only his extraordinary command of diction, but also his constant awareness of human implications. His very diffuseness springs from his constant sense of how people think and feel while they hear and read. In all this he is typically the orator.

DE ORATORE

The title *De oratore* exactly expresses the subject. Cicero is discussing rhetoric, indeed; he is writing *de arte oratoria;* but always, as Aristotle in his first book, from the point of view of the speaker. It is worth insisting on that the practitioner here coincides with the philosopher, and both with the theory and practise of rhetoric in the best days of the ancient tradition. The training of the public speaker, this tradition consistently repeats, must focus the whole training of the man. The vice of the teaching of rhetoric in its decadence under the Empire [3] was so to pervert this principle as to make all training subordinate to technical skill in rhetoric; and indeed the principle has this danger of making the whole man serve rhetoric, instead of making rhetoric bring out the whole man. None the less the principle rightly conceived is fruitful; and no one has shown this more persuasively than Cicero.

The form is obviously the Platonic dialogue. The protagonists are the famous orators Crassus and Antonius, with Scævola, Cotta, Catulus, and Sulpicius as minor interlocutors. Whatever basis there may have been in the actual conversations of these historical persons,[4] the work, like its model, is fiction. It is dramatic in representing the speakers as *personæ;* but its imaginative realization goes no further. The literary device of the dialogue is used only to add concreteness to the discussion of what is always dry when it is abstract. The object is

---

[3] See below, Chapter IV. II.

[4] W. B. Owen in the introduction to his edition of Book I (Boston, 1895) makes more of this than its importance seems to warrant.

the discussion, not even incidentally the men who discuss. They talk always as orators and to promote oratory; and as orators they proceed from point to point. Plato's *personæ* are realized more dramatically. Though only Socrates is created fully, the others emerge as individuals. The movement of a Platonic dialogue is far more conversational. Not only does its form give the illusion of actual talk; its thought moves hither and yon, suggesting rather than concluding, seeking yet other approaches and departures, not marching but questing. Cicero raises questions, indeed, but as they are raised by the public speaker who has predetermined the answer and the stages by which we are to reach it. For all the ease and skill of its dialogue, *De oratore* proceeds by paragraphs as definitely as *De lege Manilia*.

Though rhetoric is necessary to every educated man for effective communication, and especially to every aspiring youth (*laudis cupidus*), how rare are good orators! The reason is the wide scope. Oratory demands knowledge not only as *eruditio*, but also in relation to human will (*animorum motus*), It demands expressiveness in a wide range of style and delivery. What more noble? The orator is a principal supporter of the State. So begins Crassus (I. i–viii); but Scævola demurs, unwilling to grant either that states have been established and maintained by orators or that the orator is accomplished in every sort of utterance and of culture.[5] Here the question is posed, Is oratory a special art or a comprehensive study? Though abstractly it may be both, though the one view does not exclude the other absolutely, practically the emphasis of the training will be determined by a choice between the two.

As if to forestall restriction, Crassus begins with the widest extension. He will not agree to exclude [6] from the scope of oratory public management, instruction, even research. Of the Greeks who urge this, he says, Plato is a refutation of his own

[5] *In omni genere sermonis et humanitatis perfectum,* I. ix. 35 [6] I. xi.

doctrine, being himself an orator. Democritus, Aristotle, Theophrastus, Carneades, show the force of oratory; Chrysippus, the lack of it. Sound without substance is folly.[7] Even legal pleading demands more than is taught by the rhetoricians. The orator's effectiveness depends on knowledge of human emotions; and they are a field of philosophy. Though he may leave it to the philosophers as *cognitio*, he must know it [8] as applied to presentation. To make philosophy effective, you must have rhetoric. [Does this finally leave the point, which is that rhetoric needs philosophy?] "What the philosophers dispute in their corners without any urgency of application, and so in thin and feeble talk, the orator will set forth in such a way as to please and move."[9] Socrates used to say [10] 'Everybody is eloquent enough on what he knows'; but the truth is rather that neither can any one be eloquent on what he does not know, nor can he be eloquent on what he does know unless he know also the art of rhetoric."

"Therefore,[11] if we seek to define and embrace the force of oratory as both general and special, he methinks is an orator, worthy of so responsible a title, who will say whatever falls to him for presentation with wise forecast of the whole, order, style, memory, and a certain dignity of delivery."

It is disconcerting to arrive, after all, at the traditional parts of rhetoric. For the definition resolves itself into this:

1. *prudenter*, with wise forecast of the whole   = *inventio;*
2. *composite*,[12] with skill in arrangement   = *dispositio;*
3. *ornate*, with command of enhancing words   = *elocutio;*
4. *memoriter*, with sure memory   = *memoria;*
5. *cum actionis dignitate*, with dignity of delivery   = *actio.*

[7] I. xii. 51.   [8] I. xiii. 55.   [9] 56.   [10] 63.

[11] I. xv. 64. *Quam ob rem, si quis universam et propriam oratoris vim definire complectique vult, is orator erit mea sententia, hoc tamen gravi dignus nomine, qui, quæcumque res inciderit quæ sit dictione explicanda, prudenter et composite et ornate et memoriter dicet cum quadam actionis etiam dignitate.*

[12] Wilkins (note *ad loc.*) evidently takes *composite* in a general sense as referring to composition (*dispositio, collocatio*); for he says: "The defini-

But the traditional five parts of rhetoric are more than the table of contents of the manuals (*artes*). They constitute what we now call in college schedules a group of studies; and Crassus is contending for the group as a whole. What he has been insisting on is the importance and the scope of that first part which, in the long history of rhetoric, teachers have most often and most dangerously neglected, *inventio*, the investigation, analysis, and grasp of the subject-matter. He adds [13] that the orator, though in any given case he may gather his information from authorities, will express this information as no expert can express it; and he repeats that in one branch of knowledge he must himself be an expert, namely in human nature.

The practical difficulty of such a conception of oratory, rejoins Antonius,[14] is that we have not leisure to realize it. And if we had, should we not better spend our time on the practise of speaking? The manuals,[15] he adds somewhat evasively, have nothing to say about justice, temperance, etc.; they talk of introductions and perorations. The main thing[16] is that the orator should appear to his auditory to be the sort of man that he wishes to appear. That is the result of dignity of life, about which theories of rhetoric have no more to say than about the means by which men are moved [Crassus might have retorted by citing Aristotle's whole second book]. No rhetorician[17] was ever even a tolerable orator; many orators

tion includes all the five main divisions of oratory," and *dispositio* is not otherwise mentioned. But for the apparent intention to include all five parts, *composite* would more readily suggest *compositio*, which is the technical name for sentence movement, one of the subdivisions of *elocutio*. *Compositio* is consistently used in this special sense; but whether *composite* is so meant here or not, Cicero intended four of the five parts, if not five; and that suffices to establish his allusion to the traditional division. The issue between Crassus and Antonius has little to do with *dispositio;* it concerns the scope of *inventio*.

For the division of rhetoric see pages 21, 65, the table in foot-note 1a to Chapter V, and Wilkins's introduction, page 57.

[13] I. xvi.   [14] xviii.   [15] xix. 86.   [16] 87.   [17] xx. 91.

have never studied rhetoric.   The materials of rhetoric [in the large sense of material urged by Crassus] are too indeterminate[18] for an art.

"I call him a master [19] who can speak keenly and clearly to an average audience from the average point of view; but I call him eloquent [20] who more wondrously and largely can enhance and adorn what he will, and hold in mind and memory all the sources of all things that pertain to public speaking."

But what pertains to public speaking? How widely should the training for it range? The definition of Antonius obviously stresses *elocutio*. Whether he means to make this the main concern of the orator depends on whether he includes among his "sources" the fund of knowledge urged by Crassus. The context seems to show that he does not. To put his definition beside that of Crassus above is to see that its intention is narrower. It specifies no more than style, first as the amplitude and vividness that enhance a particular passage, and secondly as the orator's general virtuosity.

Crassus returns to the charge with a summary [21] of the actual training.   The student should practise [22] not only extempore speaking from outline, but also writing.   The writing that he advises here is not for the casting of a given speech in a particular form, but for education in range and control of expression.   To this end he recommends also wide reading.   The study of law, he adds,[23] should be both of technical detail and also of larger aspects and relations.

Antonius stands his ground.   His second definition of the orator is substantially a repetition of his first, merely sharpening the contrast.

---

[18] 92.   [19] *disertus*.   I. xxi. 94.

[20] *Eloquentem vero qui mirabilius et magnificentius augere posset atque ornare quæ vellet, omnisque omnium rerum quæ ad dicendum pertinerent fontis animo ac memoria contineret.*

[21] I. xxv–xxxv.   [22] xxxiii. 149 seq.   [23] xxxvi–xlvii.

"But the orator [24]—and he is the subject of our inquiry—I do not define as does Crassus, who has seemed to me to include knowledge of all sciences and arts within the orator's single function and name. I think him an orator who can use words agreeable to hear and thoughts (*sententiis*) adapted to prove in cases both forensic and deliberative; . . and I would have him also skilled in voice, gesture, and manner."

Lest there should seem to be a begging of the question in the word *sententiis*, which means thoughts and therefore may seem to imply the studies urged by Crassus, *sententia* should be understood rather of the brilliant expression of a single idea than of a line of thought or of intellectual grasp in general. That neither of the latter is intended here is shown by the context.

Because certain orators, Antonius resumes, have been masters of other things than oratory it does not follow that these other things belong to oratory. The most that can be said is that, to attain eminence in oratory, one must have heard, seen, and read much. Neither an orator's knowledge of human nature nor his use of this knowledge in speaking is scientific. Nor must the orator be a lawyer any more than he must be an actor. Mastery of law, of acting, of history, of other things, is, indeed, an advantage; but it is not a necessity to oratory. If the orator is to be, as Crassus has described him,[25] one who can speak in ways adapted to persuade, he must sacrifice many other studies in order to master his own proper art.

/ One closes the first book with the idea that both Crassus and Antonius are right. The two men, even more than the two views, are complementary. The views are irreconcilable only when pushed to the extreme; and in extreme form either the extensiveness of Crassus or the intensive-

[24] xlix. 213. *Oratorem autem, quoniam de eo quærimus, equidem non facio eundem quem Crassus, qui mihi visus est omnem omnium rerum atque artium scientiam comprehendere uno oratoris officio ac nomine; atque eum puto esse qui et verbis ad audiendum iucundis et sententiis ad probandum accommodatis uti possit in causis forensibus atque communibus: hunc ego appello oratorem eumque esse præterea instructum voce et actione et lepore quodam volo.* [25] lxi. 260.

ness of Antonius may become a *reductio ad absurdum*. Normally rhetoric is both extensive and intensive, both a comprehensive study of life and a specific art, even as the means of persuasion are both extrinsic and intrinsic. Doubtless Cicero meant to leave this impression; for he gives full weight to the theory of Antonius here, makes him the mouthpiece in Book II for the specific lore of *inventio*, which corresponds to the knowledge urged in Book I by Crassus, and makes Crassus in Book III the spokesman for style. But certainly Cicero sympathizes, and wishes us to sympathize, with Crassus. It is Cicero, not merely Crassus, who pleads that the teaching of the orator be not the imparting of tricks, nor mainly of technic in a wider and worthier sense, but the gradual bringing to bear of the whole man. He saw in the focusing of rhetoric on style a typical danger for teaching. The danger was present, apparently, in the teaching of his own day; it was serious in the time of Tacitus; it was epidemic in the schools of *declamatio* that spread along the Mediterranean and taught some of the fathers of the Church. The view of Antonius, uncorrected by the view of Crassus, is imperfect theoretically; practically it leads to the typical vices of the teaching of composition; historically it has branded a stigma on the word rhetoric and all its derivatives.

The view of Crassus, too, has its dangers: the danger of vagueness and dissipation, the danger of pretentiousness and sometimes of sciolism. But apparently these dangers can more readily be met and counteracted, and must be risked; for the history of rhetoric seems to show that his is the right emphasis and the more fruitful idea. Speaking and writing are less a profession even for orators and men of letters, much less for educated mankind in general, than a life. Though the same may be said of engineering, though all technical education involves general education, yet in learning to speak and write the technic is smaller in proportion to the general training. The training of Roman youth in oratory was at its best education for leadership. In this education composition was both end and means. It has been so always, it is so to-day, in the hands of its best teachers. The specific application is to open in the teaching of composition manifold relations. It thrives on what we now call correlation; it dwindles in segregation. For we may learn from Cicero to give rhetoric the same abundant relations to human affairs as he urges his orator to seek in all his oratory.

Because it has most of the Ciceronian message Book I has been the most studied and probably the most fruitful. The division of Book II is conventional. After glancing at the fields of oratory and the component parts of a speech and urging imitation, it treats *inventio* [26] and *dispositio* [27] under the usual heads and briefly summarizes *memoria*.[28]

Oratory, says Antonius, is essentially either deliberative or forensic; for Aristotle's third division, occasional oratory, is not so much a separate field as a particular direction and a fundamental habit of thought. Cicero is quite unconvincing here. Perhaps his own habit of introducing into forensic the ways of occasional oratory, as in his *Archias*, blinded him to the significance of Aristotle's third category.

The traditional *exordium*, *narratio*, etc., Antonius finds to be rather elements than parts, since the particular function of each is not confined to one place. From this perfunctory rehearsal we are awakened by suggestive advice to teachers.[29]

Those who really teach rhetoric are engaged less in drill than in promotion of the spirit that wins success.[30] "Therefore

[26] xxiv–lxxi.   [27] lxxii–lxxxv.   [28] lxxxvi–lxxxviii.   [29] xx. 84.
[30] *Animus acer et præsens et acutus idem atque versutus invictos viros efficit.*

I will train, if I can, so as first to discern what the pupil can do. Let him be imbued with literature; let him have read and heard something; let him have learned the rules; I will provoke him so far as is feasible to his utmost in voice, force, spirit. If I perceive that he can reach the heights, I will beg him, and if he seems also a good man, I will conjure him, to revise; so much social value do I attach to this technical skill for both the outstanding orator and the good man. But if, do what he will, he is going to remain mediocre, I will let him do what he will, and especially not nag him; if he is going to be positively offensive or ridiculous, I will tell him to close his lips or try something else. For neither can we ever desert the student of exceptional ability nor deter the one who has at least some ability. . .

"To begin at home,[31] Catulus, I first heard Sulpicius here in an unimportant case when he was a stripling. Though he showed physical equipment of voice, presence, gesture, his speech was rapid, hurried—a matter of temperament—and somewhat effervescent and superabundant—a matter of youth. I did not scorn him. I am glad to see youth exuberant. As with vines, it is easier to prune than to cultivate. You should have seen the change in him when next I heard him after he had studied Crassus."

The first specific counsel, then, is for the teacher promotion; for the student it is imitation, such as Sulpicius's of Crassus, not mere copying of mannerisms, but such as produces [32] schools of eloquence from the example of great orators.[33]

Under *inventio* the first task is the investigation of the facts.

"But finally [34] to bring the orator whom we are forming to actual cases . . . we will teach him first—laugh if you will—to know them thoroughly and deeply. This is not taught in

[31] xxi. 88.   [32] xxii.

[33] Tacitus (*Dial.* 34) says that the older method (of Cicero's time), supplanted in his own time by the schools of the *declamatores*, was apprenticeship.   [34] xxiv. 99.

school; for the cases assigned to boys are easy. For example: 'The statute forbids a stranger (*peregrinus*) to climb a wall; [this man] climbed; he repulsed the enemy; he is brought to trial.' No labor to know a case of this sort; for rightly nothing is taught [in school] about studying a case. But in the forum one has to know documents, contracts and agreements, decrees, the lives of the parties. Through carelessness in getting such knowledge men who in their anxiety to appear much in demand undertake too many cases often lose.[35] Not only so, but they may be suspected of bad faith or of incompetence.

For my part,[36] I take pains to learn the case from the client himself, alone, that he may talk more freely, and to debate against him, that he may defend himself and advance whatever arguments he has thought out. When I have dismissed him, I quite dispassionately take three parts: my own, my opponent's, the judge's. Whatever arguments promise more help than embarrassment I settle on, rejecting others in the same way. By this plan I manage to think at one time and speak at another.[37] Some speakers have the confidence to do both at once; but I am sure that they too would speak somewhat better if they recognized the advisability of setting aside one time for thought, another for speech."

Though this is a conventional topic, and though its application here is legal, it is none the less instructive generally; and it might directly improve the teaching of argument and the practise of debate in our colleges.

The second heading under *inventio* is also conventional, the *status*, or determination of the main character of the case and the main issues. The *status* was determined in the classical system by applying certain traditional questions. The *status legalis* may be set aside as applicable only to legal pleading. The *status rationalis*, or *status* considered in the general aspects of reason as an affair of common argument, was determined by asking oneself how

[35] xxiv 101.   [36] 102.   [37] 103.

far the debate hinged (1) on fact, on whether such-and-such things had happened, or (2) on definition, the facts being generally admitted, or (3) more broadly, on the interpretation of admitted facts and definitions. Though most cases need to be looked at from all these three points of view, in most there will be found a decided predominance of one; and forecast of this will direct the emphasis of the whole argument, will tell where to throw one's weight. This one is the *status* of that case.

In the Latin terms:
(1) if the main question is *an sit*, the *status* is *coniectura*, or *status coniecturalis;*
(2) if it is *quid sit*, the *status* is *finis*, or *status definitivus;*
(3) if it is *quale sit*, the *status* is *qualitas*, or *status generalis.*

Though Cicero's discussion [38] is necessarily conventional, he has keen practical suggestions. As to (2), which in his order is third, Antonius says:

"We are often advised to define the crucial term briefly;[39] but that is puerile. What we need is not a brief or abstract definition, as of terms like *law* or *state* defined according to the rule of neither too little nor too much. In the case I have mentioned neither Sulpicius nor I attempted definition of that sort. Rather each of us dilated on treason with every means of amplification. For mere definition, in the first place, is often snatched out of your hands if a single word be objected to or added or omitted; in the second place, by its very nature it smacks of teaching (*doctrina*) and almost childish practise; and finally, it cannot enter the perception and mind of the judge, for before it is grasped it slips past."

But the case must be surveyed also as to its ἦθος and its πάθος.

"Then I most carefully consider [40] both the appeal *of* my client's character and my own and the appeal *to* the feelings of

[38] xxiv–xxvi, 104–110. For the more detailed presentation of Quintilian see Chapter iv, page 74.   [39] xxv. 108.   [40] xxvii. 114.

those whom I address. So every theory of speaking seeks persuasion [41] through (1) establishing the facts, (2) winning the sympathy of the audience, and (3) arousing those of whom the case demands action." . .

"Teachers,[42] indeed, have divided cases into several kinds and have provided a fund of arguments for each kind. This is adapted to the education of the young; for as soon as a case is posed, they know where to find arguments for it. Nevertheless not only is it slow-witted to pursue rivulets, not discerning the fount, but it is becoming to our age and habit to summon what we wish from the source whence all things flow."

The lore of preliminary analysis is concluded with a brilliant summary under three questions of Cicero's own: [43] (1) what kind of case is it in general (*naturam causæ*), i. e., of fact or of interpretation? (2) on what does it turn, i. e., what is the point but for which there would be no debate? (*quid faciat causam; id est, quo sublato controversia stare non possit*)? (3) why is it disputed? how does the dispute arise (*quid veniat in iudicium*)?

The transition from argument to the other means of persuasion, from *probare* or *docere* to *conciliare* and *movere*, is the caveat of Antonius against the current division of cases into general and particular [44] as a capital error. Theoretically every particular case must have general relations; practically, if oratory is not to lapse into mere accumulation of details, the orator must have the habit of bringing these general relations to bear. Antonius adds the further caveat that the whole system of the *status* is merely analytical. It is logical; and logic shows only how to judge arguments, not how to find them.[45] The sources of arguments (*sedes argumentorum*) [46] are therefore more important.

---

[41] Hendrickson (Amer. Journ. Philol. xxvi. 260) finds this three-fold division first here. The usual terms are *docere, conciliare, movere*.

[42] xxvii. 117.   [43] xxx. 132.

[44] xxxi. 133.   [45] xxxviii. 157.   [46] xxxix. cf. above, xxvii. 117.

As to *conciliare* and *movere* [47] Cicero says only the usual things, perhaps because *inventio* in these aspects is rather to be promoted by exhortation than imparted by new categories.

Men take a decision oftener through feeling than through fact or law.[48] They are moved by evidences of character in the speaker and in his client.[49] Orators must have a scent for an audience, for what people are feeling, thinking, waiting for, wishing. To arouse feeling, the orator must have it himself.[50] He need not feign it; it arises naturally from his imaginative sympathy, as on the stage.[51] Emotional appeal is not to be made suddenly; it is to be led up to and down from;[52] and it demands full force of delivery.[53] The only way to rebut feeling is by feeling. Cicero adds the usual sections on wit and humor.[54]

The treatment of *dispositio* [55] gives little specific counsel toward the achievement of that sequence in which Cicero himself excelled.

In general, *dispositio* has to consider: how to make the most of the stronger points without seeming to slur the weaker; whether the case will prevail more readily through argument or through appeal, through direct proof or through refutation; how to cover retreat at need by making sure that the case, if it cannot be won, shall at least not be damaged. [To translate this doctrine into the terms of modern manuals, the first general consideration of *dispositio* is emphasis, both as proportion of space and as progressive iteration of main points.]

The traditional order [56] (*exordium*, *narratio*, etc.,) is natural; but the real problem is the arrangement, or sequence, of the proof and the weighing of arguments rather than the counting of them. [This is a practical caveat against the tyro's idea that he can prevail by sheer force of numbers. To be effective, an argument must be more than a series; it must be a line. Its progression is more than arithmetical; it is rather geometrical.]

[47] xlii–lxxi.   [48] xlii. 178.   [49] xliii. 182.   [50] xlv. 190.
[51] xlvi. 191.   [52] xlix–liii. 213.   [53] liii. 214.   [54] liv–lxxi.
[55] lxxii–lxxxv.   [56] lxxvi.

Appeal to feeling [57] should be rather pervasive than located in particular divisions. The strongest arguments should be put first and last; the exordium composed after the rest of the speech, in order to be the more carefully adapted [58] and more essentially related to the plaintiff,[59] the defendant, the case, or the judges. The *narratio*,[60] though concise, must be ample not only for vividness, but even for clearness. Constructive argument and refutation are to be considered together as a whole [i. e., debate is always at once destructive and constructive].

Without making panegyric [61] a separate kind of oratory, we can see that deliberative speeches offer more scope in that direction than forensic. Cicero adds general topics for panegyric.

The chapters on *memoria* [62] begin with the familiar story of Simonides, to make the obvious point that what furthers memory is order. Visual associations, Cicero thinks, are strongest, and can be used to recall even sentences. But verbal memory is less important. The orator's memory is of things.[63]

In Book III Crassus discusses style (*elocutio*). About a third of the book [64] amplifies the theme that rhetoric is inseparable from philosophy. What follows is a conventional treatment of the choice of words (*electio*) [65] and the movement of sentences (*compositio*),[66] with a few chapters on delivery.[67] These latter topics are handled so much more explicitly in *Orator* that only the first part claims analysis.

By style we mean generally diction that is idiomatic, clear, vivid, and apt.[68] Idiom and clearness we may take for granted. "All elegance of speaking, though it is polished by the study of grammar, is promoted by reading aloud orators and poets.[69]

[57] lxxvii.   [58] lxxviii.   [59] lxxix.
[60] lxxx.   [61] lxxxii–lxxxv.   [62] lxxxvi–lxxxviii.
[63] lxxxviii. 359. *verborum memoria, quæ minus est nobis necessaria . . . rerum memoria propria est oratoris.*
[64] xv–xxxvi.   [65] xxxviii–xlii.   [66] xliii–liv.
[67] lvi–lxi.   [68] x. 37.   [69] 39.

. . . If there be a certain Roman and urban tone, in which there is nothing to offend, to displease, or even to attract notice, nothing to sound or smell foreign, let us follow this and learn to flee not only country roughness but also foreign bravado.[70] . . . women more easily keep the pure tradition."

"That scheme of thought and expression and force of speaking the ancient Greeks used to call philosophy.[71] . . . For that ancient teaching appears to have been the preceptress alike of living rightly and of speaking well. Nor were the teachers separate; the same masters formed morals and speech." [72] From the scorn of Socrates for rhetoric arose the unnatural separation of rhetoric from philosophy . . "that divorce as it were of the tongue from the heart . . that one class of persons should teach us to think, another to speak, rightly." [73]

Philosophy has suffered by this separation. The Cyrenaic philosophy remains incomplete by dissuading from public life. The Stoic philosophy, though it declares eloquence to be virtue and wisdom, makes wisdom practically unattainable; and the dry abstractness of address cultivated by the Stoics is quite ineffective. Rhetoric, on the other hand, has suffered by being reduced to maxims of pleading. In a word, training in rhetoric, to be adequate, must include philosophy; and philosophy remains ineffective without rhetoric. This, of course, is the ideal; but it is not practically impossible; for we are not saying that the orator must be a philosopher, only that he must know philosophy.[74]

Therefore style must not be conceived either as the controversial acrimony of the forum or as conventional adornment borrowed by ignorance. The style must become the thought, not weary the audience by display; and the very idea of enhancing implies a store of thought.[75]

The futile distinction made by rhetoricians between a particular case and a general has this bearing on style, that eloquence consists in bringing to bear on every question those fundamental human aspects which can be exhibited only through large knowledge; for copiousness of style comes only

[70] xii. 44.   [71] sapientiam. xv. 56.   [72] 57.
[73] xvi. 61.   [74] xvii–xxiii.   [75] xxiv–xxvii.

from copiousness of thought. The Greeks gave oratory to philosophy, philosophy to oratory. Our Roman ancestors aspired to knowledge in all fields that touch civil life. The greatness of the arts has been diminished by division and separation.[76]

These twenty chapters are a brilliant instance of what the ancients meant by amplification. Logically they do little more than iterate the truism that style is inseparable from substance; but actually they make the truism live. Cicero is an admirable example of his own definition of the eloquent as those "who speak with clear distinctions, lucid order, amplitude, brilliance of matter and manner, and in prose weave something of the spell of verse—in a word, who enhance." [77] "Immortal gods! said Catulus, what a variety of things, Crassus, you have embraced! what force, what abundance! and from what poverty have you dared to lead the orator forth and establish him in the kingdom of his fathers!" [78]

[76] xxviii–xxxv.   [77] xiv. 53.   [78] xxxii. 126.

ORATOR

Cicero's *De oratore*, though it covers all five parts of rhetoric, is most ample as to *inventio*. His *Orator* is complementary in that it is largely devoted to *elocutio*.[79] Like the earlier work, *Orator* is specifically limited to deliberative and forensic oratory. Occasional oratory, or panegyric, though he declines again to treat it as a separate field,[80] Cicero recognizes as the "nurse of that orator whom we wish to form," especially in sentence skill.[81] *Inventio* [82] and *dispositio*,[83] as depending more on foresight than on eloquence, are barely summarized. *Elocutio* occupies three-fourths of the discussion.[84]

Orator has been less attractive than *De oratore* for the reason that it is more compact and more technical. None the less it has a cogency and a felicity even more characteristically Ciceronian. Few men writing on style have shown in their own styles so much precision and charm. *De oratore* keeps the fluency of dialogue; *Orator* shows more of Cicero's own mastery of the oratorical period.

The division of style into three kinds (*genus tenue, genus medium, genus grande*) [85] has been much discussed as to its origin.[86] Whatever its origin, it is dubious as philosophy and has been vicious as pedagogy. Cicero applies it later [87] to the three tasks, or objects, of oratory: to prove, to win

[79] Sandys notes that the avowed object is "criticism, and not direct instruction." This, however, is part of Cicero's literary method and of his habit of scorning the manuals. As to his main topic, *elocutio*, he writes *doctrina* as definite as that of *De oratore* on the other parts; and though his headings are not all conventional, his outline and order are thoroughly systematic.

[80] 37, seq.   [81] 40, *verba iunxisse;* cf. 77, *vinculis numerorum;* 208.
[82] 44, seq.   [83] 50, seq.   [84] 61–236.   [85] 20–23.
[86] See the articles by Hendrickson cited in the first foot-note to this chapter.   [87] 69.

sympathy, to move. He adds [88] that the orator should excel in all three directions. But this hardly warrants a division of style into three kinds; for actually the teacher too ready to classify, or the student too ready to think of style as separable and additional, may thereby deviate his whole study. Historically the trail of the three styles has been baneful. For inculcating style perhaps the least fruitful means is classification.[89]

But Cicero's discussion of style, though grouped at first by this classification, ranges beyond it.

DIGEST OF *ORATOR*, 61–236, ON STYLE [90]

Style (61) is the very mark of the orator. The diction of the philosophers (62–63) has neither the force nor the pungency of oratory; for the philosophers (64) are limited to abstract discussion, as the sophists (65) to decoration, and the historians (66) to a somewhat diffuse smoothness. The style of poetry (67) differs not in speed or vividness, but in boldness of diction (68) and in sometimes being pursued for sheer values of sound.

The three styles of speaking [91] arise from the orator's three objects: (69) to prove, to please, to move. Aptness, then, demands adjustment not only to the speaker (71) and the audience (72), but also to the object. What is proper to the plain style (*genus tenue*, 75)? This sounds so ordinary that it seems easier than it is; for, though not strong, it must be sound. It is untrammeled by cadences (77), is free without rambling, and neither fits word to word nor avoids the pleasant negligence of one elaborating matter rather than manner. It avoids peri-

---

[88] 100.

[89] One could wish that Cicero had been content with his two-fold division in *Brutus*, xxiii. 89: *cum duæ summæ sint in oratore laudes, una subtiliter disputandi ad docendum, altera graviter agendi ad animos audientium permovendos.*

[90] The digest of the whole *Orator* at pages lxxiv–lxxvi of the edition of Sandys need be neither repeated nor revised. Assuming this, I have added here certain significant rhetorical details, translation of some important passages, and the connection of the topics.   [91] See above.

odic structure (85) and dramatic delivery (86); but admits a careful use of wit (87–90). The median style (*genus medium*, 92), adjusted to the winning of sympathy (*conciliare*), aimed at the ἦθος of the audience, has as its chief character *suavitas;* as its chief exponent, Demetrius of Phalerum. The high style (*genus grande*, 97), aiming at πάθος, though it is the acme, is not to be pursued exclusively; for the perfect orator must be master of all three (100); the three may be modified (103), combined, and varied; and variety is necessary (109) both in any given speech and as a habit.

After a summary, 113–139, of the orator's necessary knowledge, especially of the other parts of rhetoric, Cicero passes to his main topic, harmony. Explaining (140–148) the importance of this, he defines it in its simplest aspect of euphony (149); negatively as the avoidance of hiatus, stops, and other awkward combinations, positively as balance, symmetry, the rounding out of the phrase by correspondence (165).

The rest of *Orator*, about one third (l–lxxi, 168–236) is devoted to prose rhythm under four heads: (a) origin, (b) cause, (c) nature, (d) use. Under the first Cicero develops a rhetorical doctrine of rhythm from Thrasymachus, Isocrates, and Gorgias. As to the second, its cause (177–8), he says: "The ear, or the mind through the ear, contains in itself a certain natural measure [92] of all spoken sounds." The third heading, the nature of rhythm, is treated at greater length (liii–lx, 179–203). Analyzing rhythm to show that it has an effect distinct from that of mere euphony, Cicero goes on to examine what this effect is (183). Since there is a distinct rhythmical effect in prose, it can be explained, though it appeals to sense, not to reason, and though it is less obvious and less essential than in verse. It is lacking (186) in earlier writers, Herodotus for example.[93] It has to be sought as a final grace of prose (186). "If there is (187) prose stinted and concise and other prose dilated and fluent, the difference must arise not

[92] *Mensionem*, 177. The word in a similar passage at 67 is *mensura*.

[93] Because, says Sandys, their style is unperiodic, and there can hardly be rhythm without periods. He cites the famous passage from Aristotle discussed above at page 27, and notes Quintilian's demur as to Herodotus. This is a fair inference from Cicero's context; and, indeed, the ancients generally considered prose rhythm as oratorical rhythm. The narrative

from the nature of letters (*litterarum*), but from the variety of intervals, long and short; and since prose is now steady, now shifting, according as it is woven and blended with these intervals, the nature of the difference (or of this variety) must reside in the rhythm (*numeris*, 187)." [94]

Prose being unmetrical, however, are its rhythms (188) still the same as those of verse? The feet must be the same; but what rhythms are available in prose? That any foot is possible appears in that we often fall carelessly into meter. Prose consists largely of iambs; but we often lapse into less familiar meters. It is plain, then, that prose feet are the same as poetic.

Some think iambic, as being most like real life (191), more suited to simple narrative; dactylic, to the dignity with which it is associated in heroic verse. Ephorus prefers the pæan or the dactyl to the spondee or the trochee because the latter are either too slow or too rapid. Aristotle, finding the heroic too grand for prose, the iambic too colloquial (192), and the trochaic too tripping, approves (193) the pæan. This is to be preferred as being less readily metrical (196); but it should be varied by other measures. Iambic is most frequent (197) in the plain style, the pæan in the grand style; but all should be mingled for variety. "Thus the hearers will hardly notice the snaring of their delight [in sound] and the pains to square the speech. These will be the less apparent if the words and thoughts are weighty; for those who are listening to these and liking them—the words, I mean, and the thoughts—while their attention and admiration are thus fixed do not notice the rhythm, though they would be less pleased without it." (197). Prose is rhythmical not (198) by never varying—that would be verse—but by movement neither limping nor fluctuating, but even and constant. Prose rhythm, therefore, is more difficult than verse. The rhythm of the period (199), in order to make such a close as the ear desires, must be marshalled

rhythms of imaginative prose were naturally not much discussed separately in a time when prose fiction was undeveloped. The nearest approach to these in oratory was in panegyric. But Dionysius with more discernment praises the *compositio* of Herodotus. (See below, Chapter v.)

[94] The translation is closer to that of Colin than to that of Sandys. The point—and if it is obvious, it is often forgotten—seems to be that variety in prose depends on rhythm.

that way from the start. Prose rhythm may arise, without rhythmical intention, from the harmonizing [95] of the phrase.

The use (204) of rhythm is most extensive in panegyric (207); in the other fields it enters when panegyric enters, or when statement of facts demands rather dignity than poignancy, often also in amplification, and most frequently in the peroration (210). For variety change (211) from the statements grouped and rounded in periods to statements detached (*incisa* and *membra*). Debate, more than exposition, needs speed. The cadence, or close (*clausula*, 215) may be in any one of several modes. The dichoreus, preferred in Asia (212), is admirable; but any one cadence palls. A full period (221) consists of four parts, or clauses (*membra*), i. e., is about the length of four hexameter verses; and is held together by *nodi continuationis*. When we wish to shift to detached short sentences (*membratim*), as we must often do in forensic, we pause, and break the rhythm that might suggest artifice. But even in such shorter reaches (223) we need rhythm, whether they be *incisa, membra,* or short periods; and these may be supported by a longer period, ending in a dichoreus or a spondee. The shorter reaches demand freer measures. They are of most force in forensic (225), especially in proof and refutation. Nor is any sort of speaking (226) stronger than to strike with two or three words, sometimes even with one, and then to interpose a rhythmical period.

Rhythm is not merely beautiful (227), but, like the beautiful motions of athletes, useful. Pursuit of it must avoid the appearance of artifice, padding (231) to round the cadence, the laming of the movement by too many short reaches, and monotony. Proof of the value of rhythm may be made by dislocating [96] the sentence movement of a good orator without changing the words, or conversely by rearranging the sentences of a careless orator (233). Those who affect to de-

---

[95] *concinnitas* (201). Cicero does not say explicitly what I have summarized in the last sentence above; but I think he implies it. He does not hint what Stevenson brings out in *Some Technical Elements of Style in Literature,* that subconscious rhythmical predilection may be a cause, or a determining factor, in adaptation.

[96] Dionysius of Halicarnassus exhibits this specifically with telling effect in the first part of *De compositione verborum.* See below, Chapter v.

spise rhythm (234) are unable to master it. Calling themselves Attic, they ignore the rhythm of Demosthenes. If
they prefer a loose style, let them follow it if they can show
even in their parts the beauty that is lacking in the whole (235),
or if they can compose in any other style; but the perfect orator (236) is master of all his art.

Cicero's treatment of rhythm in oratory, though sometimes vague and as a whole unsatisfying, is important
historically. Its very extent and care show that for the
orator, no less than for the theorist, rhythm in the classical
tradition was a main consideration. It was not something
additional, a final grace of style, but an essential element
of oratorical effectiveness. Moreover it was a primary
and controlling consideration in all that revision which is
spent on the shaping of sentences. The oral and auditory
ancients taught sentences more largely as movements in
time than do the writing and visual moderns. They
are thus the more instructive to those whose ears writing
and print have trained imperfectly. In every case, of
course, ancient or modern, the unit is logical, the expression of a thought; but whereas modern manuals generally
confine themselves to terms of syntax, the ancient rhetoric
is constantly aware of the effects of rhythm. Its analysis
of these, though it leaves much to be desired in scientific
accuracy,[97] serves at least to direct attention and stimulate
imitation; and more than the modern logic of the sentence
it seems to promote fluency.[98]

[97] For scientific analysis, with a succinct review of previous investiga-
tions, see W. M. Patterson, *The Rhythm of Prose*, New York, Columbia
University Press, 1916. For the *clausula* in particular see the summary
of Zielinski in Sandys, *Companion to Latin Studies*, 655; Quintilian below,
page 79; and M. W. Croll, *The cadence of English oratorical prose*. Studies
in Philology, 16:1, University of North Carolina, January, 1919.

[98] That the classical rhetoric has so little to say of narrative rhythms
is due not so much to the limited scope of ancient narrative as to the fact
that these rhythms are considered properly in poetic. See page 30.

CHAPTER IV

THE TEACHING OF RHETORIC

The pedagogy of rhetoric, more constant and more pervasive than that of most subjects still taught, demands historical interpretation, and thus extensive and consecutive survey.[1] Summary of its history has conveyed little of its vitality; but analysis of two cardinal documents will show, first, what the constant tradition of teaching was typically throughout the great classical centuries, and secondly what the teaching of rhetoric was destined to become, with almost equal constancy and pervasiveness, during the centuries of decadence. For each of these traditions there is fortunately, besides much other testimony, a typical text. Quintilian, writing long after rhetoric had ceased to function as an instrument of assembly government, nevertheless comprehends its best older tradition and the whole scope of its classical development in a great work of pedagogy, *De institutione oratoria* (about 95 A. D.). Seneca the Elder, who died about the time of Quintilian's birth, had already recorded from memory and notes in his *Controversiae* that particular application of the ancient schooling which in the generation before Quintilian was already infecting the old rhetoric, and through which the teaching of both Greek and Roman schools was to be dwarfed and perverted. Quintilian, though writing later than Seneca, preserves ancient rhetoric as a ripe whole; Seneca, though earlier, isolates the germ of its decay.

[1] Historical studies are relegated to a later volume.

I. QUINTILIAN ON THE TEACHING OF RHET-ORIC (*DE INSTITUTIONE ORATORIA*) [2]

A. TABULAR VIEW [3]

1. preliminary studies (προγυμνάσματα, I–II. x)

a. earliest lessons in speech	I. i–iii
b. studies with *grammaticus* (*ante officium rhetoris*)	
(1) in diction as usage	iv–vii
(2) " " " style	viii
(a) lectures on poetry (*prælectio*), with reading aloud (*lectio*)	
(3) in composition	ix
(a) retelling of fables	
(b) paraphrase of poetry	
(c) formal amplification of maxims (*chria*, χρεία)	
(4) in contributory subjects (music, geometry, astronomy)	x
(5) in enunciation (lessons from an actor)	xi

[2] The long and wide influence of Quintilian will be discussed in a later volume. It is briefly indicated by Sandys, *History of Classical Scholarship*, vol. I, and traced more specifically by Ch. Fierville in his admirable French edition of Book I (Paris, 1890), which also offers the best biography and bibliography. Much of the introduction in W. Peterson's edition of Book X (Oxford, 1891) is devoted to Quintilian's literary criticism.

The two modern English translations are (1) by J. S. Watson in the Bohn Library (Oxford, 1891, and probably earlier), and (2) by H. E. Butler in the Loeb Classical Library (London, 1921–2). Both occasionally miss the significance of technical terms. The former, providing summaries and many of the valuable notes of Spalding and Capperonier, is the more useful.

[3] Since Quintilian's survey includes all the cardinal terms of classical rhetoric, the corresponding Greek terms have been added for convenience of reference.

Compare the valuable analysis of the treatise *Ad Herennium* (current in the middle age as Cicero's) in the introduction to Wilkins's edition of Cicero's *De oratore*, vol. I, pages 56–64.

c. studies with *rhetor* (*prima apud rhetorem elementa*)
   (1) learning from his example   II. i–iii
   (2) exercises in composition   iv
     (a) rehearsal of events
       (x) summary of the plot of a tragedy or comedy
          (*fabula, argumentum*)
       (y) summary of historical events (*historia*)
     (b) elementary analysis of statements of fact
       (x) analysis of legends
       (y) analysis of history
     (c) elementary panegyric (*laudatio*) and parallel (*comparatio*)
     (d) amplification of typical propositions (*loci communes, theses*)
   (3) *rhetor's* analysis of models (*prælectio*)   v
   (4) speeches from assigned outline (*præformata materia*)
                             vi, vii
   [(5) advice to teachers on correction and promotion]
                            viii, ix
   (6) speeches on hypothetical cases (*declamatio*)   x
     (a) deliberative (*suasoriæ*)
     (b) forensic (*controversiæ*)

2. definition of rhetoric (II. xi–III. v)

a. function and scope   xi–xxi
b. origin and earlier development   III. i, ii
c. the five parts of rhetoric   iii
   (1) investigation (*inventio*, εὕρεσις, discussed III. vi–VI. v)
   (2) plan (*dispositio*, τάξις, discussed in VII)
   (3) style (*elocutio*, λέξις, discussed in VIII, IX)
   (4) memory (*memoria*, μνήμη, discussed in XI. ii)
   (5) delivery (*pronuntiatio, actio*, ὑπόκρισις, discussed in XI. iii)
d. the three fields of oratory   iv
   (1) occasional, panegyric (*demonstrativum*, ἐπιδεικτικόν; see chapter vii)
   (2) deliberative (*deliberativum*, συμβουλευτικόν; see chapter viii)
   (3) forensic (*iudiciale*, δικανικόν; see chapters ix–xi)

    e. the three aims of oratory   v
        (1) to inform (*docere*)
        (2) to win sympathy (*conciliare, delectare*)
        (3) to move (*movere*)

3. investigation and handling of material (*inventio*, εὕρεσις,
    III. vi–VI. v; *dispositio*, τάξις, VII)

    a. the nature of the case (*status*, στάσις)
        (1) in law (*status legalis*)
        (2) in reason (*status rationalis*) as having for its main issue
            (a) fact (*an sit, status coniecturalis, coniectura*, στοχασμός)
            (b) definition (*quid sit, status definitivus, finis*, ὅρος)
            (c) morals or policy (*quale sit, status generalis, qualitas*,
                ποιότης).
    b. the parts of pleading (IV. i–VII)
        (1) components
            (a) exordium (προοίμιον)   IV. i
            (b) statement of facts (*narratio*, διήγησις)   ii
            (c) excursus, proposition, division   iii–v
            (d) proof (*confirmatio*, ἀπόδειξις; as including appeal, πίστις)
                (x) evidence   V. i–vii
                (y) argument   viii–xi
                (z) order   xii
            (e) refutation (*refutatio*, λύσις)   xiii
                (x) destructive enthymeme
            (f) peroration (*peroratio*, ἐπίλογος)   xiv
        (2) pervasive elements   VI. i
            (a) appeal
                (x) imaginative   ii
                (y) humorous   iii
            (b) debate (*altercatio*)   iv
            (c) judgment (*iudicium, consilium*)   v
        (3) plan (*dispositio*, τάξις)   VII

4. style (*elocutio*, λέξις, VIII, IX)

    a. choice of words (*electio*, ἐκλογή, including figures)
                                           VIII. i–IX. iii
    b. sentence-movement (*compositio*, σύνθεσις)   IX. iv

5. training for facility (*firma facilitas*, X, XI)

a. reading to foster speaking	X. i
b. imitation	ii
c. writing for practise	iii
d. revision	iv
e. translation and other exercises	v
f. preparing the speech	vi
g. speaking the speech	vii
(1) adaptation	XI. i
(2) memory	ii
(3) delivery	iii

6. the orator himself

a. moral force and philosophy	XII. i, ii
b. knowledge of law and history	iii, iv
c. physique	v, vi
d. dealings with clients	vii–ix
e. styles of oratory	x
f. when to leave the platform	xi

B. The Terms

Quintilian's survey is in the traditional terms of classical rhetoric. These demand the more attention because translation has often missed the specific meanings attached to recognized technical terms. "Institutes of Oratory," never precisely rendering his title, is now almost meaningless. *Institutio Oratoria* means The Teaching of Rhetoric and announces not so much a manual for students as a survey for teachers. Of the pedagogical terms, *grammatica* and *grammaticus* may still be rendered "grammar" and "grammarian" only if they are understood to have wider scope. *Prælectio* (I. viii) describes the habitual introductory exposition of a passage of poetry by *grammaticus*, or less commonly of a passage of oratory by *rhetor* (II. v). *Materia*, meaning generally "material," means often technically (II. vi. vii) a prescribed outline, as French *matière* still does in pedagogical use. *Declamatio* (II. x) was quite different from "declamation." It was speaking, usually extempore, on an assigned hypothetical case, and grew, as will appear below, from an exercise for boys to an exhibition of virtuosity by men.

Of the five traditional parts of rhetoric (III. iii), the first, *inventio*, does not mean "invention"; it means, in Aristotelian language, the discovery of all the extrinsic means of persuasion, or more simply, survey of the material and forecast. *Dispositio* (*collocatio*) refers not to the arrangement of details, but to the plan of the whole. *Elocutio* means "elocution" in the sense borne by that word before the nineteenth century. It is sufficiently rendered by "style," and is always conceived in two aspects: (1) *electio*, the choice of words, including "figures of speech"; and (2) *compositio*, the arrangement of words in clauses and sentences, including rhythm and harmony—in a word, sentence-movement. *Compositio* does not mean, though it is often translated, "composition" in the wide sense now current. For the latter the term is *dispositio*. *Memoria* ranges far beyond memorizing. It embraces the speaker's whole command of his material in the order of his constructive plan and in relation to rebuttal, and was most stressed for speeches unwritten. *Pronuntiatio* and *actio* cover the whole field of delivery, including all that is now often called "elocution," from the placing of the voice to the handling of the body.

In detail, *status* (III. vi), meaning generally and simply "status," refers technically to a classifying system for determining "the nature of the case" (see 3. a, in the tabular view above). Of its three divisions, *coniectura*, having nothing to do with "conjecture," denotes a main issue of fact; *finis*, a main issue of definition; *qualitas*, a more general issue of morals or policy. *Narratio* (IV. ii) means never "narration" in the sense assigned by recent text-books, always either "statement of the facts" or, more generally, "exposition." These and other technical terms have been guarded, in the tabular view above and in the interpretations below, by adding the Latin originals.

C. TYPICAL DOCTRINE

(1) *Elementary Exercises*

The tradition of *grammatica* as having the twofold function of forming right speech and of expounding poetry [4] continued for centuries.[5] Traditional also are the first exercises in composition.[6] A chapter (x) on the concurrence of other studies toward a rounded education,[7] and one on elocution (xi), close a preliminary pedagogy so suggestive as to be still studied to-day.

(2) *Declamatio*

The counsels to *rhetor* (II) imply a warm atmosphere of promotion and a general habit of collaboration.

"The teacher himself should speak something—nay, many things a day—for auditory memory. Though reading aloud may supply a plenty of examples to imitate, nevertheless the living voice gives ampler nourishment, especially the voice of

[4] recte loquendi scientiam et poetarum enarrationem, I. iv. 2. ratio loquendi et enarratio auctorum, quarum illam *methodicen*, hanc *historicen* vocant, I. ix. 1.

[5] John of Salisbury, for instance, discusses it about 1159 in *Metalogicus*, Migne, 850 C. D.

[6] Προγυμνάσματα. The widely used compend of them by Hermogenes (late second century) includes myth, tale, chria, proverb, analysis destructive and constructive, commonplace, encomium, comparison, characterization (ἠθοποιία), description (ἔκφρασις), thesis, and the proposal of a bill.

[7] orbis ille doctrinæ quam Græci ἐγκύκλιον παιδείαν vocant, I. x. 1.

the teacher, whom the pupils, if they be rightly taught, at once love and respect. . . . Thus while mastery comes through writing, critical faculty will come through hearing." **II. ii.**

The teacher should frankly and fully show how. His criticism should beware of setting up inhibitions. To be promotive, he should find something to praise, and, besides explaining why he would have this out or that changed, should illuminate by interposing something of his own. Sometimes it will be helpful to give whole treatments which the boy may imitate without losing faith in his own (II. iv). In short, the teacher's *declamatio* should be a model for his students (II. v).

" In this teachers have shown a divergence of method. Some of them would develop orally the outlines that they gave their pupils to speak from, not content to guide by the [assigned] division. Not only would they amplify argumentatively, but also emotionally. Others, giving only a sketch, would after the pupils' speeches treat what each one had scanted. Some topics, indeed, they would elaborate with no less care than when they themselves were the orators. Either method is useful; neither, I think, should be separated from the other; but, if there must be a choice between the two, it will more avail to have shown the right way in advance than to recall from their error those who have already fallen." **II. vi. 1-2.**

The same promotive guidance appears in the assigning of outlines (*materiæ*), less and less ample as the pupils advance, for written composition (II. vi). This writing was generally for practise, not for casting a particular speech in form to be memorized. Sometimes, says Quintilian, the boys may recite what they have written out; but generally learning by heart is better spent on the orators and historians than on their own work (vii).

The *declamatio* recommended by Quintilian is speaking from outline on hypothetical cases. The more elementary assignments, for deliberative speeches, were called *suasoriæ;* the more advanced, for forensic speeches, *controversiæ.* Both he treats only as school exercises. Within these limits he recommends *declamatio* as an important pedagogical discovery.

" So soon as [the youth] is well taught and sufficiently exercised in these first tasks, themselves not small, but as it were members and parts of greater ones, let the time demand the essaying of deliberative speaking and forensic on assigned outlines. Before I go into the method of these, I must tell briefly what *declamatio* has as its idea, which is at once the most recent discovery and far the most useful. For it at once embraces almost all the exercises just discussed and offers the nearest likeness to actuality. Therefore it has become so popular as to be in the opinion of many sufficient of itself to develop eloquence. Nor can there be found any mastery in consecutive discourse which is not related to this exercise in speaking. True, the actual practise has so declined by the fault of teachers that among the chief causes corrupting eloquence have been the license and ignorance of *declamatores;* but we may use well what is essentially good.

"Let the outlines of the fictitious cases assigned be therefore as like as possible to actuality; and let the *declamatio,* so far as possible, imitate those pleas for which it was invented to prepare. Wizards, pestilence, oracles, stepmothers more cruel than those of tragedy, and other topics even more imaginary, we seek in vain among real law cases. What, then? Are we never to permit a young man to elaborate themes outside of statistics, even poetical ones, such indeed as I myself have mentioned, that he may have room, take some pleasure in the assignment, and enter as it were into the body [of the party he defends]? That used to be all very well; but at least let such [exercises] be grand and swelling without being silly and to critical eyes ridiculous." II. x. 1–6.

Evidently the *declamatio* that Quintilian recommends is not the *declamatio* that he heard about him. He wishes to recall to its original purpose what was already out of hand. Originally, he implies, it defined that general practise in debating which must have been as common in the ancient teaching as in modern universities. But already, as he also admits by implication, it had become quite different. Already it was established both as a special exercise and as a special form of public speaking. With the narrowing of the field of public discussion, the large old rhetoric surveyed by Quintilian had been narrowed more and more toward an artificial combination of forensic ingenuity with dramatic imagination. Instead of training youth to lead in public policy and to secure justice for individuals, *declamatio* had become an end in itself, the rhetor's own kind of oratory. As an exhibition of skill it was his easiest means of winning pupils, and of holding them by letting them exhibit themeslves. The inherent vice of artificiality, which Quintilian admits by implication, he nevertheless assigns entirely to perverted educational practise. He would recall *declamatio* from invention to actuality, and from display to exercise. That his warning was already too late is evident from Seneca (see section II of this chapter). Meantime one of the chief opportunities for perversion will be found in the *prosopopœiœ* described next.

The pervasive classical inculcation of appropriateness (see also XI. i) was carried into *declamatio* through specific exercises known generally as *prosopopœiœ* (προσωποποιίαι). Their idea was an imaginative entering into the character, the emotional as well as the intellectual habit, of the person for whom one was speaking (*fictœ alienarum personarum orationes*, VI. i. 25). In more elementary form, sometimes called *ethopœiœ* (ἠθοποιίαι) they bade the student say what Priam must have said to Achilles, or Sulla on renouncing the dictatorship, or some

other character of history or fiction on a critical occasion;
and they began even with the boy's amplification of fables
and myths.[8] As applied to *declamatio* (*suasoriæ* and
controversiæ) they are thus described by Quintilian:

"Therefore *prosopopœiæ* seem to me far the most difficult,
since they add to the other tasks of deliberative *declamatio*
(*suasoria*) the difficulty of characterization (*persona*). For the
same arguments must be urged in one way by Cæsar, in another
by Cicero, in another by Cato. But the practise is most useful,
either as a twofold task or as of the greatest interest to poets
also or to future historians. To orators it is even necessary.
For the many orations composed by Greeks or Latins to be delivered by others had to adapt what was to be said to the
speaker's habit of life. Did Cicero think in the same way, or
assume the same character, when he wrote for Pompey as when
he wrote for Ampius and others? Did he not, discerning the
fortune, the rank, the deeds of each of them, express the very
image of every one to whom he was giving voice, so that they
seemed to speak beyond themselves, indeed, but still as themselves? Nor is a speech less faulty for deviating from the person than from the case to which it should be adapted. Admi-

---

[8] Thus Hermogenes on the exercise of retelling myths: "Myths are
sometimes to be expanded, sometimes to be told concisely. How? By
now telling in bare narrative, and now by feigning the words of the given
characters. For example, 'the monkeys in council deliberated on the
necessity of settling in houses. When they had made up their minds to
this and were about to set to work, an old monkey restrained them, saying
that they would more easily be captured if they were caught within en-
closures.' Thus if you are concise; but if you wish to expand, proceed in
this way. 'The monkeys in council deliberated on the founding of a city;
and one coming forward made a speech to the effect that they too must
have a city. "For see," said he, "how fortunate in this regard are men.
Not only does each of them have a house, but all going up together to
public meeting or theater delight their souls with all manner of things to
see and hear.'" Go on thus, dwelling on the incidents and saying that the
decree was formally passed; and devise a speech for the old monkey."
Προγυμνάσματα, ed. Rabe, 2-3.
The exercise is still used in French schools, and for older pupils is carried, as by the ancients, into a sort of historical fiction.

rably, therefore, Lysias, in what he wrote for the untrained, is seen to have been faithful to their actual style.

"But *declamatores* [9] especially have to consider what befits each character; for the forensics (*controversiæ*) that they speak as advocates do are very few. Usually they become sons or fathers, rich, old, harsh, mild, avaricious, even superstitious, timid, or mocking, so that even comedy actors hardly conceive more ways of life on the stage than they on the platform. All these [exercises] may be regarded as *prosopopœiæ*. I have brought them under the head of *suasoriæ* because the only difference is in [the assumption of] character, although the exercise is sometimes extended also to *controversiæ*.[10] III. viii. 49–52.

[9] Though the word seems to refer rather to the masters than to the pupils, the whole passage none the less clearly indicates the nature and scope of the exercise for students. The dramatic skill of a *declamator* is described again in similar terms at X. i. 71; the use of *prosopopœia* in the peroration of legal pleading, at VI. i. 25–27.

[10] *Suasoriæ* and *controversiæ*, Quintilian adds, should not be treated as essentially different. So far as *prosopopœia* goes, they differ hardly at all; and otherwise they differ mainly in degree, *controversiæ* being more difficult.

Besides the consecutive discussion of *declamatio* in chapter x of Book II, much of which is quoted above, Quintilian has many incidental references and allusions. At IV. ii. 29, he defines *declamatio* as *forensium actionum meditatio*, "exercise in pleading", and he implies the same definition in *ad declamandum ficta materia* (I. x. 33) and in *fictas ad imitationem fori consiliorumque materias* (i. e., *controversias suasoriasque*, II. iv. 41). Steadfastly ignoring its use as a form of public speaking, he consistently treats it as a school exercise. He implies that *declamatio* embraced a large part of actual teaching when he complains (II. i. 8) that it is forecast by *grammaticus*, and calls *rhetor* (II. i. 3) *declamandi magister*. He says repeatedly that it depends largely on imaginative realization of character and emotion (VI. i. 25–27; X. i. 71; and the passage on *prosopopœiæ* quoted above). He admits the use of it as an exhibition of virtuosity (*in ostentationem*, II. x. 10), but satirizes this (II. xx. 3) by the anecedote commemorating the futile skill of a man who could throw grains through the eye of a needle. Though he regards it as a gymnastic profitable for mature speakers in providing variety and relief (X. v. 17), he has no patience with the common practise of keeping up indefinitely what is properly a school exercise (XII. xi. 15). Finally he repeats explicitly and implicitly his warning that *declamatio* should be kept close to actuality; and in a long passage (V. xii. 17–22) concluding his discus-

(3) *Status*

Quintilian's chapter (III. vi) on *status* is one of his most important, both as specific doctrine and as typical of ancient method. He has simplified a pedagogical device which, while it had been hampered by too analytical subdivision, had long vindicated itself as one of the most effective applications of the ancient theory of systematic guidance. *Status*, meaning the essential character of the case as it appeared to preliminary survey of all the material and all the bearings, had come to denote a uniform system for determining that essential character by leading questions. To gauge the sufficiency of his preparation and the line of his argument, to bring to bear not only his particular investigation, but the whole fund of his experience, the student was to ask himself what the case meant to him as a whole. He must interpret it as resting mainly on one of three issues: (1) of fact (*an sit*); (2) of definition (*quid sit*); or (3) of general considerations, as of right or expediency (*an recte sit*). The first was called *status coniecturalis*, or *coniectura;* the second, *status definitivus*, or *finis;* the third, *status generalis*, or *qualitas*.[11] Even if

sion of the *sedes argumentorum*, he indignantly condemns its perversion into prettiness as an emasculation of oratory.

Lucian, whose satire does not spare rhetors, makes specific mention now and then of *declamatio*, using the term μελέτη or μελετᾶν: *Demonax*, 33, 36; *Rhetorum præceptor*, 17. One passage is very like Quintilian's in the text above: "But the chief exercise and the aim of the art of dancing, as I said, is acting, which is practised in the same way by rhetors, especially by those who cultivate the so-called *declamationes*. Their art is the more applauded for its adaptation to the assigned characters and for its consonance with the persons introduced, whether princes, tyrannicides, poor men, or farmers." *De saltatione*, 65. Some of his satires, e. g., *Tyrannicida*, *Abdicatus*, and some of the *encomia*, sound like mock *declamationes*.

[11] Watson's (Bohn) translation quotes (foot-notes to pages 212–13 of volume I) Capperonier's tabular summary of the doctrine of *status* found

two of these entered, or all three, one must always be the focus.

The first *status* (*coniecturalis, an sit*) is most frequently determining in criminal cases at law; but it may be determining in any debate involving history, for instance on the question of the recognition of Anglican orders by the Roman or the Eastern Church, or on the question of the historical justification of the fifteenth amendment to the Constitution of the United States. Whether it is to be determining must usually be forecast by experiment; for the ancient system presupposes that all three *status* will be tried in preparation before one is chosen. Actually many arguments against the validity of Anglican orders have interpreted the *status* as *coniecturalis*; i. e., they rely mainly on establishing certain facts of the English Reformation. Others have chosen *status definitivus*. Though neither excludes the other, one, according to the ancient system and by the very conditions of public address, will always be for that particular speech *the status*. There can be no cogency without unity.

Erskine's defense of Lord George Gordon in a trial for treason was based on the second *status* (*definitivus, quid sit*). The facts alleged he admitted. That Gordon was concerned in a riot he did not challenge. *Status coniecturalis* he simply waived. He organized his case to show that what Gordon admittedly did could not be construed as coming within the term treason.

In the defence of Orestes, a familiar ancient assignment, the *status* could not, except by mere ingenious perversion, be *coniecturalis*. The facts of his killing of Clytemnestra and of her previous killing of Agamemnon had to be admitted. The *status* might, indeed, be *definitivus* for some one who cared to split hairs about what we now call murder or homicide; but naturally it was the third (*generalis, an recte sit*). Orestes was justified on the ground of the sacred duty to avenge the murder

in Quintilian, Cicero, the treatise *Ad Herennium,* and Hermogenes. For Cicero see also pages 49–51 above.

Jæneke's Leipzig dissertation (1904) *De statuum doctrina ab Hermogene tradita* compares by tabular view (pages 23–4, 120–1) the system of Hermagoras, as it is inferred from Cicero, Quintilian, and St. Augustine, with that of Hermogenes.

of his father. *The* issue was whether even a criminal mother should be executed by her own son.

College debaters defending the maintenance of the Monroe Doctrine settled on the third *status*. The forcing of the second by their opponents they found themselves prepared to rebut. The issues of democracy, protection, peace seemed to them vital as offering valid arguments for and against, i. e., as being real clashes of actual opinion; and all these issues fell under *status generalis*. *Status coniecturalis* could never be made determining. *Status definitivus* would lead to quibbling costly for opponents who should raise it. *Status generalis* held *the* issue.

This sort of forecast, surveying the whole trend, the ancients regarded as so vital that they reduced it to a system. The classified *status* is typical of their pedagogy of rhetoric. Their teaching of *inventio* did not stop with investigation; it promoted reflection directly and guided it so systematically that no essential aspect could be ignored. Such questioning for focus and line in our day of statistical accumulation is not less, but more valuable.

(4) *The Parts of a Speech*

The traditional parts of an oration Quintilian discusses (IV–VI) under their traditional subdivisions. The exordium (IV. i), for instance, may be drawn from the case, from the persons, from the occasion, or from rebuttal of one's opponent; and its threefold aim is to remove prejudice, to win attention, and to open the way for understanding.[12] But Quintilian often constructively recombines the traditional items, and often interprets them from teaching experience. The statement of facts (*narratio*, IV. ii) is not limited to pure exposition; even

---

[12] The maxim was *reddere auditores benevolos, attentos, dociles.* The classical lore on the third of these functions is surveyed by F. P. Donnelly, S. J., in *A function of the classical exordium,* Classical Weekly, V. 204–7, New York, May 11, 1912.

rehearsal may contribute to persuasion. Its cardinal
virtue of clearness he reasserts in rebuke of those students
whom an itch to be always impressive makes impatient
of the obligation.

> "When they have experienced the whole range, they will
> find nothing in eloquence more difficult than to say what every
> hearer thinks he would have said himself, because it seems to
> him not good, but true." IV. ii. 38.

That the statement of facts should be brief does not permit its being either abrupt or meager. That it should
sound true implies that it should be in character, i. e.,
that it should be dramatically consistent and convincing,
and also that it should lead into the argument. Similarly
practical are the warnings against making the division
(IV. v) too minute and against letting it hamper emotional appeal or interrupt progressive coherence. To his
conspectus of the ancient classification of proof (V) Quintilian adds (xiii) the following shrewd maxims for rebuttal:

> Defense demands more skill than attack.
> The system of *status* has one of its main uses in refutation.
> Rebuttal often consists largely in breaking down analogies.
> Never rebut what your opponent did not say.
> Neither be too anxious nor fight over every item.
> Peroration should be more than recapitulation; it should
> take occasion from the adversary. VI. i.

(5) *Plan*

Quintilian's discussion of *dispositio* (VII) is like that of
other ancient treatises in confining itself to plan in general.
Without specific doctrine for the promotion of cogency
as progressive coherence, it carries forward the system of
status as determining the main line of argument. That the
ancients appreciated and practised what is now taught in

American schools and colleges as the lore of paragraphs
is evident in their best composition, notably in the orations
of Cicero.   The decline from such progressive coherence
among the later *declamatores* is one of the marks of decadence (see section II, below).   But how the lore was
taught we are left to infer.   The elementary working out
of what is now unfortunately called a detached paragraph,
i. e., of a single short composition, is prescribed in the
chria (I. ix) much as in modern manuals; but that does not
touch the art of composing a sustained speech *by* paragraphs.   In the cogency of mounting by stages we miss
the typical systematic instruction.   Some of this must
have been inculcated through assigned outline (*materia*,
page 67 above), some of it by the rhetor's oral teaching.
Quintilian's instruction as to the close of the exordium is a
clear hint of what is now taught as paragraph emphasis.

"The proem should put last that to which the beginning of
what follows can most conveniently be linked."   IV. i. 76.

There are, indeed, other hints; but that so important an
aspect of composition should not be a distinct topic even
in Quintilian's constructive pedagogy leaves the ancient
lore of *dispositio* too analytical to be sufficient for modern
teachers.

(6) *Style Analyzed*

Quintilian's long discussion of style (*elocutio*, VIII–XI)
opens with one of his best sayings, "let care in words
be solicitude for things"; [13] and the whole introduction

[13] Curam ergo verborum rerum volo esse solicitudinem. VIII, proem,
20.   The passage goes on: "For generally the best words are inseparable
from their things, and are discerned by their own light.   But we look for
them as if they were always lurking and hiding.   So, forgetting that they
must be near the subject-matter, we seek them elsewhere and, when we

is an admirable answer to the old quibble about form and substance. If he thereupon proceeds for two books by the usual categories, he at least avoids the subdivision that had become excessive, and provides a convenient guide to the voluminous classical lore of *elocutio*.[14] Typical is his introduction, under sentence-movement (*compositio*, IX. iv), to the doctrine of sentence close (*clausula*).

[" Though rhythm must be pervasive] it is more demanded in closing cadences (*in clausulis*) and more obvious; first, because every thought has its own conclusion and demands a natural pause to separate it from the beginning of the one that follows; and furthermore, because the ear, having followed an oral sequence, having been guided by the current of flowing prose, is more critical when that movement stops and gives time to consider. Neither hard, therefore, nor abrupt should be the place where the attention takes breath and is renewed. Here is the dwelling-place of prose; here is the point to which the audience looks forward; here speaks the orator's whole merit." IX. iv. 61–62. (The text of the last sentence is dubious; but the general intention of exalting the importance of the *clausula* is clear.)

(7) *Style Promoted*

Having followed the usual analysis of style, Quintilian proceeds (X) to constructive promotion, to the ways of gaining secure control (*firma facilitas;* see the tabular view, page 66). "We who contemplate oratorical power, not mountebank volubility, have to inculcate both range

have found them, lay hold of them by force. A higher spirit is needed for essaying eloquence; for if she is in sound health throughout her frame, she will not think her care should be spent on manicuring and hairdressing." Fronto, on the contrary, praises the young Marcus Aurelius for digging up words, "ut verbum ex alto eruas et ad significandum adcommodes," ed., Haines, I. 6.

[14] For Aristotle's treatment see above page 24; for Cicero's, pages 53, 57; for those of Dionysius and "Longinus," Chapter V.

and discrimination" (*copia cum iudicio*, X. i. 8). So the vivid impressions that come through the ear should be supplemented by critical reading. The reading of poetry promotes concrete realization, heightening of style, emotional appeal, and aptness in characterization. [15] From imitation Quintilian passes (X. iii) to writing for practise in style. Since this, like deep plowing, is for a better yield, he goes into specific counsels.

Repeat what you have just written, both for connection and to warm up afresh. Fluency comes from habit, not from haste. You will not learn to write well by writing rapidly; you will learn to write rapidly by writing well. Lolling and looking at the ceiling will not answer; you must follow a plan (*ratio*). Rapid extempore draft (*silva*) has this disadvantage, that subsequent revision, though it may amend words and rhythm, is likely to leave the superficiality (*levitas*) that has arisen from hasty crowding. Better exercise prevision, and so conduct your work (*opus ducere*) from the beginning that revision shall be polishing, not entirely making over.

Dictation, by either urging or delaying the natural pace of composition, leads to crude, random, or inept expression. It is neither writing nor speaking; for it has neither the accuracy of the one nor the impetus of the other. Incidentally it precludes those motor activities which help composing when one is alone. [16]

Though solitude is best—night, the closed door, the single light—since you cannot always have it, learn abstraction. X. iii. 3–28, paraphrased.

In transition Quintilian observes that meditation (*cogitatio*, X. vi) for speaking without writing can go so far as to fix not only the order of points, which is enough,

[15] in rebus spiritus et in verbis sublimitas et in affectibus motus omnis et in personis decor. X. i. 27.

[16] For an interesting note on dictation as practised by a professional orator, see H. von Arnim, *Leben und Werke des Dio von Prusa*, page 140.

but even the connection of words. The value to the speaker of practise in writing is to make channels (*formæ*) for such meditation. Since meditation must always leave a margin for improvisation, the plan must be such as may be easily left and resumed. In other words, to give the speaker secure control, the plan must be progressive. Iterating this in the next chapter,[17] Quintilian adds that the other main means to extempore power is concrete realization.[18]

Writing gives speaking precision; speaking gives writing ease (X. vii. 29). From this summary of their general relations in education, Quintilian passes to the use of writing in the preparation of a particular speech.

"Busy pleaders commonly write the most essential parts and the beginnings [i. e., of paragraphs, so as to be readier to pick up the constructive pattern after weaving in rebuttal impromptu]. The rest of their prepared matter they grasp by meditation; and what arises suddenly they meet extempore." X. vii. 30.

Brief notes to be held in the hand are admissible, but not what is advised by Lænas, to write out the whole speech and then sum it up in outline.[19] X. vii. 32, paraphrased.

The secure control that Quintilian seeks to promote, that *firma facilitas* which is the subject of the whole tenth book, is evidently quite different from mere fluency. With the gift of gab in boys he has long ago expressed his impatience. "Impromptu garrulity, without the

[17] via, X. vii. 5; intendendus animus . . usque ad ultimum, X. vii. 16.
[18] imagines, X. vii. 15.
[19] The interpretation is substantially that of Luigi Valmaggi: "Insomma il precetto di Quintiliano è questo, che occorre o recitare a memoria o improvvisare sia pure su appunti presi meditando il discorso, ma è d'uopo evitare assolutamente una miscela dei due sistemi." *Osservazioni sul libro x di Quintiliano*, in Atti della reale accademia delle scienze di Torino, 37: 228.

meditation that the master intends, almost without hesitation in rising to speak, is really the brag of a mountebank" (II. iv. 15).   He not only presupposes, he specifically inculcates, most careful preparation.

(8) *Memory*

In this preparation the importance that he gives to writing, not only for general practise, but for the composition of a particular speech, may seem greater than is warranted by experience.   Even so he is far from supporting those who represent classical oratory as having been generally written and memorized.[20]   That the urgencies of public address could be met by that method is *a priori* a difficult assumption; and even the spread of the oratory of display in his time, and his own professorial fondness for finish of style, did not lead Quintilian to urge memorizing generally and unreservedly.   Rather what he offers

[20] Our modern habits of writing and reading hinder our comprehension of the speaking and listening ancient world. Especially are we liable to misinterpretation of the idea of writing in the ancient rhetoric. This contemplated primarily general training in style. It also included some written preparation for a particular speech, and finally the writing out of some speeches, especially speeches on occasion, in full. But that this last was the general ancient practise has never been sufficiently supported and is *a priori* improbable. The writing out of speeches after they had been spoken, and the common ancient practise of writing speeches for other men to learn and deliver, are not in point, and must be kept apart from the question of written preparation. The traditional quarrel between the ancient oratory which relied more and that which relied less on writing is admirably summed up by Van Hook, *Alcidamas versus Isocrates; the spoken versus the written word*, in the introduction to his translation of the attack of Alcidamas *On those who write written speeches*, Classical Weekly, XII, 89–94, New York, Jan. 20, 1919. Though there is ground for difference of opinion in interpreting what we can learn of the habit of Demosthenes or of Cicero, there is no ground for assuming that the ancient counsels of care in preparation generally imply writing out. Quintilian, who leans toward written preparation, is by himself almost sufficient testimony to the contrary.

under *memoria* (XI. ii) has the usual wide ancient scope. It should be read in its connection with what he has already taught (X. vi. vii, page 80 above) about *cogitatio*.

"All training rests upon memory . . . It is the power that makes available funds of examples, laws, decisions, opinions, precedents, funds which the orator ought to have in abundance and at command. Rightly is it called the treasury of eloquence.

"Those who plead much ought not only to retain surely, but to discern [bearings] quickly, not only to grasp what has been written by reading it over and over, but to follow the sequence of points and words in what has been [merely] thought out,[21] to remember the points made on the other side, and, instead of rebutting them seriatim, to bring them in where they will be opportune. Nay, extempore speaking seems to me to rest upon no less vigor of mind.[22] For while we are saying one thing, we have to be considering what we are going to say. So while thought (*cogitatio*) is always questing beyond what is [actually on the carpet], whatever it finds meantime it deposits, so to speak, in the memory; and the memory, as it were a third hand, transmits what it has received from forecast (*inventione*) to expression (*elocutioni*)." XI. ii. 1–3.

Devices and exercises for training and applying such a faculty (XI. ii. 8–35) are summed up (36) under the two principles of *divisio* and *compositio*, definiteness of outline and definiteness of sentence movement. The former is thus iterated for the third time (see X. vi. vii) as essential. The importance of the latter lies in the fact that the mind more readily retains settled rhythms (39). As verse is easier to memorize than prose, so periodic rhythms than unperiodic.[23] Thus Quintilian faces finally

[21] *Cogitatis*, with obvious reference to *cogitatio* in X. vi. vii.

[22] Note that *memoria* is vigor of mind, and that it is first, as often, applied to extempore speaking.

[23] For Aristotle on this aspect of the period (*Rhetoric*, iii, 1409 b), see 27 above.

the question of learning by heart. That it was a question, even for Quintilian, shows that classical practise was divided, as modern practise is, by differences both in talent and in the field of habitual exercise.

"From this diversity of talents arises the question whether the preparation of a speech should go so far as learning by heart (*ad verbum sit ediscendum dicturis*), or only far enough to grasp the force of each point and the order (*an vim modo rerum atque ordinem complecti satis sit*). As to this doubtless no rule can be proclaimed as universal. With a memory strong enough, and with time enough, I should like to hold every syllable. Otherwise it is idle to write [the speech out. Such power] is to be secured especially in boyhood, and memory to be trained to that habit, lest we learn to excuse ourselves. Therefore to be prompted or to refer to notes is a fault, because it encourages slackness, and there is no secure hold without some anxiety not to lose. By prompting or the use of notes the impetus of delivery is interrupted, the speech halting and abrupt; and he who speaks as if he were reciting forfeits the whole charm even of what he has written well by betraying that it has been written [i. e., memorizing, to be effective, must be perfect].

"Memory can even give such an impression of impromptu talent that we seem not to have brought the speech from home, but to have laid hold of it on the spot; and that is a great advantage both to the orator and to his case . . .

"But if memory is less tractable, or if time does not suffice, tying oneself to words will be useless, since the forgetting of a single one may lead to awkward hesitation, or even to silence. It is far safer, having firmly grasped the substance, to give oneself freedom of expression." XI. ii. 44–48.

D. Scope and Plan

The comprehensive program announced by Quintilian in his proem is carried through. No other ancient treatise is so exhaustive.[24] Including all the traditional topics, he

[24] See the tabular view above (page 63, with foot-note 3) and Quintilian's own review and forecast in the proem to Book VIII.

proceeds upon the classical theory of systematic guidance, but makes the important contribution of pedagogical order. For his plan is progressive. Though sometimes anxiously analytical in subdivision, he is constructive in making his main line not the survey of the subject, but the development of the student. The traditional five parts of rhetoric stand out clearly; but they cover only about half of the space, and they do not determine the plan. Rather Quintilian proceeds from less to more, from boyhood through adolescence to manhood. His idea is to widen and deepen the practise of public speaking as it opens more and more to the growing speaker. Aristotle's philosophy of rhetoric begins with the speaker as theoretically the efficient cause; Quintilian's pedagogy ends with the speaker as practically the efficient result. So, before entering upon definitions, he devotes two books to practical exercises, beginning not with the subject, but with the boy.[25] So, after he has defined the field and scope, he expounds *inventio* as in practise it expands, and links it with *dispositio*. So the two books in which *elocutio* is traditionally analyzed are followed by the two that show practically how it may be achieved; and these two are the culmination, the final application of all the preceding doctrine. His *Institutio* is faithfully what its title proposes, a pedagogy of rhetoric.

That it keeps its place in the history not only of rhetoric, but of education is due, of course, to Quintilian's cogency; it is due also to the largeness of the subject. Rhetoric, for the fortunate few who alone could aspire to leadership, comprised most of the higher systematic education. The

[25] How deliberate and consistent is his order appears, for instance, at the opening of II. xi, where the definitions begin: Iam hic ergo nobis inchoanda est ea pars artis ex qua capere initium solent qui priora omiserunt.

scope so brilliantly vindicated by Cicero [26] is taken by Quintilian as a matter of course. Thus his work is in more than one aspect a general pedagogy. Thus also rhetoric itself, to fulfil his demands and follow his methods, must keep his conception of bringing to bear the whole man. The narrowing of rhetoric in practise arose from the narrowing of public life and meant the narrowing of education.

[26] See Chapter III, pages 38, 46.

II. DECLAMATIO IN SENECA,[27] TACITUS, AND PLINY

A. DECLAMATIO

The *declamatio* exhibited by Seneca, though already established, was fairly new at Rome.[28] Cicero, writing about the time of Seneca's birth, still uses *declamare*, *declamatio*, and *controversia* [29] in their older general senses. His approval of practise speaking on hypothetical cases was apparently of something like our modern "moot courts." *Controversiæ* of the Senecan sort he knew only in their incipiency.[30]

Tacitus, writing his *Dialogus de oratoribus* about 81 A. D., a few years before Quintilian's *Institutio*, shows clearly that the specialized *controversiæ*, from being common, had become pervasive almost to the extent of monopoly.

[27] The best edition is *Sénèque le rhéteur, controverses et suasoires*, traduction nouvelle (with expository introduction), texte revu (in fine print at the bottom of each page), Henri Bornecque (Lille), 2 volumes, Paris (Garnier), 1902.

The best discussion is also by Bornecque, *Les déclamations et les déclamateurs d'après Sénèque le père*, Travaux et mémoires de l'Université de Lille, nouvelle série, I. Droit, Lettres—fascicule 1, Lille, au siège de l'Université, 1902 (bibliography, index of authors cited other than Seneca, catalogue raisonné of *declamatores*).

Incidental and more general discussion will be found in standard treatises on Roman literature of the Empire, in G. Boissier's *La fin du paganisme*, and in his *Tacite*, pages 200–240.

Peterson's translation of the *Dialogus* of Tacitus is published in the Loeb Classical Library.

[28] For a summary of the earlier Greek history see Bornecque, *Déclam.*, 40.

[29] E. g. *De orat.* I. 140.

[30] Commentabar declamitans—sic enim nunc loquuntur. *Brutus*, 310. On this point Seneca has no doubt:—Declamabat autem Cicero non quales nunc controversias dicimus, ne tales quidem quales ante Ciceronem dicebantur, quas thesis vocabant. Hoc enim genus maxime, quo nos exercemur, adeo novum est, ut nomen quoque ejus novum sit. Seneca, *Controversiæ*, I. præf. 12.

From the older, Ciceronian position of comprehensive
training his Messalla derides *declamatio* and all its works.

"As to this [education of an orator] the great men of the past
had made up their minds. To bring it about they discerned the
need not of *declamatio* in the schools of the rhetors, nor of exer-
cising tongue and voice in imaginary *controversiæ* without specific relation to actuality, but of filling the mind by the technic
(*artibus*) of discussing (*disputatur*, i. e., discussing after the
manner of the philosophers) good and evil, honor and dishonor,
justice and injustice; for this is the orator's subject matter
(*subiecta ad dicendum materia*)." Tacit. *Dial.* 31, 1.

[The dialogue, which of course gives more than one point of
view, but none the less clearly shows the position of Tacitus,
proceeds from such general studies to the old custom of appren-
ticing oneself to an experienced orator (31–34), and then contrasts the modern habit as follows.]

"But now our striplings are drawn off into the schools of
those who are called rhetors. How little, just before Cicero's
time, these teachers pleased our ancestors is evident from the
fact that the censors Crassus and Domitius bade them close, as
Cicero puts it, their 'schools of impudence.' Well, as I started
to say, the boys are drawn off into schools in which it would be
hard to say whether the place itself, or their fellow students, or
the sort of exercise, is likely to do their talents more harm.
The place has no respect, since every one is equally unskilled;
the fellow students give no impetus to progress, since boys
among boys and youths among youths speak and are heard
with equal carelessness; but the exercises are in great part positively thwarting. For two sorts of themes are handled with
the rhetors: *suasoriæ* and *controversiæ*. Of these the *suasoriæ*,
as being easier and demanding less foresight (*prudentia*), are
left to the boys; the *controversiæ* are assigned to those of more
power. My word! what assignments! and how incredibly composed! It follows, moreover, that *declamatio* may be applied
to an assignment far removed from actuality. So it comes to
pass that they pursue with great words rewards for tyrannicides, or the choice to be made by ravished maidens, or incests
of matrons, or whatever is argued as often in school as sel-

dom in the forum. When they come before real judges—"
. . . Tacit. *Dial.* 35, 1-7.

What Quintilian deplores, then, in the practise of *declamatio* Tacitus shows to have been none the less common. All the more significant is the slight and as it were unwilling consideration that Quintilian gives to these fashionable aspects. Even while he insists on the value of *declamatio* for general training, he deprecates that wide departure from actual pleading in themes, conception, and style which Seneca records as a matter of course and Tacitus derides as habitual. The use of *declamatio* by mature speakers not for exercise, but for exhibition, he passes over incidentally in a few sentences as a perversion. Its undoubted prevalence he admits sadly as something that a serious teacher should ignore.[31] Both the scorn of the historian and the reservations of the teacher spring from the older, larger tradition of rhetoric. To this both Tacitus and Quintilian discerned in *declamatio* a menace. How far their fears were justified will appear in later narrowing and perversion. Meantime they have supplied for interpreting the collection of Seneca not only the ancient standard, but also the necessary information.

B. CHARACTER AND SCOPE OF SENECA'S COLLECTION

Seneca's *Controversiæ* [32] is a collection of the *declamationes* made by celebrated rhetors. Though Seneca may well have used published material, his extensive reports, as it were verbatim,[33] at once attest the grasp of the ancient

[31] See above, pages 70–73 and foot-note 10. The objection of Petronius, *Satyricon* i. 2, is less specific.

[32] Seneca the Elder (sometimes called the Rhetor, circ. 56 B. C.—39 A. D.) made the collection in his last years.

[33] Bornecque, *Déclam.* 25, thinks that the *Controversiæ* may be taken as substantial reproductions.

memoria and suggest, amid considerable variety, a fund of
stock cases. To exhibit the rhetors' skill by competition,
his plan is to show side by side different treatments of the
same theme. He interpolates specific, and, in the prefaces
to the several books, general criticism. Though he does
not offer his collection of models explicitly as a comprehensive guide, his pervasive implication is that *declamatio*
exhibits the cardinal virtues. Rhetoric might with more
safety tend to monopolize education so long as it had its
old comprehensiveness; but as it was narrowed, it tended
to put the cart before the horse. "Give your mind to
eloquence," says Seneca; "from this you can range easily
into all arts." [34] The idea is almost opposite educationally
to Cicero's view that eloquence is nourished by all studies;
and the eloquence exhibited by Seneca is itself much
smaller than that intended by Cicero.

(1) *Subjects for Suasoriæ*

Suasoriæ were deliberative; *controversiæ*, forensic.
Though in actual practise the one field of oratory seems as
difficult as the other, in pedagogical use *suasoriæ* were
generally assigned as elementary exercises, the boy's
first extended compositions with the rhetor.[35] The seven
surviving specimens of Seneca's collection are on the following themes:—

1. Alexander debates whether to embark on the ocean.
2. The three hundred Spartans sent against Xerxes debate,

---

[34] *Controv.* II, præf. 3. J. W. H. Walden quotes a similar counsel from
Libanius, *Ep.* 248: καὶ σύ τοι τὸ ἄρχειν ἔχεις ἀπὸ τοῦ δύνασθαι λέγειν.
The Universities of Ancient Greece, page 78, foot-note.

Bornecque, *Déclam.* 135, sums up the situation as follows: "la rhétorique, devenue l'étude unique, perd, du même coup, le contact avec la
réalité . . . et elle dépouille à peu près toute valeur comme moyen
d'éducation oratoire et général."

[35] Tacitus, *Dial.* 35–5, quoted above, page 88. Quintilian, II. iv. 25.

after the flight of the expeditionary forces from the rest of Greece, whether they too shall flee.

3. Agamemnon debates whether to sacrifice Iphigenia, when Calchas has declared that the Trojan expedition cannot otherwise set sail with the consent of the gods.

4. Alexander the Great debates the entry into Babylon after the auguries have warned that danger lurks for him there.

5. The Athenians debate whether to remove the monuments of their victories over the Persians, Xerxes having threatened to come back unless they do so.

6. Cicero debates whether to appeal to Antonius for mercy.

7. Cicero debates whether to burn his writings, Antonius having offered him immunity on this condition.[36]

That the subjects seem to have been always historical reminds us that Roman deliberative oratory was barred from its natural field of the living present. Thus restricted, it is meager even for a school exercise.

(2) *Subjects for Controversiæ*

The cases assigned for the *controversiæ* of older students, though more various, were even more removed from actuality. The list of those used by Seneca to exhibit the skill of the rhetors themselves fully justifies the exclamation of Tacitus,[37] *quales, per fidem!* Posed as available for argument on either side—a rhetor would sometimes espouse now one side, now the other—they are difficult,

[36] C. T. Cruttwell translates the second of these at page 335 of his *History of Roman Literature*.

The subjects mentioned incidentally by Quintilian are similar:— Deliberant Patres conscripti an stipendium militi constituant. III. viii. 18. Deliberant Patres conscripti an Fabios dedant Gallis bellum minitantibus. 19. Deliberat C. Cæsar an perseveret in Germaniam ire, cum milites passim testamenta facerent. 19.

Pompeius deliberavit Parthos, an Africam, an Ægyptum peteret. 33. Deliberat Cæsar an Britanniam impugnet. VII. iv. 2.

[37] *Dial.* 35. 5, quoted above, page 88.

subtle, sensational, often so dubious as to preclude quotation, always remote. On their face they were chosen and iterated by men who desired sensation, prized ingenuity, and had turned the art of persuasion to advertisement.

A Disinheriting Uncle (I. 1)

"Children who refuse support to their parents are liable to imprisonment."

Two brothers quarreled. The son of one of them, in spite of his father's prohibition, supported his uncle, who had fallen into poverty. Disinherited on this account, he made no legal protest. He was adopted by his uncle. Through a legacy the uncle became rich. The father began to be in want. The son supported him in spite of the uncle's prohibition. He was disinherited. [Speak for either the young man or the disinheriting uncle.]

The Pirate Chief's Daughter (I. 6)

[A young man] captured by pirates wrote to his father for ransom. He was not ransomed. The pirate chief's daughter induced him to promise marriage if he got his freedom. He promised. She left her father to follow him. He has returned to his father and has married her. An orphan heiress comes along. His father bids him repudiate the pirate chief's daughter and marry the heiress. When he refuses, he is disinherited. [Defend either the father or the son.]

An Oath of Husband and Wife (II. 2)

A husband and a wife made an oath that if anything happened to either, the other would die. The husband, traveling abroad, sent a messenger to his wife to announce that her husband had died. She threw herself from a cliff. Having recovered, she is bidden by her father to leave her husband. She refuses. She is disinherited. [Speak for either the wife or her father.]

Poison Given to a Maniac Son (III. 7)

A father has given poison to a son who was raging mad and did violence to himself. The mother brings action for cruelty. [Speak for either the father or the mother.]

Crucifixion of a Slave who Refuses Poison to his Master (III. 9)

A sick man has asked his slave to give him poison. The slave has not given it. The master provides in his will that his heirs shall crucify the slave. The slave appeals to the tribunes. [Speak for either the appellant or the respondent.]

An Exiled Father Excluded from his Lands (VI. 2)

"Aiding an exile with shelter or food is prohibited."
"The penalty for homicide shall be exile for five years."

The father of a son and a daughter was found guilty of homicide and exiled. He used to come to one of his properties near the frontier. The son learned this and punished the overseer. The overseer excluded the father. The father began to go to his daughter's. Tried for harboring an exile, she was acquitted on the plea of her brother. The five-year period having expired, the father disinherits the son. [Speak for either the father or the son.]

Against such subjects, against others equally subtle and unreal, even indecent and perverted, both Tacitus and Quintilian protest in the name of education. Training for actual pleading, they urge, is not to be had from tyrannicide, rape, incest, wizards, pestilence, and stepmothers. Seneca leaves no doubt that such subjects were typical; but he expressly repudiates the assumption that *controversiæ* should be exercises to train for the bar.[38] That

[38] Deinde res ipsa diversa est: totum aliud est pugnare, aliud ventilare. Hoc ita semper habitum est, scholam quasi ludum esse, forum arenam. III. præf. 13.

The same point of view is taken by Pliny in the letter (*Epist.* II. 3) quoted below.

The following *controversia* was assigned to the young Marcus Aurelius

declamatio was quite different not only in his view, but in fact, there is no room to doubt. The difference between what Tacitus and Quintilian urge on principle and what they themselves, as well as Seneca and Pliny, record as practise is decisively sharp. It is the difference between the old rhetoric and the new. Even in Seneca's time, much more in that of Quintilian, *declamatio* was measured as a special form of public speaking. As such Seneca seems to regard it with complacency. That he thinks it self-sufficient and self-justifying seems evident from his pains to give its oral triumphs the permanence of written record. *Declamatio* might be cursed by the older tradition as bad education, or justified as originally good by ignoring what it had become. None the less it had gone quite out from the old rhetoric, and had been accepted and widely applauded as an end in itself.

That it perverted schooling, as Tacitus complains, was partly due to its inevitable tendency to turn the school into an auditorium. The rhetor remained, indeed, a teacher; but even in teaching he offered himself as a model.[39] The transition was easy to offering himself to the public as an orator in the latest style of oratory. While this was one of the few ways left under the Empire for appeal to a large audience, it was also one of his chief means of publicity. What the rhetor was thus to become throughout the Roman Empire may be clearly forecast from Pliny's account of Isæus.

by his master Fronto: "I have sent you an outline; the case is serious. A consul of the Roman people, laying aside his robes, has donned a coat of mail and among the young men at the feast of Minerva has slain a lion in the sight of the Roman people. He is denounced before the Censors. Put into shape and develop." *Correspondence of Fronto*, ed., with a translation, C. R. Haines, London and New York (Loeb Classical Library), 1919, vol. I, page 210 (see the further correspondence on this theme, pages 212, 214).

[39] See above, page 69.

(3) *Pliny on Isæus*

Great as is the reputation that had prepared me for Isæus, I found him greater. He has in the highest degree mastery, abundance, fertility. He speaks always extempore, but as if he had long written. The diction is Greek, nay Attic; the prelude, neat, simple, winsome, or grave and lofty. He asks for several *controversiæ*, and lets the audience choose, often even the side. He rises; his robe is right; he begins. Instantly everything is ready, and ready almost equally. Deep thoughts respond at once and words, but what words! chosen and refined. From his impromptus gleam much reading and much writing. He introduces aptly, states the case lucidly, argues keenly, sums up strongly, in style is superb. In a word, he instructs, charms, moves; [40] and which he does best you hardly know. The enthymemes are frequent, and so are the terse and finished syllogisms, an achievement difficult even for writing. His memory is incredible. He resumes what he has spoken extempore, and does not slip on a single word. Such control he has attained by study and practise; for day and night he does nothing else, hears nothing else, says nothing else. Past his sixtieth year, he is still only a schoolman; and nothing is more ingenuous than that sort of man, or more unsophisticated, or better. We who are crowded at the bar and in real cases learn, even against our will, much cunning. The school and the auditorium, with their made-up cases, are inoffensive and innocuous—and none the less happy, for old men especially. For what is happier in old age than what is pleasantest in youth? Therefore I account Isæus not only most eloquent, but also most blest; and if you have no desire to know him, you are made of stone and iron. So come, if not for other reasons, if not on my account, at least to hear him. Have you ever read of the man of Gades who was so stirred by the name and fame of Livy that he came from the ends of the earth to see him and, once having seen him, forthwith went his way? ' Tis crass, uncultured,

---

[40] For all its informality, Pliny's letter runs, as it were inevitably, into the traditional channels of the formal parts of a speech (*proœmiatur, narrat, pugnat*) and the three ends of oratory (*docet, delectat, afficit*). Indeed, it shows throughout a familiarity with rhetorical technic, and assumes a like familiarity on the part of its recipient.

stupid, almost base, to think no more highly of an experience than which nothing is pleasanter, or prettier, or more refined. You will say, "I can read no less eloquent orators here." Yes; but there is always a chance to read, not always to hear. Besides, the living voice, as the phrase goes, is far more moving. For though what you read may be more vehement, yet what is fixed by the delivery, the mien, the bearing, the very gesture of a speaker abides deeper in the mind. Else we give the lie to the story of Æschines, who when he had read aloud to the Rhodians a speech of Demosthenes, and every one was admiring it, is said to have added: "What if you had heard the beast himself? " And Æschines, on the testimony of Demosthenes, had a most brilliant delivery. None the less he admitted that the man who had begotten that speech delivered it far better. All this goes to prove that you should hear Isæus, if only to say that you have heard him.

Pliny, Epist. II. 3.

In essentials this description applies to the *controversiæ* preserved by Seneca. The Greek rhetor Isæus whom Pliny heard at the end of the first century is recognizably like the Roman rhetors whom Seneca heard some hundred years before.[41] A century had only fixed the type as a distinct form of oratory, and extended its vogue. Succeeding centuries repeated it, in Greek and in Latin, throughout the Roman world. Meantime Tarsus may have taught *declamatio* to its most famous citizen. Certainly St. Jerome knew it well. "We have been rhetoricated," he says with grim humor, "and have played a bit in the way of the *declamatores*." [42] Indeed, the rhetoric that

[41] H. Keil's editio maior of Pliny's Letters (Leipzig, 1870) dates the second book A. D. 97–100, within a few years of Quintilian's *Institutio*. For Isæus see Philostratus, *Vit. Soph.* i. 20, and Juvenal's satirical phrase "Isæo torrentior" (I. iii. 74).

[42] "Rhetoricati sumus, et in morem declamatorum paululum lusimus," quoted by Labriolle, *Histoire de la littérature latine chrétienne*, Paris, 1920, page 470. *Lusimus* corresponds to Seneca's description of *declamatio* as *ludus* (foot-note 38 above).

came first and most actively to the Fathers of the Church must have come through *declamatio*.[43] Its influence as late as the fourth century on St. Augustine throws into sharp relief his ignoring of it in his rhetoric for preachers, the fourth book of *De doctrina christiana*. With such real work of oratory *declamatio* has nothing to do.

C. Seneca's Classification and Treatment

Instead of giving his specimens entire, Seneca divides them by a threefold critical classification: (1) *sententiæ*, (2) *divisio*, (3) *colores*. The treatments of the same case by different *declamatores* are thus compared specifically as to (1) the significances, (2) the analysis, (3) the imaginative handling.

(1) The term *sententiæ* might imply such interpretations as were significant because they were leading. Taken thus, it suggests the saliences which mark, stage by stage, the development of a single, controlling interpretation. But *sententiæ* was used familiarly of such interpretations as were valuable rather separately than together, for themselves rather than for the furthering of a progressive development—in a word, aphorisms, or epigrams. The latter sense had become the more common, and in fact is what Seneca exhibits. His *declamatores* seem more concerned to strike now and strike again than to urge on. Though they still distinguish the formal parts (proem, statement, etc.),[44] they are no longer preoccupied with the

---

[43] The history of *declamatio* as a direct and an indirect influence is reserved for a later volume. It is summarized suggestively by Bornecque in both the introduction to his edition of Seneca and his treatise cited in foot-note 27. Walden's ample summaries of the work of Libanius (4th century) in his *Universities of Ancient Greece* corroborate what Bornecque says of St. Augustine.

[44] See Pliny's letter on Isæus above.

onward march of the older tradition. For the cogency of progressive development they have substituted the momentary effectiveness of striking summaries.

(2) Seneca's *divisio*, the analysis of the case, shows similarly not the stages of a consecutive order, but merely the components of an arbitrary classification. Given such cases as were posed, even the *divisio* called for ingenuity. Its preliminary *quæstiones* sometimes suggest an ingenious and perverted application of the traditional *status*.[45]

(3) Under *colores*[46] Seneca exhibits the imaginative development. Meaning generally the tone, or cast—in a large sense, the style, *colores* means specifically in Seneca's collection (1) descriptive amplification, and (2) dramatic characterization. Even the descriptions were more than concrete realization of the facts; they were imaginative elaborations.

> Quintus Haterius, on the side of the father [in the case of the pirate chief's daughter, above, page 92] evoked a very fine picture. In the abrupt style habitual with him he began to describe, as if he heard the tumult, how everything was laid waste and ravaged, the farms given to the flames, the peasants' flight; and, when he had amplified the terror, he added: "Why shudder, young man? 'Tis the arrival of your father-in-law."
>
> Seneca, *Controversiæ*, I. 6. 12.
>
> [Fabianus] was apter at *suasoriæ*. The local color of places, the courses of rivers, the sites of cities and the habits of their

[45] E. g., I. præf. 21; II. iii. 11. See also Bornecque, *Déclam.* 51. For *status* see above, page 74.

[46] The long and intricate history of *colores*, extending, with that of its Romance cognates, through the middle ages, must be postponed; but its interest may be divined by merely glancing at the successive uses recorded in a few dictionaries. The importance of exploring the term has been urged again by Fletcher in his "*True Meaning*" *of Dante's Vita Nuova*, Romanic Review, XI. 119.

peoples, no one described more amply. Never did he pause for lack of a word. His soothing speech would flow about everything with swiftest and easiest course. *Ibid*. II. præf. 3.

More boldly and ingeniously imaginative was the characterization. The case itself being fictitious, the treatment might go the whole length of fiction. At least the *declamatio* must so enter into the motives, and especially the emotions, of the parties as to make them *dramatis personæ;* at most he might go so far as to supply his imaginary dialogues with a plot.[47] Thus a guilty son is staged in dialogue with his father:

> I shall die. I shall die.
> Perhaps. I shall not weep.
> Heart, why quiverest thou? Tongue, why tremblest? Eyes, why are ye dulled? It is not yet the thirtieth day.
> You beg for life? I gave it; and you have lost it.
> It is your will that your son should die.
> My will? No, your madness, your blind and rash desire, yes, and her father, too soon overborne by your prayers.
>
> Seneca, *Controversiæ*, II. 3. 1.

That such dramatization is obviously an extension of the school *prosopopœiæ* [48] shows how pervasive was the preoccupation with imaginative development. "Asinius Pollio used to say that the *color* was to be exhibited in the statement of facts, and carried out in the arguments."[49] What was left of the old rhetoric? The interpretations demanded by *sententiæ* and *divisio* were at least intellectual;

[47] For the literary influence of this habit of oral fiction see Bornecque, *Décl*.

[48] See above, page 71.

[49] Seneca, *Controversiæ*, IV. iii. 3. Doubtless Quintilian had such perversion of *narratio* in mind when he wrote: "[*The narratio*] should be neither dry and starved . . . nor again winding and seductive with far-fetched descriptions, into which many are led by imitation of the license of poetry." II. iv. 3.

but the main interpretation, the goal and measure of skill, was imaginative. The surest way to fame was through *colores*. Through *colores* what had once been useful as a school exercise was artificially extended, and forensic was turned into a form of occasional oratory.

Sententiæ, divisio, colores, epigrams, ingenious analysis, imaginative development, seem a poor substitute for the traditional five parts of rhetoric. Especially impoverishing was the restriction of the ancient *inventio*. With investigation supplanted by fiction, debate lost its typical training and its typical power. With the shift of emphasis to imagination, rhetoric was confused with poetic,[50] to the impairing of both. Nor was *dispositio* furthered by *sententiæ* and *divisio*. Salience, instead of being used to further consecutiveness, became an end in itself. The whole was sacrificed to the parts. *Elocutio*, thus left to itself, tended inevitably toward an art of display. The history of rhetoric has no more striking proof that style, when cultivated in artificial isolation, goes bad.

So wide a departure suggests a divergence in conception, a divergence older and deeper than the particular innovations of *declamatio*. Beside Aristotle's conception of rhetoric as the art of giving effectiveness to truth there had persisted the conception of it as the art of giving effectiveness to the speaker. Though the two conceptions are not mutually exclusive, the dominance of the one or of the other tends either to give rhetoric those manifold relations and that constant answer to reality which mark its great ancient achievements, or on the other hand to narrow it toward virtuosity and display. The large peda-

[50] See the section on Ovid in Chapter VII below. Bornecque sums up the tendency acutely as "pénétration réciproque de la poésie et de la déclamation," *Déclam.* 115.

gogy of Quintilian is animated by the Aristotelian conception. The other conception, brilliant in Gorgias and his like, had already animated not only the *declamatores* at Rome, but that larger "second sophistic" [51] which became pervasively the rhetoric of the imperial centuries, in Greek and in Latin, throughout the Roman world. Ancient rhetoric offers the historic example, then, of a divergence that has remained typical.

[51] The development of this history is reserved to a later volume.

CHAPTER V

THE LITERARY CRITICISM OF RHETORIC

Criticism is inevitably a part of teaching. The teacher's holding up of models involves both analysis of them and appreciation. The differentiation of the critic from the teacher is roughly that his judgments are not applied immediately to tasks of composition, that he rather defines or extends theory than promotes practise. His estimate of the professional writer is not directly brought to bear on the advancement of the amateur. He stops with appreciation; the teacher tries to carry this over into imitation. But the differentiation of the two functions has never been complete; and in classical times it went only a little way. Quintilian, who was typically the teacher, is included with respect in histories of criticism. Dionysius of Halicarnassus classifies his acute appreciations of orators and poets under text-book headings, and puts forth his treatise on style, as does the great unknown "On the Sublime," for instruction. Both are what we now call critics. The classification of Dionysius does not hinder his critical appreciation; the classification of the great unknown merges into a kindling enthusiasm.

Probably most of the literary criticism current in the last years of the Republic and the first centuries of the Roman Empire came from grammarians and rhetoricians.[1] It is worth while, nevertheless, to consider separately from

[1] For Cicero, see Chapter III, for Quintilian and Tacitus, Chapter IV; for Dio Chrysostom and Apuleius, Chapter VIII.

the manuals and methods of instruction those treatises which were written rather to educate appreciation than to further the tasks of the schools. Outstanding among these are the *Brutus* of Cicero and the *Dialogus* of Tacitus; but the two most specific and significant in doctrine are the ones mentioned above: Dionysius of Halicarnassus on Sentences (*De Compositione Verborum*), and the unknown author on the Heightening of Language (*De Sublimitate*). In some respects complementary, the two together offer a clear view of style in the classical conception.

A. DIONYSIUS OF HALICARNASSUS ON SENTENCES

The most specific and systematic rhetorical treatise of Dionysius[1a] deals with sentence movement, or *compositio*[2]

[1a] For biography and bibliography of Dionysius see Roberts, W. Rhys, *Dionysius of Halicarnassus, the Three Literary Letters*, Cambridge, 1901, pages 1–50, 209–219. To the latter should be added: Egger, Max, *Essai sur la critique littéraire et la rhétorique chez les grecs au siècle d'Auguste*, Paris, 1902; Mætzke, Karl, *De D. H. Isocratis imitatore*, Wratislaw, 1906; Kremer, Emil, *Ueber das rhetorische system des D. von H.*, Strassburg, 1907; Geigenmüller, Paul, *Quæstiones Dionysianæ de vocabulis artis criticæ*, Leipzig, 1908; Nassal, Franz, *Æsthetisch-rhetorische Beziehungen zwischen D. von H. und Cicero*, Tübingen, 1910; Hubbell, H. M., *The Influence of Isocrates on Cicero, Dionysius, and Aristides*, Yale University Press, 1914.

The best edition of the *De compositione verborum* is that by Roberts, W.

[2] That it deals with this exclusively, not with composition in general, is clear from both the Greek title and the Latin. The terms σύνθεσις and *compositio* are technically specific. They do not mean style in general, which in the classical treatises includes also choice of single words (ἐκλογή, *electio*). Much less do they mean *composition* in our larger modern sense, for which the ancient term is *dispositio, collocatio*, or more generally οἰκονομία. Dionysius makes the distinction quite clear at the opening of his treatise, and holds to it throughout. In this sense is to be taken the title of the admirable translation of Rhys Roberts, *Literary Composition*, as is shown by his rendering elsewhere *The Arrangement of Words* (page 8 of his edition of *Three Literary Letters*).

(see pages 25, 53, 67, 79). This, he makes bold to say in his second paragraph,[3] is the aspect of composition most profitable for the study of youth.

Rhys, *Dionysius of Halicarnassus on Literary Composition* (text, introduction, translation, notes, glossary, appendices), London, 1910. A current summary of the *De compositione* will be found in Roberts, *Three Literary Letters*, pages 8–19; a more detailed summary, with a tabular analysis, in his edition, pages 1–10; a commented summary in Egger, pages 67–111.

The rhetorical system of Dionysius is tabulated from all his works by Ammon, George, *De D. H. librorum rhetoricorum fontibus*, Monachii, 1889. In English equivalents, the pertinent parts of his analysis are as follows:

A. subject-matter
    I. investigation (inventio)
       selection (iudicium)
    II. arrangement (dispositio)
       1. division
       2. order
       3. revision and elaboration
B. style
    I. choice of words (electio)
       1. precision
       2. imagery
    II. sentence movement (compositio)
       1. nature
       2. force
                     a. in phrases
       3. processes   b. in clauses
                     c. in periods
                     a. melody
       4. charm and beauty   b. rhythm
                     c. variety
                     d. aptness
               a. strong
       5. kinds   b. smooth
               c. blended
       6. verse and prose

Kremer (see above), whose analysis, though less detailed, is substantially the same, collates from all the writings of Dionysius his doctrine

---

[3] i. 66. The Roman numerals in these foot-notes refer to chapters; the Arabic, to the pages of the Rhys Roberts text. The Rhys Roberts translation is used with modifications.

There is need . . of oversight and guidance . . . for a choice
of words at once pure and noble . . and a sentence movement combining charm with dignity. . . .   The chief heads
under which I propose to treat the subject are the following:
what is the nature of sentence movement and what force it has;
what are its aims and how it attains them; what are its generic
varieties, and what is the distinctive feature of each, and which
of them I believe to be best; and still further, what is that poetical something, both pleasant on the tongue and sweet to the
ear, which naturally accompanies the sentence movement of
prose, and wherein lies the force of that poetical method which
imitates unpoetical speech and succeeds thoroughly in the
imitation, and by what method each of these two may be
attained.[4]

Sentence movement, moreover, Dionysius thinks to
be more important than the choice of words.[5]   He supports this assertion first by analyzing a passage from the
Odyssey.[6]

on the several topics and gives foot-note references to Aristotle, Cicero,
and others.

Nassal (see above), pointing out that Dionysius and Cicero agree
strikingly in many points, argues that they have for common source in
these cases a Greek treatise written during the years between the time of
the *Lysias* of Dionysius and of the *De Oratore* of Cicero and the time of
the *Demosthenes* of Dionysius and of the *Orator* of Cicero, and that this
common source is very probably Cæcilius of Calacte.

Geigenmueller (see above) supplies a collation of critical terms with
valuable comparisons.

Nassal (page 11) quotes from Doxopater a definition of rhetoric ascribed to Dionysius: "Rhetoric is the artistic mastery of persuasive
discourse in communal affairs, having as its end to speak well."   (Usener,
Fragment I.)   The definition is sound and striking, but for the lame and
impotent concluding phrase.   As reported by Maximus Planudes (quoted
by Ammon, page 1), the definition is substantially the same, but has
amplified this concluding phrase with a clumsy twist from Aristotle.
Whether the definition belongs to Dionysius or not, the tradition shows
his fame as a rhetorician.

[4] i. 68–70.   [5] iii. 74.

[6] iii. 76–78 (Odyssey, xvi. 1–16).

Everybody would, I am sure, testify that these lines cast a spell of enchantment on the ear, and rank second to no poetry whatsoever, however exquisite it may be. But what is the secret of their fascination, and what causes them to be what they are? Is it the choice of words or the sentence movement? No one will say "the choice"; of that I am convinced. For the diction consists, warp and woof, of the most ordinary, the humblest words, such as might have been used off-hand by a farmer, a seaman, an artisan, or anybody else who takes no account of elegant speech. You have only to break up the meter, and these same lines seem commonplace and unworthy of admiration. For they contain neither noble metaphors nor *hypallages* nor *catachreses* nor any other figurative language; nor yet many unusual terms, nor foreign or new-coined words. What alternative, then, is left but to attribute the beauty of the style to the sentence movement?

In like manner he urges concerning a passage from Herodotus: [7]

Here again no one can say that the grace of the style is due to the impressiveness and the dignity of the words. These have not been picked and chosen with studious care; they are simply the labels affixed to things by Nature. Indeed, it would perhaps have been out of place to use other and grander words. I take it, in fact, to be always necessary, whenever ideas are expressed in proper and appropriate language, that no word should be more dignified than the nature of the ideas. That there is no stately or grandiose word in the present passage, any one who likes may prove by simply changing the harmony. There are many similar passages in this author, from which it can be seen that the fascination of his style does not after all lie in the beauty of the words, but in their combination.

Not content with analysis, Dionysius proceeds [8] to enforce his point by garbling. Fine passages of verse and of prose, without any change of words, are dislocated to show that their force resides not in these words taken

[7] iii. 84 (Herodotus i. 8–10).   [8] iv. 84.

singly, but in the sentence order, or movement. The method is ingenious. It is even telling. Any teacher who shall thus put side by side a fine passage of English prose and the same words in a different order will make his students aware of literary effects to which they should not remain deaf.[9] The connotation of pace and tune may be further exemplified by comparing, for instance, a tale of Chaucer's with the version made by Dryden.[10]

The method is interesting, striking, to some extent revealing. What does it reveal? That suggestiveness is not only through the imagery of single words, but through their sound in combination; that a large part of the connotation which we call style is sentence pace. This is generally so little discerned that Dionysius may be pardoned for magnifying it; and he further guards himself by recording his intention of writing a treatise also on the choice of words. Occupied in the present treatise exclusively with their combination, he naturally brings out the importance of this as vividly as possible. Is the effectiveness of style in the choice of words, or in their combination? Here he seems to answer, "In their combination." [11]

But effectiveness of expression resides primarily in neither *electio* nor *compositio*, secondarily in both. Primarily it is the writer's keen sense of the ways of nature and of man, his receptivity and insight. Then it is con-

[9] See, for example, my *Writing and Speaking*, pages 376–378; *College Composition*, pages 184–188.

[10] That this sort of analysis may be carried even further is suggested by R. L. Stevenson's *Some Technical Elements of Style in Literature*, which is partly along the lines followed by Dionysius.

[11] That this is generally more important he explicitly affirms in his *Demosthenes*, chapter li. Reviewing the traditional five parts of rhetoric, he puts οἰκονομία (*dispositio*) above εὕρεσις (*inventio*), and σύνθεσις (*compositio*) above ἐκλογή (*electio*).

crete expression, the choice of words of sensation, the
speaking in terms of light, sound, color, motion, attitude,
gesture. Such words, whether figurative in the technical
sense or literal, may be called imagery. Or, in other fields
of composition, it is an illuminating precision. Finally,
that effectiveness which we call style comes from apt and
beautiful rhythms, from that *compositio* which is the subject of this treatise. In a word, style is a complex. That
compositio is an important element Dionysius does well to
show, for this is not obvious and is commonly neglected;
but that *compositio* is *the* cause, or even that it is generally
more important than the other elements, can hardly be
demonstrated. Undoubtedly Homer's verse weaves much
of his spell;[12] but surely his words, though often, as
Dionysius says, ordinary, have none the less that specific
concreteness which characteristically makes epic vivid.
In the following passage that he quotes from Herodotus,
where the separable charm of the sentence movement is
made more obvious by playing as it were in the wrong
tempo, he might claim even more. Surely the dialogue
method is important for vividness and economy, and this
too is a matter of *compositio*. But is the *compositio*, for
all its charm, the main cause? Who shall determine?
The impression is a complex in which each element
counts—the choice of details, the choice of words, the
arrangement or movement—and in which we can hardly
assign an exact proportion to any one. Certainly the beat
and tune of prose are part of its connotation, its effect on
the reader. Doubtless also—though here we lack sci-

---

[12] Rhys Roberts's use of imitative renderings to make this point is of
course necessary; but readers unfamiliar with Greek rhythms should beware of inferences based on an assumption of equivalence between Greek
metrical habits and English.

entific analysis to confirm our impression [13]—they are demanded subconsciously by the composing emotion of the author as he speaks or writes. Nevertheless Dionysius is an early instance of a danger lurking in statistical analysis of literature, perhaps also of a danger lurking in the treatment of style—much more of a single element of style—as a separate entity. Being a teacher, Dionysius doubtless thought that there was little danger in over-emphasizing the importance of pace with young students. They are too likely to be quite unaware of it to be corrupted by pedagogical exaggeration.

That "thin and bloodless talk" with which Cicero [14] taxes the philosophers Dionysius thinks to be due to defective *compositio*.

> The main difference between poet and poet, orator and orator, is in aptness of sentence movement. Almost all the ancients gave this much study; and consequently their poems, their songs, and their discourses are things of beauty. But among their successors, with few exceptions, this was no longer so. In time it was at last entirely forgotten; and no one thought it to be indispensable or even contributory to beauty of discourse.[15]

Having established the importance of adapting sentence movement, Dionysius proceeds to show that such adaptation is little hindered by *a priori* consideration of logic.

> I used to think that we ought to follow nature as far as possible in adjusting the parts of a discourse . . . for instance, to put nouns before verbs . . the essential before its modifiers . . . This idea is plausible; but I came to think it was not true.[16]

[13] This is the contention of Stevenson in *Some Technical Elements of Style in Literature.*

[14] *De Oratore*, I. xiii. 57. [15] iv. 92. [16] v. 98.

Does Dionysius mean that logic offers no norm for the order of words? [17] Hardly. Rather he shows by his instances that word order has little to do with philosophical or logical classification. The order in a given sentence is not determined abstractly by the logical idea of putting the subject before the predicate, or the substance before the accident. It is guided partly by rhythm; and it is widely variable.

The variability that he shows in the Greek word order is wider than in English. In both languages it is controlled by usage, by what is habitual and therefore expected; and this fact seems to be ignored by Dionysius. Even a Greek could not shape a sentence at his own will without reference to the habit of the language. But in this respect Greek usage, because the Greek could rely on showing sentence relations by inflection, was less restrictive than English usage. For English, then, it is not true to say that there is no sentence norm, no normal or natural order. That the norm is not determined by logic in the sense of abstract analysis is true for either, or any, language; but in modern languages, much more than in Greek, it is restricted by usage. Every careful translator has found his efforts to convey Greek style hampered by the inferior variability of modern sentence habits. Taken more generally, however, the contention of Dionysius is sound and suggestive. It is that the order of words in a sentence is not predetermined by logic, that it is freely adaptable, and that this adaptation constitutes a large element in effectiveness.

Having thus vindicated the right of the speaker or

[17] Henri Weil's classic essay on the order of words in the ancient languages has been translated into English by C. W. Super, Boston, 1887. The rationale of word-order is discussed in Spencer's *Philosophy of Style*.

writer to deal with the order of his words artistically, unfettered by logic, Dionysius proceeds to inquire in what artistic shaping consists.

The functions of *compositio* [the tasks of sentence movement] seem to me to be three: (1) to discern what goes naturally with what to make a beautiful and satisfying combination; (2) to know how to make systematically out of these potential agreements a better harmony; (3) if revision is still necessary, whether abridgement, expansion, or alteration, to know how to work out the adaptation as the potential values demand. The scope of each of these I will explain more clearly by using certain analogies from the industrial arts with which all are familiar: house-building, ship-building, and the like. When a builder has provided himself with the material from which he intends to construct a house—stones, timbers, tiling, and all the rest—he then puts together the structure from these, studying the following three things: what stone, timber, and brick can be united with what other stone, timber, and brick; next, how each piece of the material that is being so united should be set, and on which of its faces; thirdly, if anything fits badly, how that particular thing can be chipped and trimmed and made to fit exactly. And the shipwright proceeds in just the same way. So, I say, they also should work whose task is to compose sentences well.[18]

To simplify the language of Dionysius by borrowing from music a metaphor which, though it does not cover his whole intention, is true so far as it goes, the three tasks of the shaper of sentences are: (1) to hear the tune, (2) to follow the tune, (3) to correct the tune. The first depends on the speaker's awareness, his sensitiveness to words; the second depends on his technical ability to carry out what is thus suggested, to sustain and enhance; the third, more specifically technical, is to revise in detail.

On its face this division is new. Not only has it nothing

[18] vi. 104.

to do with other divisions which apply to style in general, being limited to sentence movement, but it also differs from earlier divisions of this item by being synthetic. Its point of view is not that of a critic analyzing what has been already composed, but of a speaker or writer composing. It is practical.

Is it practicable? At the very outset of the exposition the analogy of the building arts is disconcerting. Even when allowances are made for the strict limitation to building, the exclusion of all that we now call architecture, the description still seems hardly exact. And, its exactness assumed, is it applicable? Is the analogy sound? Both the *Rhetoric* and the *Poetic* of Aristotle in speaking of sentences generally avoid analogies from the static arts. The *Poetic* even rules them out at the start by its classification of the arts; and Aristotle's analogies for sentences are drawn not from building, but from walking, running, and breathing.[19] Dionysius both assumes and asserts the same point of view: "The science of public speaking is, after all, a sort of musical science, differing from vocal and instrumental music in degree, not in kind." [20] And generally his discussion, like Aristotle's, is in terms of rhythm. Why, then, this analogy with arts that Aristotle regarded as lying in quite another field? The famous analogy in the *De Sublimitate* [21] of building with solid blocks is not, in its context, so remarkable; for it is applied less restrictively to *compositio*. Is a shaper of sentences like a builder?

Is he like a builder in the process that Dionysius puts first, the discerning of inherent compatibilities in his material? The question is not of the subject-matter or conception of a whole work, but of component parts or

[19] See above, pages 28, 29.   [20] xi. 124.   [21] Section x.

details. Doubtless an author may be somewhat vaguely considered as discerning potentialities in this material; but what is the material? Is it words in the sense that the builder's is stone or wood? Can an author find inherent compatibility in words as a builder in the strength, texture, shape, or color of his stone? His material is ideas and images. His choice of particular words for these is doubtless affected by connotations of sound; [22] but must it not be primarily suggested and finally determined by the sense? Can word combinations be considered as in themselves beautiful and satisfying, as really having compatibilities of sound? An author who followed Dionysius literally might launch himself into mcllifluous nonsense. Dionysius is speaking figuratively; but is his figure really suggestive? We may well remember that more modern analogies drawn from the static arts of mass and line have been misleading for the consecutive art of words.

The distinction between Dionysius's two remaining items may seem slight until we remember that the division is not analytical into elements, but synthetic into processes that are consecutive in time. Given the primary and general equipment of sensitiveness, the writer may enhance while he is writing and then afterward revise. In fact, there is a typical difference between following the flow of thought and imagery and sound, and then correcting it, between composing and revising. That the two should be distinct, and that both should be guided partly by sound, is counsel practically helpful.

In fact, once he proceeds to apply his second and third headings in detail, Dionysius is more convincing. The righting [23] of a sentence by transposing phrases or clauses is in practise, and should be in theory, a first counsel of

[22] See above, page 60 and foot-note 95.   [23] vii.

sentence emphasis. A defect of modern text-books is to set forth this important process as if it were purely logical. Dionysius follows the ancient tradition in making it rhythmical; and he also clarifies it by specific instances. He proceeds [24] to the varying of the rhythm by lengthening or shortening. Here his preoccupation with rhythm tends to obscure other considerations. That a sentence is a logical unit, and that a given statement is left single or combined with its neighbor according to its logical bearing on the whole passage,[25] he seems to ignore or take for granted. Again, the lengthening of a clause to fill out the rhythm risks bombast. On the other hand, some of the additions that he quotes as unnecessary to the idea are not superfluous for the image; their value is not mainly rhythmical. But so far as it goes this chapter is suggestive.

Distinguishing [26] charm ($\dot{\eta}\delta o\nu\dot{\eta}$) from beauty ($\tau\grave{o}$ $\kappa a\lambda\acute{o}\nu$), Dionysius finds [27] that they arise from four qualities: melody, rhythm, variety, aptness. Melody is an affair of pitch and inflection. The passage,[28] besides being a precious hint as to the Greek scale, is a useful reminder that English—and especially American—speech too often ignores variety of pitch. Similarly the treatment of rhythm as quantitative [29] should remind us that in our own habit it is predominantly accentual. These differences in habit of speech, while they suggest resources unused, should none the less warn us against transferring the distinctions and counsels of Dionysius bodily from Greek to English. Of those that are equally applicable to both languages is the general advice [30] to seek variety and aptness less in the choice of words, where there can be

---

[24] ix. [25] See my *College Composition*, page 69.
[26] x. The same distinction is made in his *Demosthenes*, xlvii.
[27] xi. [28] xi. 126. [29] xi. 128. [30] xii. 130.

little latitude, than in their combination. Indeed, it is hardly too much to say that aptness of style, though abstractly it includes precision and imagery in the single word, is more largely than most of us realize an effect of rhythm, and that variety, except when in oral utterance it includes pitch, consists in rhythm exclusively.

Distinguishing [31] the letters as vowels or consonants, Dionysius finds Greek speech sounds to be neither more nor less than twenty-four. His phonetic analysis of these is specifically according to the position of the vocal organs in utterance. The following discussion [32] of the quality of syllables in combination, of effects hard, smooth, or sweet in sound apart from sense, is doctrine oftener accepted as an idea than tested.[33]

> . . Syllables, which are combinations or interweavings of letters, preserve at once both the individual properties of each component and the joint properties of all, which spring from their fusion and juxtaposition. The sounds thus formed are soft or hard, smooth or rough, sweet to the ear or harsh to it; they make us pull a wry face, or cause our mouths to water, or bring about any of the countless other physical conditions that are possible.
>
> These facts the greatest poets and prose-writers have carefully noted, and not only do they carefully arrange their words and weave them into appropriate patterns, but often, with curious and loving skill, they adapt the very syllables and letters to the emotions which they wish to represent.
>
> [Passages from Homer are quoted as examples.]
>
> Such lines are to be found without number in Homer, representing length of time, hugeness of body, stress of emotion, immobility of position, or similiar effects, simply by the manipulation of the syllables. Conversely others are framed to give the impression of abruptness, speed, hurry, and the like.[34]

[31] xiv.   [32] xv–xvi.
[33] In English it is urged specifically by Stevenson in *Some Technical Elements of Style in Literature*.   [34] xv. 154–156.

That such associations are natural is obvious, Dionysius thinks, from onomatopœia, the earliest and simplest form of sound-connotation in words. But he does not shrink from pushing his doctrine far beyond this to the conclusion that sound effects both subtle and various may be achieved, and should be consciously sought, by literary art.

> The conclusion is inevitable, that style is beautiful when it contains beautiful words, that beauty of words is due to beautiful syllables and letters, that language is rendered charming by the things that charm the ear in virtue of affinities in words, syllables, and letters. . . .
>
> If, then, it were possible that all the parts of speech by which a given subject is to be expressed should be euphonious and elegant, it would be madness to seek out inferior ones. But if this be out of the question, as in many cases it is, then we must endeavor to mask the natural defects of the inferior letters by interweaving and mingling and juxtaposition.[35]

The following instances of poetic effects gained by apt combinations of proper names that have no such suggestions singly will remind English readers of certain sonorous passages in Milton.[36]

That the connotation of such combinations is due to their syllabic quality, however, as distinct from their rhythm, Dionysius hardly succeeds in establishing. The doctrine is flatly denied by Lewis.

> A certain learned and well-known student of verse says that (for example) gutturals and sibilants express "amazement, affright, indignation, contempt," and he cites as an illustration a passage from Paradise Lost.

[35] xvi. 160, 166.
[36] It may remind some elder readers also of a story once current concerning a pious old lady who in reading her Bible found emotional satisfaction in the "blessed word Mesopotamia."

> Out of my sight, thou serpent; that name best
> Befits thee with him leagued, thyself as false
> And hateful; nothing wants but that thy shape
> Like his and color serpentine may show
> Thy inward fraud.

One objection to this kind of doctrine is that it makes people think they have no ear for verse, for after careful reading they are still uncertain whether they can detect the effect described. Another objection to it is that it is not true. Compare with the lines quoted this little song from Browning's Pippa Passes:

> The year's at the spring,
> And day's at the morn;
> Morning's at seven;
> The hill-side's dew-pearled;
> The lark's on the wing;
> The snail's on the thorn;
> God's in his heaven—
> All's right with the world.

This is shorter by four syllables than the passage from Milton, but it has the same number of gutturals and two more sibilants; yet fancy describing it as an expression of "amazement, affright, indignation, contempt!"

For another illustration, in one of the standard manuals of versification it is pointed out that the surd mutes (p, k, t) "help to convey the idea of littleness, delicacy, and sprightliness," and that the short vowel i is fitted to express "joy, gaiety, triviality, rapid movement, and physical littleness." To illustrate both assertions, Mercutio's account of Queen Mab is cited:

> She comes
> In shape no bigger than an agate stone, . . .
> Drawn by a team of little atomies.

Here the effect is perhaps easier to recognize, and even an obtuse reader thinks he follows the reasoning; but compare Browning's lines:

> The wroth sea's waves are edged
> With foam, white as the bitten lip of hate.

The "bitten lip" has as many surd mutes and short i's as the "little atomies"; but it fails to express sprightliness, gaiety, or triviality. . .

The fact is, of course, that all this analysis of sounds proceeds upon a false assumption. When you say Titan you mean something big, and when you say tittle you mean something small; but it is not the sound of either word that means either bigness or littleness, it is the sense. If you put together a great many similar consonants in one sentence, they will attract special attention to the words in which they occur, and the significance of those words, whatever it may be, is thereby intensified; but whether the words are "a team of little atomies" or "a triumphant terrible Titan," it is not the sound of the consonants that makes the significance.[37]

Rhythm is discussed in the same order, first [38] by classifying feet as iambs, trochees, dactyls, etc., then [39] by analyzing their effects singly and in combination. "A simple rhythm or foot has not less than two syllables nor more than three." [40] This is commonly accepted for meter; but does it hold for the rhythms of prose? Moreover that the foot is the rhythmical unit, whether in Greek or in other languages, is oftener assumed than proved. Rhythmical effects, in English at least, seem to be not so much of feet as of measures, whether verses or clauses. Unless the foot is actually a unit, for the composer or for the hearer—and this is at least doubtful—such analysis as that of a noble passage from the funeral speech in the second book of Thucydides [41] lays too much stress on the components—spondees, anapests, etc.—and not enough on the *compositio*, or pace of the sentence. By way of contrast to Thucydides, Plato, and Demosthenes, Dionysius pillories Hegesias of Magnesia.[42]

[37] Charlton M. Lewis, *The Principles of English Verse*, New York, 1906, page 131.   [38] xvii.   [39] xviii.   [40] xvii. 176.
[41] xviii. 178.   [42] Stevenson makes similar use of Macaulay.

Variety of rhythm [43] is discussed more generally, without instances, and as an introduction to rhythm in prose.

> Prose diction has full liberty and permission to diversify the *compositio* by whatever changes it pleases. A style is finest of all when it has the most frequent rests and changes of harmony; when one thing is said within a period, another without it; when one period is formed by the interweaving of a larger number of clauses, another by that of a smaller; when among the clauses themselves one is short, another longer, one roughly wrought, another more finished; when the rhythms take now one form, now another, and the figures are of all kinds, and the voice-pitches—the so-called "accents"—are various, and skillfully avoid satiety.[44]

Aptness,[45] or appropriateness to the actors and the action, is analyzed rather as imitative smoothness or roughness in detail than as the speed of the whole stanza or paragraph. Dionysius says nothing, for instance, of the staccato effect of frequent predication. His text is the famous stone of Sisyphus from the eleventh book of the *Odyssey*. Finally [46] Dionysius classifies sentence movement into three typical modes: [47] the rough (αὐστηρά), the smooth (γλαφυρά) or florid (ἀνθηρά), and the blended (εὔκρατος). Certain accidental likenesses to the familiar threefold classification of style [48] should not obscure the fact that we have here something different, a classification not of style in general, but of *compositio*. The first mode Dionysius defines as seeking rather the force of each part than the harmony of the whole. The words stand out separately, without fear of hiatus or other clashing of sounds, and without care for periods.[49] The aim is rather a direct

---

[43] xix.   [44] xix. 196.   [45] τὸ πρέπον, xx.   [46] xxi.
[47] Dionysius uses the same classification in his *Demosthenes*, xxxvi.
[48] See above, page 56.   [49] xxii. 212. One thinks of Carlyle.

stirring of emotion ($\pi\acute{a}\theta os$) than a pervasive suggestion of character ($\mathring{\eta}\theta os$). This sterner, elder mode, quite different from "the showy and decorative prettiness of our day," [50] he exemplifies, with his usual minute analysis, from Pindar and Thucydides. The second, or smooth mode [51] is periodic in its sentences and nicely articulated in its clauses and phrases.

It tries to combine and interweave its component parts, and thus give, as far as possible, the effect of one continuous utterance. This result is produced by so nicely adjusting the junctures that they admit no appreciable time-interval between the words. [52]

Aiming at the easiest transitions within the period, it is careful to distinguish between periods. The parts coalesce; the units stand out. [53] This is in line with the doctrine of Aristotle, [54] and is admirably exemplified by the practise of Cicero. Dionysius's instances are Sappho and Isocrates. The third, or blended mode [55] Dionysius labors in vain to distinguish from the other two. Ingenious as are his analyses of the three modes, even sometimes suggestive, they fail to establish the reality of the classification. We can discern in the distinction between his first two a carrying out—perhaps an undue extension—of Aristotle's distinction between the unperiodic style and the periodic. [56] His third mode seems to be not a mode at all, but merely a reminder that neither of the other two can be used exclusively or pushed to excess.

As to the distinction of prose rhythms from verse [57] Dionysius quotes with approval Aristotle's dictum [58]

[50] xxii. 216.   [51] xxiii.   [52] xxiii. 234.   [53] xxiii. 236.
[54] Rhetoric III. ix. 1409 a. See above, page 28. Aristotle's εὐσύνοπτος may have suggested the περίοπτος of Dionysius.
[55] xxiv.   [56] Rhetoric, ibid.   [57] xxv, xxvi.
[58] Rhetoric, III. viii. 1408 b. See above, page 26.

that prose should be rhythmical without becoming metrical. It seems plain none the less that his own taste is for rather marked rhythms even in prose, and that he would encourage students to go a long way toward meter. Before he closes his book upon this consideration, he raises quite frankly the question of how far its analyses have practical value.

I have a presentiment that an onslaught will be made on these statements by people who are destitute of general culture and practise the mechanical parts of rhetoric unmethodically and unscientifically. . . Their argument will doubtless be: "Was Demosthenes, then, so poor a creature that, whenever he was writing his speeches, he would work in meters and rhythms after the fashion of clay-modellers, and would try to fit his clauses into these moulds, shifting the words to and fro, keeping an anxious eye on his longs and shorts, and fretting himself about cases of nouns, moods of verbs, and all the accidents of the parts of speech? So great a man would be a fool indeed were he to stoop to all this niggling and peddling." If they scoff and jeer in these or similar terms, they may easily be countered by the following reply: " First, it is not surprising after all that a man who is held to deserve a greater reputation than any of his predecessors who were distinguished for eloquence was anxious, when composing eternal works and submitting himself to the scrutiny of all-testing envy and time, not to admit either subject or words at random, and to attend carefully to both arrangements of ideas and beauty of words: particularly as the authors of that day were producing discourses which suggested not writing, but carving and chasing—those I mean of the sophists Isocrates and Plato. . . . What wonder, then, if Demosthenes also was careful to secure euphony and melody and to employ no random or untested word or thought? " [59]

The defense is sufficient abstractly, though it does not quite meet the fact that in practise both teachers and

[59] xxv. 262.

students of rhetoric have not infrequently frittered away
much time in minute analysis of *compositio*. Such analysis
easily becomes over-minute, easily deviates from the
paramount consideration of the idea or the image. That
it is properly the work of revision, not of the first draft,
Dionysius often implies, but might well have stated explicitly. So applied, given common sense and the honest
determination to say what one means, analysis of prose
rhythms is distinctly valuable and often necessary.

B. The Great Unknown on Imaginative Diction

"Longinus on the Sublime" [1] will for many years continue to name the most captivating of ancient treatises,
though its author, whoever he was, was not the rhetorician
Longinus, and though its subject is wider than our word
sublime. The Latin *sublimitas* translates precisely enough
the ὕψος of the Greek title; but our words *sublime* and
sublimity are reserved for special application to such
lofty passages as we quote from Dante and Milton.
Sappho's love poem, quoted by the author as a typical
instance, though we feel at once its vivid beauty, we

---

[1] The edition of W. Rhys Roberts (Cambridge, 1899; second edition,
1907), bearing this traditional title, has, besides text and translation, an
introduction on the authorship, contents, and character, and several
valuable appendices: A. textual; B. linguistic (beginning this scholar's
collation of Greek rhetorical terms); C. literary (with a table of contents
and a list of quotations located and arranged alphabetically by authors);
D. bibliographical.

Other modern English translations are: by H. L. Havell, with an introduction by Andrew Lang (London, 1890; reprinted by Lane Cooper in
Theories of Style, New York, 1907); by A. O. Prickard, with a brief introductory essay on the authorship and character, a digest by chapters, and
four appendices: I. Specimen Passages Translated from Greek Writers of
the Roman Empire on Literary Criticism; II. The Treatise on Sublimity
and Latin Critics; III. Passages Translated from Bishop Lowth's Oxford Lectures on Hebrew Poetry; IV. Additional Note on Paraphones.

should not call sublime. The Greek word is more general. Meaning literally height, it includes in this treatise all such effects of style as lift us, as move us beyond comprehension or assent to sympathy or resolve. But though the meaning is clear, an equivalent English term is still to seek. *Elevation* has unfortunate suggestions of the rhetorical; *height* is too vague; *heightening*, though nearer, is not generally used in this sense. Falling back on such a periphrasis as *heightening of style*, we become aware that our word *style*, as used generally and untechnically, is not far from the author's intention. Though in text-books and works of criticism it is often extended, in ordinary parlance it means that very heightening, or lift, which is discussed by the Great Unknown. So we shall convey his intention as fairly as seems feasible by translating his title *Style*.

In the following digest Roman numerals indicate the chapters, or sections.

The heights of style are such passages as please always and please all.

(i) The heights of authorship are seen in eminence and excellence of words. Experience in subject-matter (*inventio*) and cogency of order (*dispositio*) are effects of the whole; but the orator's power flashes in his happy moments of style (*elocutio*). (ii) Nor because we see genius here are we to think that style is beyond art. (iii, iv) [Contrast] the turgid, the pretty, the frigid, (v) faults arising from the search for novelties. (vi) Though judgment of style is the final fruit of much experience, we must attempt definition of heightening. (vii) Count those passages wholly beautiful and true instances of the heights of style which please always and please all.

The first source of height in style is intellectual power of conception.

(viii) Of such heightening (1) the first and strongest source is intellectual power of conception; (2) the second, emotion. These are native; the remaining three are acquired: (3) handling of figures, (4) noble diction, and (5), what includes the other two, sentence movement (*compositio*). (ix) The force of the first (i. e., conception), and also its waning, we feel in Homer, whose *Odyssey* lapses into narrative from the dramatic power of the *Iliad*. (x) The realization of this first source in actual composition means compression, the bringing together of significances with no insignificances to interrupt. (xi) Oratorical amplification, which is complementary to this, of itself never rises to the heights. (xii) Heightening of style is single and intensive, as in poetry or in the orations of Demosthenes; amplification is iterative and extensive, as in Plato or Cicero. (xiii) Plato, however, shows the way to mastery—imitation, (xiv) a way which even we may follow.

The second source is emotion. (This is not treated here in its place as a separate section, but is implied throughout what follows.)

The third source is handling of figures.

(xv) For weight, grandeur, and energy the right language is imagery. In oratory the purpose of this typically is intellectual; in poetry, emotional; but oratory too may use it for emotional effect. [xvi—xxix. Discussion of figures.] (xxx—xxxi) Beautiful words are essentially the light of thought; and homely words have their expressiveness. (xxxii) Abundance of figurative language may proceed from emotion and kindle it. Even extended and detailed metaphor may be stimulating.

The fourth source, noble diction, means more than constant excellence.

(xxxiii) Better eminence with some faults than a lower plane without them: Homer than Apollonius, Archilochus than Eratosthenes, Pindar than Bacchylides, Sophocles than Ion, (xxxiv) Demosthenes than Hyperides, (xxxv) Plato than Lysias, and, in general, force than elegance. (xxxvi) But though the achievement due to art is typically that of the lower plane, the success of never failing, the assurance of technical mastery, still this does not make art the less important. [xxxvii—xxxviii. Further on figures: metaphor, hyperbole.]

The fifth source is sentence movement (compositio).

(xxxix) The fifth of the elements that combine to give height is *compositio*. Having already in two other treatises gone exhaustively into the theory of *compositio*, I will treat it here only in general. The pervasive emotional effect of rhythm need only be insisted on; it is too evident to require proof. (xl) That it is separately distinguishable as a cause of heightening can be seen in many authors, most strikingly in Euripides, who is a poet rather of *compositio* than of thought. (xli–xlii) Conversely, a wrong rhythm may drag down or distract, (xliii) as may also a descriptive detail that interrupts or jars.

That orators rarely attain the heights of style means that they live unworthily.

(xliv) Why have we now few authors that reach the heights? Is the cause political, the decay of democracy? Rather it is moral; it is our materialism.

Compared with the orderly *a priori* progress of Dionysius, this treatment seems at once less systematic; and though the manuscripts show gaps, some apparently of considerable length, we have enough of the treatise to conclude that the whole was rather suggestive than logically divided and consecutive. But through it all runs the controlling idea that the higher reaches of style are, in cause and in effect, imaginative. Discussing oratory, the author is all the while drawing instances from poetry; and this means more than in the treatise of Dionysius. The scope is larger. Not only does he range far beyond *compositio*, which occupies only five of his chapters; he is looking in general less to technic and more to motive. What lifts the orator, and makes him lift his hearers, is first intellectual power of conception, then emotional power of sympathy. These are the springs. They work out in imaginative diction and rhythmical pace; but that few orators lift us by these means is due fundamentally to a general lack of idealism.

The contribution, then, of this unknown critic consists

in illuminating the bearing of poetic on rhetoric, the importance of imaginative realization even for purposes of persuasion. The distinction between rhetoric and poetic he never blurs; in fact he contrasts the two explicitly; but he brings out, more clearly than any other ancient author, their interdependence.

First, he precludes any undue separation of thought from emotion by making conception, in Homer as well as in Demosthenes, intellectual. His word νόησις reminds one that Aristotle conversely brings rhetoric into poetic by making thought, διάνοια,[2] one of the elements of tragedy. Then further he shows throughout that style at its height, in Demosthenes as well as in Homer, is imaginative realization, that where we feel ὕψος, sublimitas, even in the field of rhetoric, we find the typical language of poetic. Such passages, he says in his first chapter, do not merely persuade us; they carry us out of ourselves.

This is clearest in chapters x–xv, which show how power of conception works out in the typical movement (x) of poetic, then (xi–xiv) in that of rhetoric, and then (xv) in their common ground of diction. These chapters, the core of the treatise, confirm by artistic divination the philosophical analysis of Aristotle, and range beyond diction into composition. How, he inquires, are we to lift oratory to the heights? Even as Sappho, he answers, makes us in a single poem feel love; that is, by selecting those characteristic actions which are most salient and gathering them into a single body. "Do you not marvel how she seeks to gather soul and body into one, hearing and tongue, eyes and mien, all dispersed and strangers before?"[3]   Poetry gives us the truth of life by bringing

[2] *Poetic,* 1450 a.   [3] x.

into organic continuity what is revealing and significant. What life disperses and interrupts, poetry focuses and brings into emotional sequence and momentum. Its essential processes are to realize these saliences imaginatively and to unify them. "It is survey*of the high points, and composition (σύνταξις) for unity." [4] A simple modern instance is Browning's "Meeting at Night."

This, the treatise goes on (xi–xii), is the typical method of poetic. The parallel (σύνεδρος) method of rhetoric is the converse; it is amplification. Poetry suggests in a flash; oratory iterates and enlarges. The one is intensive; the other, extensive. The one is compressed; the other, cumulative. Now none of the many and well-known means of amplification is self-sufficient. They all fall short without what we have called heightening. True, amplification and height of style may seem (xii) to amount to the same thing, since the object of both is by definition to invest the subject with greatness; but they differ in method.

> Height means direct lift (διαρμα); amplification implies multitude. Therefore the former is often in a single idea (νόημα), whereas the latter always implies quantity and abundance. . . So Cicero differs from Demosthenes in grand passages. The [force of the] one is in sheer height; of the other, in volume. . . The fire of the one is like lightning . . of the other, like a conflagration. [5]

So much for height as proceeding from the whole conception and movement. To return now to diction:

> Weight, grandeur, and energy are furthermore most readily achieved by images (φαντασίαι), or, as some call them, bodyings-forth. . . [By these terms are meant] specifically those

---

[4] xi, at the end. The ἐκεῖνο of this parenthesis in xi refers to x.
[5] xii. A similar comparison is made by Quintilian, X. i. 106.

cases in which, moved by enthusiasm and passion, you seem to see the things of which you speak, and to put them under the eyes of your hearers. As imagery means one thing with the orators and another with the poets, you must have observed that with the latter its function is vivid suggestion; with the former, precision.[6] Nevertheless both uses of imagery appeal to emotion. [Euripides in a passage quoted from *Orestes*, 255] saw the Furies himself, and what was imaged in his mind he almost compelled his hearers to see. [In another passage, from the lost *Phaëthon*] would you not say that the soul of the writer mounts the car with the driver, takes the risk with him, and with the horses has wings?[7]

Imaginative diction, then, is not primarily a trick of words; it is a visualizing habit of thought. It is sympathetic insight, even to the extent of feeling with Phaëthon's horses their wings.

[In poetry imagery may even range beyond what is convincing;] but in oratory it is always best when it holds to reality and verisimilitude ($\check{\epsilon}\mu\pi\rho\alpha\kappa\tau\sigma\nu$ $\kappa\alpha\grave{\iota}$ $\check{\epsilon}\nu\acute{\alpha}\lambda\eta\theta\epsilon\varsigma$) . . . What, then, can the image do in oratory? Much else, doubtless, it can add to speeches in energy and emotion; but infused into arguments drawn directly from facts it not only persuades the hearer, but also makes him its slave. [Instances from Demosthenes and Hyperides] While he is arguing from the facts, the orator has expressed them in images. He has given his very premise ($\lambda\hat{\eta}\mu\mu\alpha$) a force beyond persuasion. As by a law of nature, in all such cases we always hear the stronger. So we are drawn away from the argumentative [value] to that which is imaginatively striking, in which the facts [as mere evidence] disappear in excess of light.[8]

Imaginative realization of facts, the author is saying, which is essentially poetic, has its use also in rhetoric. That use is normally intellectual, for precision, for making an idea luminous. But there is a further use that is emo-

[6] In English the familiar contrast is between Shakspere's figures and Bacon's. [7] xv. [8] xv.

tional. Besides making ideas clear, imagery in oratory, as
well as in poetry, makes facts live. Thus it is not merely
stylistic beauty; it has its function at the very base of
oratory, in the subject-matter, in the very facts. Make
the audience visualize these facts, see them, hear them,
live in them by imagination, and you have done something
more effective than marshaling them as evidence and
urging your inferences. By the imaginative illusion of
actuality the audience is not merely convinced; it is captured. In such passages, rather than in reasoning, oratory
reaches its heights.[9]

The following chapters (xvi–xxxviii) on figures, carrying
into detail the fundamental principle of imaginative
realization, are handled less originally and less suggestively
than the principle itself. Perhaps we are the less patient
with the details of imagery because we have been made to
see vividly the scope of imagination. Classification of
imagery, which seems inevitably to produce the most
tedious chapters in rhetorics, lacks for us moderns what
is most characteristic of this ardent and original spirit,
constructive suggestion. But at least he abstains from
carrying it into minute analysis. Even these his most
technical chapters are illuminated by that genius for
appreciation which brought together one of the most
significant of all collections of literary models. His own
style, too, flashes in memorable sentences:

> A figure seems best when it is not noticed as a figure (xvii).
> What is hurried and roughened by emotion, if you smooth
> out to a level by conjunctions, loses its spur and fire (xxi).
> Beautiful words are essentially the very light of thought (xxx).

[9] The bearing of delivery on this, of the art of the actor on the art of
the orator, is glanced at in the opening chapter of Aristotle's *Rhetoric*,
Book III (see above, page 24), a meager passage illumined by this doctrine of the Great Unknown.

Occasional oratory (ἐπιδεικτικός) being recognized by the ancients as the most literary of the three fields,[10] one might expect this treatise to dwell on it especially. But the author's object is not special; it is general. This and the contagion of his enthusiasm have made his book, ever since its recovery in the Renaissance,[11] a powerful influence. Its promotive quality sets it above the schematic analysis of even so discerning a critic as Dionysius. Milton must have felt in it his own creative attitude toward reading. Nor does it need to dwell on the school of Isocrates when its own most characteristic passages have themselves the very mood and method of occasional oratory.

> What, then, did those immortals see who reached at the greatest things in writing and scorned unvarying nicety? Besides many other things, this, that nature meant us men to be no low species nor ignoble; but leading us, as into a great pageant, into life and the whole order of things, to be spectators of all that she shows and contestants eager for honor, she implanted forthwith in our souls invincible passion for all that is permanently great and in our eyes more divine.[12]

Where has been more nobly expressed the mainspring of interest in literature? Great authors satisfy our longing to enter the human scene fully, to experience vicariously and to share in imagination passions and deeds greater than those of our every day. They touch the heights of style who know the heights of life. To bring oratory into this company is at once to claim for it literary height

---

[10] Aristotle, *Rhetoric*, III. xii. 1414 a. See the discussion of this passage above, page 33.

[11] See the bibliography in the edition of Rhys Roberts.

[12] xxxv. Beside this may be set for contrast the bitter satire of Lucian's *Rhetorum præceptor*, which declares the practical equipment for success in oratory to be effrontery, a loud voice, a store of strange words, stock allusions, and sheer gab.

and to insist on the relation of rhetoric to morality. The moral implications of rhetoric are stressed again in the last chapter (xliv) that remains. Aristotle had recognized them explicitly. St. Augustine, at the end of the ancient world, must reaffirm them for Christian preaching. But against the sophistic that had always threatened this ideal no antidote is more effective than the great unknown's sense of mission.

Aristotle's theory of rhetoric determines its function. Cicero dignifies even its conventional tasks as training for leadership. Quintilian surveys it as a comprehensive pedagogy. Dionysius analyzes its art. But the great unknown moves us to share that art ourselves.

CHAPTER VI

THE *POETIC* OF ARISTOTLE [1]

Veneration of Aristotle has been impatiently classed with "other mediæval superstitions," both by those who disliked authority and by those who revolted against the inlaying and overlaying of his text with centuries of interpretations. Since the Renaissance the *Poetic* has, indeed, fared in this regard somewhat as the Bible; and in both cases those deviations from the original intention are widest, perhaps, which have arisen from "private interpretation," from missionary zeal more anxious to read *into* the text than to read *in* it. What may be called on the other hand communal interpretation, the consentient application of Aristotle's ideas to the typical problems of a whole group or period, constitutes an important guide in the history of criticism. Both kinds of interpretation imply in the original an extraordinary fertility. This vitality, it is also clear, is of principles, of ideas set forth not only as classifying, but as constructive. The principles have been from time to time crystallized in rules; and some of the rules, having been found restrictive or even inhibitory,

---

[1] The best recent editions of the *Poetic* for English readers are: (1) S. H. Butcher, *Aristotle's Theory of Poetry and Fine Art*, text, translation, notes, essays, London, 1895, 4th edition 1911 (text with translation issued separately); (2) Ingram Bywater, *Aristotle on the Art of Poetry*, text, translation, introduction, commentary, Oxford, 1909. For other translations and for a select bibliography see Butcher. Lane Cooper has added to his "amplified version with supplementary illustrations for students of English," Boston, 1913, an essay (1923) on *Meaning and Influence*.

have thereupon been flung aside. But again and again a
return to Aristotle's *Poetic* for orientation of practise and
of criticism has vindicated it as constructive. It is not
what Professor Dewey has lately called a "closed system." [2] It has exceptionally little of that mathematically
abstract method which Bergson [3] found unsatisfying for
survey of human activities in time. Rather its method is
inductive. It examines how imaginative conceptions have
been so composed and so expressed as to kindle, direct, and
sustain the imagination of an audience; and its formulation is typically like what modern science calls an hypothesis, that is a generalization interpreting facts so
far as they are known, and fruitful in their further investigation.

To reinterpret the *Poetic* in 1924, therefore, should be not
merely to reconsider the drama and the epic of Aristotle's
time, valuable as this is historically, but according to Aristotle's intention to consider what makes drama, our own as
well as his, and what vitally moves it to possess an audience. Each interpretation of so fundamental a work
must have its own preoccupations. The French interpretations of the seventeenth century had an emphasis different
from that of the Italian of the sixteenth; and we in turn
must see with our own eyes. But the correction that therefore becomes necessary, lest we make Aristotle say what
we wish, lies in the text itself. Fortunately the *Poetic* is
short enough to be read attentively in two hours; and its
terms, though translated somewhat variously, sometimes
imperfectly, now and then perversely, really demand not
so much erudition as patience, attention to the context,
and some acquaintance with the processes of art. The

[2] *Reconstruction in Philosophy*, New York, 1920, chapter iii.
[3] *L'évolution créatrice*, chapter. i.

Poetic should be read consecutively as a whole and then scrutinized in its parts. Interrupted though it is here and there, in some few places even fragmentary, it nevertheless progresses as a whole.[4] As to its terms, the best precaution is to remember that they mean to express the processes of actual composition and the results of the actual representation of drama or of the actual recitation of epic. In this sense the book is practical. It is not, as Bywater implies,[5] the less theoretical; but it deals with the composing as well as with the thing composed.

That Aristotle's survey of human expression included a *Poetic* as well as a *Rhetoric* is our chief witness to a division[6] oftener implied in ancient criticism than stated explicitly. Rhetoric meant to the ancient world the art of instructing and moving men in their affairs; poetic the art of sharpening and expanding their vision. To borrow a French phrase,[7] the one is composition of ideas; the other, composition of images. In the one field life is discussed; in the other it is presented. The type of the one is a public address, moving us to assent and action; the type of the other is a play, showing us in action moving to an end of character. The one argues and urges; the other represents. Though both appeal to imagination, the method of rhetoric is logical; the method of poetic, as well as its detail, is imaginative. To put the contrast with broad simplicity, a speech moves by paragraphs; a play moves by scenes. A paragraph is a logical stage in a progress of ideas; a scene is an emotional stage in a progress con-

---

[4] I say this without forgetting that the *Poetic* as we have it is probably but a part. If a part, it is still self-consistent, as I have tried to show in the tabular view below.

[5] viii, 206, 232.   [6] See Chapter i.   [7] See page 4.

trolled by imagination. Both rhetoric and poetic inculcate
the art of progress; but the progress of poetic is distinct in
kind. Its larger shaping is not controlled by considerations of *inventio* and *dispositio*,[8] nor its detail by the
cadences of the period.[9] In great part, though not altogether, it has its own technic. The technic of drama in
Aristotle's day was already mature and was actively
developing. The technic of narrative, in epic derived
from the great example of Homer, in "mime" and dialogue still experimental, was less definite. To set forth
the whole technic, the principles of imaginative composition, in a single survey is the object of Aristotle's *Poetic*.

TABULAR VIEW OF THE *POETIC* OF ARISTOTLE [10]

*The first section moves from definition of poetic in general to
the mode of drama* (chapters i–v.)

I. The art of poetry   Chapter
  A. is one of the arts that imitate men in action
    1. belonging with instrumental music and dancing   ii
      a. as using rhythm and melody besides words
  B. has two typical modes   iii
    1. narrative
    2. drama
      a. tragedy
      b. comedy
  C. developed historically   iv
    1. from the instincts of imitation and rhythm
    2. toward
      a. idealizing what men may be
        (1) as in epic and tragedy
      b. satirizing what men are
        (1) as in lampoons and comedy
      c. differentiation of form

---

[8] See page 42.   [9] See page 27.

[10] This analysis is intended to supplement, and in some cases to emend,
the outlines of Butcher and of Bywater by bringing out the significance
of the parts in relation.

(1) drama tending toward unity of plot   v
  (a) through the successive improvements of
      Æschylus and Sophocles
(2) but keeping variety in verse.

The second section discusses plot as the mainspring of tragedy
(chapters vi–xviii)

II. In the mode of drama, tragedy
  A. (definition) is an imitation of an action   vi
    1. serious
    2. determinate
    3. in language enhanced by rhythm, melody, and song
    4. by action, not by narrative
    5. issuing in emotional catharsis
  B. is primarily plot
    1. the subsidiary elements being character, diction,
        thought, spectacle (including make-up), and
        song
    2. (definition) Plot is a course of action planned to move
        causally   vii
      from a beginning through a middle to an end
    3. Plot is thus animated
      a. not merely by one main person   viii
      b. but by such consistency
        (1) as arises from truth, as distinct from facts   ix
        (2) as is opposed to the episodic
        (3) as is necessary to the catharsis
    4. Plot may be complicated by reversal or recognition   x
      a. arising causally from the plot itself   xi
      b. and has as a third element emotion and suffering
    5. Plot is the consistent working out, in an illustrious
        personage, of some human error to its issue
      a. Prologue, episode, etc., are merely formal parts   xii
      b. Plot is not mere reversal of fortune in a character
        altogether good or bad   xiii
        (1) for consistency, plot should be single, not di-
           vided by reversal to make a "happy ending"
          (a) as in inferior tragedies
          (b) and in comedy
      c. Plot achieves catharsis by its own consistency   xiv
        (1) not by spectacular means

ment in tragedy, includes the effects produced directly by persuasive speech, as distinct from those produced by action.

D. The subsidiary element of diction, to set aside what be-   xx
longs under delivery, includes letters, syllables, connectives, nouns and verbs (with their inflection), and word-combinations.

1. Words may be classified as   xxi
a. single or double
b. ordinary or extraordinary (figurative, coined, etc.)
c. masculine or feminine

2. Virtue in the choice of words consists in being clear without being colorless   xxii
a. Though extreme or habitual deviation from ordinary use is a fault, occasional deviation is necessary to distinction
b. Though it is a great thing to use variations of diction with propriety, the greatest thing is to be master of metaphor.

The third section defines epic and compares it with tragedy (chapters xxiii–xxvi).

III. In the mode of narrative, epic
A. has some general likeness to tragedy   xxiii
1. in that its [component] stories should be single, complete, having beginning, middle, and end
a. giving the pleasure of a living whole
b. not following the method of history
(1)as inferior poets do, but not Homer
2. in that it may be simple or complex, emphasize either character or emotion, and has some of the same elements as tragedy   xxiv
B. differs in length and in meter
1. Its characteristic advantages are scope and variety
2. The respective meters are the result of experience in appropriateness
C. shows in Homer the superiority of making the characters reveal themselves without explanation
D. can make freer use of the marvelous
1. by vividness of description
2. from the fact that the causal sense is weaker in read-

I

The principle of poetic art is imitation. Its two kinds
are drama in several forms and that other kind which
ranges from epic to dialogue and which has no single
generic name. All its forms in both kinds—tragedy,
comedy, dithyramb in the one; epic, mime, dialogue in
the other—are grouped with the arts of the flute, the lyre,
and the dance, and apart from those of painting and singing. Thus begins Aristotle's *Poetic* with that chapter of
definition which, as in the *Rhetoric*, opens and illuminates
the whole subject.

As to poetic art [11] I propose to discuss what it is in itself and
in the capacity of each of its species, how plots must be organized if the poem is to succeed, furthermore the number and
nature of the parts, and similarly whatever else falls within

---

[11] ποιητικῆς. The adjective means generally active, productive, creative, *efficiens*, as commonly in Aristotle's philosophy, in Dionysius and
Demetrius, and in Plotinus. Specially it means poetic, as of diction.
The noun ἡ ποιητική (with τέχνη understood) includes all imaginative
composition in words.

the same inquiry, beginning systematically with first principles.[12]

Epic and tragedy, comedy also and the [dramatic [13]] art of the
dithyramb, and most of the art of the flute and of the lyre are
all, taken together, imitations. They differ one from another
in three respects: in the means of imitation, in the object, or
in the mode [i. e., all are essentially imitation; in imitation
they are generally alike, and in imitation they are specifically different].

For as there are those who by colors and outlines imitate
various objects in their portrayals, whether by art or by practise, and others who imitate through the voice, so also in the
arts mentioned above. All [these] make their imitation by
rhythm, by language, and by music, whether singly or in combination. Thus only rhythm and music are used in the art of
the flute, of the lyre, and in such other arts, similar in capacity,
as that of the pipes. Rhythm itself, without music, [suffices
for] the art of the dancers; for by ordered rhythms they imitate
both character and emotion and action [i. e., dancing com-
passes the whole scope of representation]. Words alone,
whether prose or verse of whatever kind, are used by an art
which is to this day without a name. We have no common
name for the mime of Sophron or Xenarchus and the Socratic
dialogue. Nor should we have one if the imitation were in
trimeters or elegiacs or some other kind of verse . . . . [For
it is not verse, Aristotle goes on to say, that makes poetry, but
imitation.]

So much for differentiation. There are some arts that use
all the means mentioned above, i. e., rhythm, music, and verse,
e. g., dithyrambic and nomic poetry and also both tragedy and
comedy; but they differ in that the first two use all the means
in combination, whereas the latter use now one, now another.
Therefore I differentiate these arts by their respective means
of imitation.

[12] Bywater (page vii), protesting against too generalizing interpretations, goes to the other extreme of undue restriction. That the treatment is philosophical and intends to suggest large inferences appears
from both its plan and its language. Certainly the *Poetic* is technical;
but no less certainly it is theoretical.

[13] The interpretation of Bywater.

To proceed surely from this opening chapter, it is evidently necessary to grasp what Aristotle means first by imitation, secondly by that nameless art which uses only words, thirdly by classifying the art of poetry with that of music and that of the dance.

By imitation Aristotle means just what the word means most simply and usually, but also and more largely the following of the ways of human nature, the representation or the suggestion of men's characters, emotions, and actions.[14] At its lowest, imitation is mimicry; at its highest, creation. The latter is often implied in the Greek word *poetic*.[15] Poetic is one of the fine arts. By whatever means, in whatever forms, it is a direct showing of life, as distinct from any account of life through experiment or reasoning. The artist enhances our impressions of life by the suggestions of music or of story, the representations of dance or of drama. All these ways are called by Aristotle imitation because they follow the movements of human life. It is noteworty that he presents imitation primarily as a constructive or progressive principle. The more obvious imitation achieved by a single phrase, a single melody, or a single dance-movement is reserved for later discussion of detail.[16] The poet is a maker, as indeed he was called by our Elizabethans as well as by the Greeks, in the sense that he is creative. Poet, poetry, poetic, all are used by Aristotle with this broad implication of creative composition,[17] of "imitating men in action."

---

[14] ἤθη καὶ πάθη καὶ πράξεις, 1447 a, where Aristotle is speaking of dancing. [15] See foot-note 11 above.

[16] In Chapter ix, 1451 b, Aristotle says: "It is evident from the above that the poet should be rather the poet of his plots than of his verses, inasmuch as he is a poet by virtue of his imitation, and it is actions that he imitates."

[17] Butcher (pages 110–124) in pointing out that the Greek phrase for

Secondly, Aristotle specifies as kinds of the poetic art tragedy and comedy, which belong together as drama, and on the other hand epic, mime, dialogue, which also belong together, but have no common name. We lack, he says, a generic name for those forms of poetic art which, however various, are alike in having for their sole means of imitation words. The generic name that Aristotle desired to cover all prose and all metrical compositions in which the imitation is through words alone is still to seek. Yet that the genus is distinct through many varieties of form is even clearer to-day than in his time. The imitation of dancing and of all forms of drama is through representation; the imitation of music without words is through suggestion. Now so is the imitation of words without music. True, the words in the latter case carry something besides imitation; they convey ideas; but in so far as they achieve imitation, they do so by suggestion, and it is this suggestive imitation that makes them poetic. What is needed, then, is a term to cover all composition in words that proceeds by suggestion. Perhaps the nearest term

the fine arts is *imitative arts* (μμμητικαὶ τέχναι or μμμήσεις), says that Aristotle applies it specifically only to poetry and music. In this opening chapter of the *Poetic* he evidently means to include dancing. That Aristotle had no thought of "bare imitation," of that reproductive copying which Ruskin confused with artistic truth, has been remarked also by other critics. Butcher adds suggestively, though not with strict reference to the text, that to imitate nature was for Aristotle not to evoke the mere background which romanticism has taught us to spell with a capital N, but to work in nature's ways. Nature (φύσις) in Aristotle is not the sensible world, but "the creative force, the productive principle." So the immediate objects of poetic imitation are human characters, emotions, and actions, not as objective phenomena, but as expressions of human will. "The common original," Butcher concludes, "is human life . . . essential activity of the soul." Though this is true to the underlying idea of the *Poetic*, Aristotle does not use any single phrase corresponding to "imitation of nature."

in modern English is *narrative*. Using narrative widely enough to include, as in common modern use it often does include, dialogue and description, we have the term that Aristotle desired. *Story* would serve if it were not often used of the plot of a play or of an account in a newspaper. *Narrative* usually connotes a distinct method. A distinguishing generic term is more important to-day than in the time of Aristotle. Modern authors have developed narrative in directions little explored by the ancients. We have thus a variety of narrative forms which was quite unknown to Aristotle. Still, through all this variety, runs what he discerned as a common controlling method, the method of suggestion. In this fundamental *Gulliver's Travels* and the *Sentimental Journey* and *The Lady of the Lake*, to take examples as different as possible, belong together; and together they belong apart from *Othello*.

Thirdly, what is the significance of grouping all these forms of poetic art with music and dancing? Painting, which even in Aristotle's day was a fine art, is mentioned only as an analogy from another group. Singing, or chanting, also is only mentioned for analogy, perhaps because it is not creative. Architecture may have been omitted as being primarily at that time a useful art; but sculpture was both a fine art and, perhaps most obviously of all arts, imitative. Though we need not assume that Aristotle intended here a comprehensive classification of the arts, it is clear that he intended to group poetic art with the arts of music and dancing. Nor is his principle of division far to seek. Clearly he regards poetic as one of the arts of movement in time, and as distinct from the static arts of line and color, balance, mass, and pose. True, music and dance entered largely into early Greek drama and were still present in the drama of Aristotle's time; but that fact does not explain the grouping together of "epic, tragedy, comedy, dithyramb, flute-playing, and lyre-playing," with the later inclusion of dancing. Aristotle does not say that these occur together; and the mention of epic precludes any such interpretation. He says that they are alike. He saw all poetic art, especially drama, as primarily an art of movement. What is implied here in the opening chapter is carried out consistently, in doctrine and in terms, through the whole book. No one should deny a certain fundamental likeness among all the arts; but the likeness is not in technic except among those arts which have like "means" of expression, such as "rhythm, language, and music." Modern application of terms from architecture and painting to drama and story has spread no little confusion. Aristotle will have us think along right lines; and, as in his *Rhetoric*, the first chapter is the most important of all. We are to think of poetic composition not as structure, but as movement.

[Chapter ii differentiates the epic and the tragic art, which idealize "men in action" by seeking higher types of manhood and exhibiting men's aspirations, from the comic art, which exaggerates human failings. Chapter iii differentiates the two typical modes of poetic imitation as the narrative and the dramatic. Chapters iv and v, starting from the common impulses toward imitation, toward music, and toward rhythm, summarize the history of tragedy and of comedy. The conclusion is that tragedy differs from epic not only in proceeding by representation instead of narrative, but by being focused on a short period of time, normally twenty-four hours; in a word, by being intensive. Thus we arrive at the famous analysis of the essentials and the elements of tragedy.]

A tragedy,[18] then, is an imitation of an action that is (1) serious and, (2) as to size, complete, (3) in language enhanced

[18] 1449 b.

as may be appropriate to each part, (4) in the form of action, not of narrative, (5) through pity and fear effecting its catharsis of such emotions. . . . Every tragedy,[19] therefore, must have six constituents, according to which we estimate its quality: plot, character, diction, thought, spectacle, and music.

The greatest of these is the plan of the actions (the plot); for tragedy is an imitation not of men, but of action and life . . . and the end [for which we live] is a certain form of action, not a quality. By their characters men are what they are; but by their actions they are happy or the reverse. [In a play] therefore they do not act in order to imitate character; they include character for the sake of the actions. Hence the actions and their plot are the end of tragedy; and the end is greatest of all. Furthermore, without action there may not be tragedy; without character there may be. . . By stringing together speeches expressive of character and well made as to diction and thought you will not achieve the tragic function. Much rather is it achieved by a tragedy which, however deficient in these, has plot and plan of actions. Besides, those things by which tragedy moves us most, scenes of reversal and of discovery, are parts of the plot. A further proof is that novices in dramaturgy can put a fine point on diction and characterization before they compose deeds; and it is the same with nearly all the early dramatists. The principle and, as it were, the soul of tragedy is plot.

Second is character . . . Third [20] is thought, i. e., the ability to say what is necessary and appropriate, which in public address is the function of politics and rhetoric. . . . Characterization is what shows habit of mind. . . Thought appears in formal reasoning.

Fourth is diction, i. e., the expression of meaning in words, which is essentially the same in verse as in prose.

Of the remaining elements, melody is the greatest of enhancements; and spectacle, though moving, is [in general] the least artistic and [in particular] has the least to do with the art of the drama.

The history of criticism involved in the successive interpretations of this much discussed section and the

[19] 1450 a.   [20] 1450 b.

following may be postponed, The immediate concern
is the meaning of the definition and the division for
dramaturgy, i. e., for the actual composition of a tragedy and for the analysis of tragedy in terms of composition. Aristotle begins with the subject-matter. The
theme itself must be tragic, and is so if it is first serious
and secondly complete within its own extent. A playwright considering the possibilities of such-and-such
material is to ask first whether it is serious. The Greek
word [21] means not solemn in the sense of sad, but such
as to interest the composer and the audience by its importance. It might be rendered *humanly significant.* The
question, Is there drama here? becomes, then, first of all, Is
there action here that will engage emotional participation?
That is the first question; for it is fundamental.

Secondly, is this action dramatically manageable as
to extent? Will it finish within the time of a drama, come
to its issue, focus; or is its interest such as to demand more
extensive development in time; in a word, is it a drama
plot or an epic plot? The epic of "much-enduring Odysseus" demands extent of time; the tragedy of Oedipus,
compression of time. *Complete* [22] here means concluded,
i. e., susceptible, within dramatic limits, of a conclusion emotionally satisfying. To be dramatic, the action
must be self-consistent and self-determining. Tragedy
is characteristically intensive.[23]

[21] Σπουδαῖος, which of persons means *earnest;* of things, what we mean
by *serious* in such phrases as a *serious proposal* and *serious consideration.*

[22] Bywater makes one item, "as having magnitude, complete in itself."
Butcher makes two items, "complete, *and* of a certain magnitude." The
former seems closer to the Greek text and, on the whole, more consistent
with the context; but both renderings give much the same meaning ultimately.

[23] The distinction has lately been pointed by Mr. Hardy's *Dynasts.*
This, whatever else may be thought of it, is not "complete as to size,"

So far our tragedy has no words; it may even do without them. Nevertheless in its higher ranges it expresses itself also through suggestive language. In the third place, then, tragedy uses the whole range of "enhanced utterance," i. e., rhythm, and occasionally music and song. In conception a tragedy must be significant and complete; in expression it may be variously suggestive.

The fourth distinction of tragedy is its characteristic movement, which is acting, not narrative. The process of drama is representation; the process of story is suggestion. Drama shows men and women doing; story tells what they did. That is essentially dramatic, then, which is best brought home by actual representation. In this regard imaginative conceptions of human life differ essentially. Some are best conveyed by the indirect but abundant suggestions of narrative; others have their poignancy only through the few direct strokes of visible action.

Finally, tragedy is defined by its effect, the tragic catharsis. Tragedy "through pity and fear achieves its purgation of such emotions." [24] It is complete, then, not only in action, but in emotion. Emotion is not merely aroused; it is satisfied; it is carried through to a release. Tragedy is thus thoroughly emotional, more emotional than any other form of art. It is emotional not incidentally, but essentially; for it offers not merely emotional excitement, but emotional satisfaction. As all art enhances by imitation our impressions of life, so

but indeterminate. Doubtless that is why it is styled an "epic-drama." Certainly, for all its "enhanced utterance" and occasionally striking dialogue, it is not, by any definition, a drama.

[24] Bywater, pages 152–161, has discussed this phrase amply, and in an appendix, 361–365, has compiled with their dates the successive critical translations.

tragedy reveals our motives and moves us onward through
vicarious experience. We yearn toward our fellows moved
as we are, only more deeply; we fear in some great crisis
what obscurely threatens us all day by day; and we know
the inevitable end not with our minds, but with our
awakened hearts.

From definition of tragedy by its essential characteristics Aristotle proceeds to enumeration of its constituents. Of these the *sine qua non* is plot. The insistence
on this is so ample and so convincing as hardly to need
interpretation. Characterization comes second. Third is
the expression of thought, as distinct from the expression
of emotion or of character. The persons of the play not
only reveal their individualities; they have also occasion
to expound or persuade, and here poetic leans on rhetoric.
For drama, though its movement is imaginative, though
it primarily expresses emotion and character, cannot dispense with logic. Fourth is diction. Here again it is
noteworthy that Aristotle puts this fourth, though tyros,
he says, can master it before they can manage plot.
Whether the diction be verse or prose he regards as negligible at this point. With the same brevity he enumerates
finally musical and scenic accompaniments. What he
enlarges upon is plot and characterization, and upon
plot as the essential and determining factor.

These distinctions made, let us thereupon discuss of what
sort the plan of the actions (the plot) must be, since this is
both the first and the greatest [constituent] of tragedy. We
have shown tragedy to be imitation of an action complete and
whole which has a certain magnitude. Though there is such
a thing as a whole without any appreciable magnitude, we
mean by a whole that which has beginning, middle, and end.
A beginning is that which does not itself follow anything by
causal necessity, but after which something else naturally is

or comes to be. An end, on the contrary, is that which itself naturally follows some other thing, either by causal necessity or as a rule, but has nothing following it. A middle is that which follows something as some other thing follows it. Plots that are well planned, therefore, are such as do not begin or end at haphazard, but conform to the types just described.[25]

Plot, then, is what makes a play "complete and whole"; it is a planned sequence of actions. Aristotle's terms connote, not space and structure, but time and causal movement. The beginning is the point at which the cause is set in motion; the end is the result; the middle is the course from the one to the other. Plot is thus a significant course of action determined by permanent impulses; it imitates, not the mere surface movements of life, but its undercurrents. It is not a "slice of life," such as the experience of this day or that, but a course of life, moving from a "serious" crisis of determining emotions, through actions that carry these emotions out, to the final action in which they are seen to issue. Plot gives us what we often miss in actual experience, and consequently seek in the vicarious experience of drama, a sense of progress to completion. Experience is interrupted and complicated; drama moves steadily on a single course. Plot is the means by which dramatic art simplifies life, in order from the facts of life to extract the truth.

Furthermore, plot means technically management of a significant course of action within a practicable time. The tragedy must be long enough to show the action as progressive, yet short enough to be grasped as a single whole. "Beginning, end, middle" are thus very practical considerations. Every playwright considers every plot

[25] vii. 1450 b.

in this aspect.   Where is he to take hold in order to make
the situation clear?   What final action is, for his conception, the inevitable end?   What are the stages between,
leading one to another, in which the action will best be
seen as a progressive course?   Without limiting his consideration to the time-rules of the actual dramatic com-
petitions of his day, Aristotle seeks

> the limit determined by the very nature of the act; the greater,
> within the limits of clearness, the finer by its scope. To define
> roughly, that scope is sufficient within which the sequence of
> events according to probability or necessity may change from
> ill fortune to good, or from good to ill.[26]

What Aristotle finds necessary is time enough to make
the action convincing, to carry out the dramatic conse-
quences to their conclusion.   Compressed within too
short a time-lapse, the plot may remain fragmentary;
stretched out too long, it may sag or trail.   "Beginning,
end, middle," then, constitute a formula for plot.

> A plot does not gain unity by being, as some think, all about
> one person. . . . .   For as in the other imitative arts, the
> imitation is unified by being of one thing, so also the
> plot, since it is an imitation of an action, must be the imita-
> tion of an action which is one and entire and whose parts are
> so composed of acts that the transposition or omission of any
> part would disjoin and dislocate the whole [That, indeed is
> what we mean by a part]; for a thing whose presence or absence
> makes no visible difference is no part of the whole.

> From what has now been said it is plain that the function of
> a poet is this, to tell not the things that have happened, but
> such things as may happen, things possible as being probable
> or necessary.   The historian and the poet differ not by writing
> in verse or in prose.   The work of Herodotus might be put into
> verse, and none the less it would be history, with verse or with-
> out.   No, the difference is in this, that the one tells the things
> that have happened; the other, such things as may happen.[27]

[26] 1451 a.   [27] viii–ix, 1451 a–1451 b.

Consistency of plot, consistency of characterization also, as Aristotle goes on to show, imply that the poet interprets. He is not merely a recorder. The acts (πράγματα) of his *personæ* are not statistics; they are parts of the consistent presentation of a single whole. Every one of them, quite differently from the acts of real life, is seen to be significant. In thus including the significant and excluding the insignificant, the poet interprets according to his conception of the springs of action. He simplifies life according to his view of causes and motives, "according to probability or necessity."

In this the poet differs from the historian more generally. Tragedy is true to life not by rehearsing what men have done, but by revealing in significant action what men do, what they must do, being the men that the dramatist shows them to be. History records a man's deeds, and reasons from this evidence; drama directly represents the doer doing what he should do "according to probability or necessity." Plot, then, implies actions shaped to a unifying consistency. It imitates life; but it imitates by creative interpretation.

Therefore poetry is something more philosophical and more serious than history; for poetry speaks rather in universals, history in singulars. By universal I mean what such or such a man will say or do according to probability or necessity. . . . It is evident from these considerations that the *poet* must be rather a *poet* of plots than of verses. He is a *poet* by virtue of imitation; and what he imitates are actions. Even if he chance to *make* [28] history, none the less for that is he a *poet;* for nothing hinders some historical events from being just what they should

[28] The verb here translated *make* corresponds to the noun *poet*. The insistence brought about by the repetition will be made clear by rendering the words italicized *creator* and *create*, or, to revive an older use, *maker* and *make*.

be according to probability or possibility, and it is [only] in that aspect of them that he is their *poet*.[29]

That dramatic composition is thus primarily the devising of a convincing sequence is seen conversely when the sequence is defective.

Of all plots and actions the episodic are the worst. By an episodic plot I mean one in which the sequence of the episodes is not determined by probability or necessity. Actions of this sort are composed by bad poets through their own fault, and by good ones on account of the players; for as they compose for competitive presentation, and stretch a plot beyond its capacity, they are often compelled to twist the sequence.[30]

The essential dramatic force, then, is sequence, steady onward movement to a convincing issue. Scenes merely episodic, however vivid or clever each may be in itself, weaken this essential force. The episodic fault, whether it arise from weakness in the composer or from an actor's insistence on having a "part" to suit himself rather than to suit the play, makes the worst plays because it is a fault at the source.

Finally on cogency of plot depend the tragic pity and fear. The catharsis depends on our feeling the issue to be inevitable. Unexpected to the actors it may be, and most strikingly; but it cannot be fortuitous. While it is surprising to them, it must be satisfying to us as the outcome of their action.

Considering the imitation as not only of a complete action, but also of events arousing fear and pity, we find these too at their height when they are [at once] unexpected [by the *dramatis personæ*] and consequential. For so we shall be more struck than by what happens of itself or by chance.[31]

["Reversal[32]" or "recognition,"[33] Aristotle goes on in

[29] ix. 1451 b.   [30] ix. 1451 b.   [31] ix. 1452 a.   [32] περιπέτεια.   [33] ἀναγνώρισις.

chapters x and xi, if the plot is so far complicated, must arise from the plot itself, not be merely added.]

Two parts of the plot, then, reversal and discovery, are such as has been shown; a third is [actual] suffering . . . action destructive or painful, such as deaths on the stage, tortures, wounds, and the like.[34]

This latter passage is tantalizingly brief. So far as the context shows, *suffering* is used here to denote single scenes of unusually violent action. Why should such a scene be called a "part of the plot"? The word πάθος is used generally—and in the plural it is used repeatedly throughout the earlier chapters of this work—to mean emotion. Emotion is not a part of the plot in the sense that reversal or recognition may be a part. Rather it is a pervasive principle and an object. *Suffering,* to translate the singular noun so, may be regarded as a part of the plot in the sense that it may be an element of tragedy. So taking it, we may suppose Aristotle to countenance here such scenes of violence as were more familiar on the Elizabethan stage than on the Greek.[35] At any rate, Aristotle here inserts a chapter [36] on the formal parts (prologue, episode, exodus, etc.), before proceeding with the methods by which the plot may be worked out.

Chapter xiii insists that the vital principle of plot is

[34] xi. 1452 b.

[35] Both Butcher and Bywater so interpret; but Butcher's rendering "tragic incident" seems hardly to meet the context. Bywater's rendering "suffering" seems preferable if we may venture to interpret it as meaning, more generally than Bywater suggests, the working out of the plot to its full emotional expression. So taken, it corresponds to the climax of pity and fear, as "reversal" and "recognition" correspond to the preceding complication.

[36] xii. 1452 b. This has been challenged as an interpolation. It is at least meager and, as it were, impatient, as is the corresponding section in the *Rhetoric* (III. xiii. 1414 b) on the formal parts of an oration.

causal consistency. This rules out mere reversal. A turning-point (περιπέτεια) is, indeed, characteristic of drama. There is usually and typically a crisis, in which the hero's fortunes turn from good to bad; but this reversal will not suffice by itself. The mere turn of fortune does not achieve the catharsis of pity and fear.

> There remains, then, the [hero] between [the typically virtuous man and the typically depraved], a man neither exceptional in virtue and righteousness nor falling into adversity by vice and depravity, but by some error, a man among those who live in renown and prosperity, such as Œdipus or Thyestes or other illustrious men of such families.
>
> The perfect [tragic] plot, therefore, must be single, not, as some say, double;[37] the change of fortune not from adversity to prosperity, but on the contrary from prosperity to adversity; not through depravity, but through great error on the part of a man either such as we have described or rather better than worse.[38]

Why this insistence on character in the midst of the discussion of plot? Why the iteration of "not through depravity, but through error"? Because, as Aristotle shows below,[39] plot implies consistency of characterization, but more fundamentally because consistency of plot has for its very beginning and mainspring the realization of a central figure like ourselves progressively winning our sympathy. The essence of plot is motivation. What moves us is never mere luck, never mere surprise, but the

---

[37] διπλοῦν. The context seems to show that this means *divided* in interest and issue, insufficiently focused. Aristotle does not mean that the plot should not be complicated; for at the opening of this chapter he says that the plot of the perfect tragedy is not simple, but complicated (μὴ ἀπλῆν ἀλλὰ πεπλεγμένην). What he adds here is that the complication should not be such as to divide our sympathy. The plot should not, indeed, be simple; but it should be single.

[38] xiii. 1453 a.   [39] xv.

causation that springs from human will. Consistency of plot means clear causation; and causation in drama is the working of will. So the first consideration is the title rôle, the main "part." He or she should be illustrious because the action is thereby conspicuous and partly known in advance; but his course of action must be moved by springs that we feel in ourselves. Macbeth is a warrior of an elder day and a king; but we, though neither warriors nor kings, feel the perversion of his manhood as like enough to our own to purify us through pity and fear.

Fear and pity may, indeed, be aroused by mere spectacle, but they may also be aroused from the very plan of the actions,[40] and the latter is superior and shows a better dramatist.

This is the second consideration of consistency. First, the best tragedy springs from a great personal will gone wrong; secondly, it springs from a compelling progress of actions, from the plot itself. It depends not on the shock of this violent deed or that, but on the causal movement of the whole.

Character is discussed in chapter xv as a distinct topic, but still with reference to plot. For throughout this section, especially from chapter xiii on, the topic is consistency.[41] Consistency, though it refers primarily to plot, must also include characterization. In general, characterization must be consistent with the morality of the individual purpose, with the moral habit of the social group, with the received idea of the person, and finally with itself.[42] In particular,

it is necessary in the characters, as in the plan of the actions, to seek always the inevitable or the probable, so that the say-

[40] xiv. 1453 b. ἐξ αὐτῆς τῆς συστάσεως τῶν πραγμάτων.
[41] See the tabular view, page 136.
[42] I follow Bywater's note, pages 227–228.

ing or doing of such-and-such things by such-and-such a person, just as the happening of this event after that, shall be inevitable or probable. Evidently, therefore, the solutions also
[as well as the complications] of plots must come about from
the plot itself, and not, as in the Medea . . . by the *deus ex
machina.*[43]

In a word, consistency of characterization is part of the
causal weaving of the plot.

Chapter xvi applies the principle of consistency to
"recognitions," or "discoveries." [44]

Best discovery of all, however, is that which arises from the
actions themselves, when the surprise comes as a natural result, as in the *Œdipus* of Sophocles and in the *Iphigenia.*[45]

Chapters xvii and xviii turn to the actual processes of
dramaturgy, to the work of the playwright. This is concerned mainly with plot; but first Aristotle urges the
fundamental necessity of visualizing.

One must compose plots and work them out in the "lines"
by putting [the scenes] before his eyes . . . and as far as
possible by acting out, even with the gestures.[46] . . . . .
His stories, whether already made or of his own making, he
must first set out in general (i. e., make a scenario), then put
in the incidents and carry out.[47] . . .
Every tragedy has both complication and solution, the
events that precede [the opening scene] and often some of those
within the play constituting the complication, and the rest the
solution. By complication I mean all from the beginning to

[43] 1454 b.
[44] ἀναγνώρισις. 1454 b. "This and the next two chapters form a
sort of Appendix; they discuss a series of special points and rules of con-
struction which had been omitted in the sketch of the general theory of
the μῦθος." Bywater, page 233. I am not convinced of an interruption
here. What seems to me the bearing of this chapter and the following on
the discussion of consistency from Chapter xiii on is indicated in the
tabular view on page 136.
[45] 1455 a.   [46] xvii. 1455 a.   [47] xvii. 1455 b.

that scene which is just before the change in the hero's fortunes; by solution, all from the beginning of the change to the end [of the play].[48] . . .

It is necessary to remember what I have said often and not make a tragedy an epic system—by epic I mean aggregative— as if one should dramatize the whole story of the Iliad.[49] . . .

The chorus too should be regarded as one of the actors, be a part of the whole and share in the action, be not as in Euripides, but as in Sophocles.[50]

Visualizing actively at every stage, the playwright is to compose his plot before he works out his lines. He is to determine his play by the method of solution, to avoid the extensiveness of epic, and to make even the chorus contributory to the plot.

The bearing of the meager observations on the logical element and on diction (xix–xxii) will be clear from the tabular view.[51] They are not distinctive except in the saying "the greatest is the being metaphorical"; [52] and they have surprisingly little on dramatic rhythms.

The third section of the *Poetic* (xxiii–xxvi) defines epic and compares it with tragedy.

As to metrical narrative, its plots [severally] should have the movement of drama in focusing on an action whole and complete with beginning, middle, and end, that [each] may give its proper pleasure as an organic unity, and not be composed as history, which has to exhibit not a single action, but a single time, whatever chanced to happen in this period to one person or to more.[53]

The general likeness of epic to drama, then, is in interpretative focus, as distinct from the chronicle method of history. Story, as well as drama, selects in order to unify.

---

[48] xviii. 1455 b.   [49] xviii. 1456 a.   [50] xviii. 1456 a.
[51] Page 138. As to whether xx is an interpolation, see Bywater.
[52] xxii. 1459 a.   [53] xxiii. 1459 a.

Moreover (xxiv) story, too, as well as drama, has its crises, its recognitions, its emotional outbursts. The epic poet, if he have something of Homer's skill, can make his characters express themselves without intruding his explanations. These are general likenesses throughout the whole poetic field. For characteristic differences, epic has the advantages of scope and variety. It gains from the marvelous, which can generally be suggested better than it can be represented.[54] These points are as significant to-day as in the time of Aristotle. Not so the defense (xxv) of epic against certain typical objections which smack more of the schoolmaster than of the critic. To argue whether a given epic story were possible or probable or promotive of good morals was in fact one of the regular elementary exercises of the later schools. The closing exaltation of drama over epic [55] is summary, indeed; but that is natural, since the points, having been made before, are here simply reviewed comparatively. The idea of intensity through unity is a logical conclusion of the *Poetic* as a whole.

II

From Aristotle's introductory grouping of drama with music and dance, throughout his long discussion of plot, runs the idea of movement. The dramatic mode of imitation is to set human life in motion before us and to heighten our sense of living by carrying it through to a significant issue. Has this idea animated other drama than the Greek? Is its vitality shown by its permanence? Is it essential? As all art heightens our impressions of

---

[54] A most striking exemplification of this is *Paradise Lost*.

[55] Sainte-Beuve, *Étude sur Virgile*, vii. page 151, disputes the superiority of drama to epic.

life and our sense of living, so the art of the dramatist in particular heightens and extends our sense of human life by vicarious experience. Its object is to make us feel human experience more widely and more intensely. All the technic of the stage, whether ancient or modern, whether simple or elaborate, has for its main object this sort of creative imitation. The dramatist tries to induce and to hold the illusion of actual experience. In so far as he succeeds, we forget that we are in the theater; we imagine that we are seeing a reality more real than we can piece out of our fragmentary glimpses at men and women; and in his greatest successes we almost pass from spectators to actors. Toward this result how important is Aristotle's idea of movement, his doctrine that plot is a progressive synthesis of actions, unified but never static?

Those who have superficially thought of Greek drama as static, who may even have pictured it as statuesque, can hardly have studied the great play of Sophocles that Aristotle offers as an example, *Œdipus the King*.

Laius, King of Thebes, and his wife Jocasta cast out their infant son Œdipus to die. But the shepherd commissioned to do away the child gave it instead to a stranger, who carried it to Corinth. There the little Œdipus, fostered by a Corinthian couple, was brought up as their son. In the strength of his manhood setting forth to make his own way, he met in a narrow pass another traveler who haughtily bade him yield passage. The dispute warmed to blows. Œdipus killed him. It was his own father Laius. Proceeding to Thebes, Œdipus found the throne vacant and the city in terror of the monster Sphinx. He silenced the Sphinx, and, hailed by the people as their deliverer, he became their king and married the widowed queen Jocasta, his own mother. But Apollo having in time sent a pestilence upon Thebes, Œdipus was besought by the people to be once more their savior. His emissary to the oracle, Creon his brother-in-law, brought back word that Thebes must put away the unclean person who had slain Laius. By searching investigation Œdipus discovered that he himself was the pollution, that he had slain his own father and married his own mother, that not only he but his children were accursed, that the outlawry which he had invoked upon the guilty fell upon his own head. Thereupon he put out his eyes in an agony of horror, after Jocasta had killed herself, and groped his way from Thebes led by his wretched daughters.

This is the legend. Its events extend over many years. Which of them shall be chosen for the stage as having most dramatic value? Which to an audience can be made most significant; and how shall these vital scenes be arranged in such continuous and progressive movement as will convey, and at the same time enhance, our sense of the movement of life? Sophocles with his own dramatic skill, but in the form typical of all the best Greek tragedy, arranged his whole action within the compass of its last poignant hours. Omitting nothing that is emotionally essential, nothing that is essential to clear understanding, he yet relegated some events to the background in order to represent fully the great crisis. He gathers together the whole visible action into an hour and a half on the stage and a half-dozen persons; and in this brief compass he unfolds that action with increasing intensity by making every scene move from the last and to the next, on to the awful close.

The Theban people, represented by the chorus supplicating their savior king, rehearses his great achievements for their deliverance. Œdipus in the strong confidence of his power and his mission stands before his palace like a god. At the end of the play he is led slowly from that palace a broken man. But the composition of the play is not mere reversal for contrast. Between the first scene and the last, action moves without haste, but without delay or interruption. The vigorous and self-reliant king chafes at the cryptic response brought from the oracle by Creon; he is indignant, then furious, at the tragic silence of the seer Tiresias. His quick intelligence scents a plot between the two. Breaking through the interposition of Jocasta, he wins from her false hopes while he gives her no less unwittingly the premonition of doom. Once suspecting, however darkly, he must know, he will know, he knows a dreadful part, he knows more, he knows all. So this great play, though it is focused on a single day, though it excludes all the past history and the development of character, is never static. It is never for a moment tableau. Because of its compression it moves not less, but more.

For that is why Aristotle insists that the dramatic action should be self-consistent, limited in scope. The object of dramatic unity is not bareness, but fulness and continuity. It is to give time for full and intense realization of what actual life merely hints interruptedly. It is to give us human life undisturbed and uninterrupted, so that we may see it clearly and whole. We are to have the illusion of actual experience, yes, but of larger and deeper experience than we can get from the mere reproduction of facts or from the cross-currents of life itself. Like every other art, drama is a simplification of life because it is an interpretation. The dramatic simplification is seen by Aristotle to consist essentially in moving from revealing crisis to revealing crisis up to a final revelation. It excludes all the accidental and the irrelevant that embarrass our actual movements; it tells what has happened through what is happening; it cuts to the quick. It takes those moments only in which a man is himself, suppressing those in which he is indistinguishable from other men. But it does not leap or halt between; it brings out our real sequences. It reveals life to us by showing the emotional connection of its great moments.

That such dramatic unity became sometimes a bondage in seventeenth-century French classical drama was due not to any defect of the Aristotelian principle, but partly to making the practise too rigidly a code, and still more to stiffening the movement into tableau. The classical French application of the principle of dramatic unity is not, as has often been pointed out, altogether Aristotelian. Least of all is it Aristotelian when it hinders dramatic movement. French classical tragedy when it is cold—and to think of it as generally cold is a prejudice—is static; it is feeble in movement. The free movement, not to say the loose movement, of Elizabethan plays, which was hailed by Hugo and other Romanticists as a deliverance from the classical code, is indeed better than tableau; but it is compatible with bad playwriting. He would be rash who should assert that Elizabethan plays are in general more effective dramatically than French classical plays. Rather, since the two traditions bring out different dramatic values, each has something to learn from the other. But it is plain that the progress of the Elizabethans in dramaturgy was in the direction of unity, of more highly organized movement. To see this we need go no farther than Shakspere. The difference between his earlier plays and *Othello* is largely a difference in unification. *Othello* by itself is sufficient proof of the value of dramatic unity for dramatic intensity. And with or without unity, with the Greek and the French focus of time or the Elizabethan lapse of years, drama demands movement from scene to scene. The value of unity is only to heighten this sense of movement.

Drama, of course, has its differences of age and of race. We are not to think that at its best it must always be Greek. One of the large differences between ancient drama and modern is, indeed, a difference of emphasis. Ancient drama relies more on plot, modern drama on characterization. The ancient playwright had above all, for his theater, to realize the emotional values of a situation by seeing that his play was well put together; the modern playwright has sometimes, in a theatre giving opportunity for facial expression, relied far more on realizing his persons, on writing what the actor calls a good part. Nevertheless, though playwriting does not always need the compactness of Greek form, many modern plays have chosen this compactness, this closely organized movement, for intensity.[56]

Undoubtedly such dramatic composition demands of the playwright definiteness of interpretation. His selection, his limiting of time and place, his leading from scene to scene, are only the technical means of realizing his emotional intention. He is trying to show us human life, not in random and interrupted glimpses, not in the jumble and discord of its surface, not in aimless and frustrated movements, but in the animating emotions of its crises. In order to represent crises, he is compelled to show us wherein they are critical; in order to give to emotion full expression, he must make it significant. Rather it is this significance which first caught his attention, which gave him the con-

---

[56] The most familiar instances are certain plays of Ibsen. Of plays recently on the stage, Bernstein's *Voleur*, Mirbeau's *Les affaires sont les affaires*, Besier's *Don*, Kenyon's *Kindling*, show that this type of dramatic movement is not confined to any particular school. Of plays that on the contrary dispense with this and rely mainly on characterization the most familiar to Americans is the dramatization of *Rip Van Winkle* used by Joseph Jefferson.

ception of his play and guided his realization. If his dramatic movement halts or lapses, the reason may lie deeper than technic in uncertainty of intention; and if on the other hand he is able to sustain it and carry it through, the fundamental reason is that his conception of its issue is strong and clear.[57]

This presumption has more than once been challenged. Why must the dramatist have an intention, a theme? Why may he not simply represent life? Represent life he not only may, but must, to the extent that he must reflect life, not reflect *on* it; but what is represented? Life in its multitudinous complexity, its unfulfilled intentions, life as it whirls past and escapes us? That is a task beyond drama. No playwright has ever represented life except as he saw it, or made his representation intelligible without interpretation. And as the dramatist has to interpret in order to compose, so the audience wishes to be led up to some issue. We desire not mere emotional excitement, but emotional release. Else the pity and fear, to use Aristotle's words, will not bring us purgation. A play shows us life in critical moments, and these are moral moments, moments of the clash of wills. Drama assumes free will, and its movement is by motives. Motivation, on which Aristotle so much insists, is to make the issue convincing. The dramatic representation of life is creative imitation largely in proportion as it thus moves to an end; and the typically dramatic end is not blind fate, but poetic justice.

Poetic justice sums up what Aristotle means by saying that "poetry is something more philosophical and more

[57] The paragraph is adapted from the author's *College Composition*, page 248.

serious than history." It means the truth revealed
beneath facts, the real cause and effect moving beneath
the surface. An audience, desiring deeper emotional
experience than it achieves through daily observation,
desires especially to see how its sharper conflicts issue.
It asks of the dramatist not only sight, but insight. It is
not satisfied with "mere reversal." "The mere spectacle
of a virtuous man brought from prosperity to adversity
moves neither pity nor fear; it merely shocks us." The
same criticism is implied in Stevenson's objection to
Meredith's *Richard Feverel*, that it "began to end well"
and then cheated us.

The convincing close, expressing the playwright's intention and resulting from the whole course of action,
is thus a fair measure of what used to be called problem
plays. It measures how far they are in Aristotle's sense
serious, how far they are penetrative and significant, in a
word how far they are tragic. Each disclosure, each
critical scene of the dramatic progress, having its full
emotional value separately and for itself, leads on to the
next. Such planning for momentum is not only Aristotelian; it is permanently dramatic.

Creative imitation of human life, thus moving us along
that course of actions which is both the means and the
measure of creative power, makes drama of all the arts
most poignant. Whether it is, as it has always seemed to
its devotees, the highest form of poetic, at least its appeal
is at once the largest and the most direct. In the very
persons of men and women it speaks to us by face and
gesture, by the message, the imagery, and the rhythm of
words, most of all by the order of its actions. Plato, indeed, would have us draw from this the moral that our
own lives should be ordered poetically, that is creatively,

that we should control and direct our lives to harmonious movement.

> For we are ourselves according to our power poets of a tragedy at once fairest and best.   Every social order [58] becomes for us an artistic creation [59] of the fairest and best life, which we say to be essentially the truest tragedy.[60]

[58] πολιτεία.   [59] μίμησις.
[60] *Laws* 817 b; quoted by Bywater on Aristotle's *Poetic*, 1450 a.

CHAPTER VII

POETIC IN ANCIENT DRAMA AND NARRATIVE

The classical practise of poetic in the two modes distinguished by Aristotle, dramatic and narrative, has a twofold significance. It has the claim of all great art for its own beauty; and it reveals certain fundamentals of literary form and literary influence. Classical influences on later art have been defined sometimes vaguely, sometimes amiss, for lack of clear grasp of classical practise. Yet the vitality of classical poetic art is hardly more proverbial than its definiteness. Without circumscribing in formulas its creative variety, we can discern quite clearly its artistic habits in these two enduring modes.

Into such a survey recent questions as to literary forms need not enter. How far a literary form may be modified or extended without losing its character, how suggestive a recognized form is to the composing imagination, are questions important rather for those modern times in which the artist is much concerned with individual self-expression than for the centuries in which he was more the spokesman of a community. Even if Brunetière's transference of the word *genre* from biology to literature be only analogy, even if Croce's denial that a literary form is directive of the artist be justified, we must still use the terms drama and epic. From Aristotle down, criticism has used them not only for convenience, but because in fact there were two typical ways of extensive imaginative composition in words, varying in detail but constant

167

essentially, and always sharply distinct. Whether these should rather be called types or modes than forms is a question for later consideration. For the purposes of the present review the terms drama and epic connote only habits of composition universally recognized.

The two discussed by Aristotle as types are in fact seen as types to persist. The habits of drama have remained typically distinct from those of narrative, and have changed far less. To add Senecan tragedy to its Greek proto-type, and to mark the distinctive traits of Latin comedy, will both fill out Aristotle's summary and show in what forms classical influences came first to modern drama. Narrative in the ancient world developed along few lines. Its poetic art long remained epic. This art was at once followed by Vergil and recreated. The Æneid is the great exemplar of all that is fruitful in literary influence. The Hellenistic art that Vergil rejected was cultivated by Apuleius and ran to seed in the Greek prose romances. Meantime it was practised with facile brilliancy by the Latin poet whom the middle ages knew better even than they knew Vergil—Ovid. Setting aside, then, all minor forms, and in the two major forms all but what is typical, we may venture to survey ancient poetic, first in Greek tragedy, with Senecan tragedy for contrast and Latin comedy for supplement, then in Vergilian epic, with Ovidian narrative for contrast and Apuleius for divergence.

I. DRAMA

A. GREEK TRAGEDY [1]

At first glance Greek tragedy strikes the modern student as finished. Its historical period is definite. It grew;

[1] All the larger histories of Greek literature appraise Greek tragedy,

it matured; it died. Its strictly dramatic influence appears to be sharply limited. Inoperative as a mode of representation, indeed almost unknown, in the middle ages and the early Renaissance, it seems at first to have been revived in modern times only for archæological reproduction, as the models of Greek architecture in museums. Even if such a view were just—and it is not—Greek tragedy would compel attention by sheer artistic em-

trace its history, and cite monographs for special study. The study of Greek tragedy as drama should begin with the plays themselves. These should be read—and with happily increasing frequency they may even be seen—before reading further about them; for they are now available not only in many editions, but also in many translations. Translation, though it must fall short or go wide of the original diction, conveys the larger dramatic movement, the characteristic dramaturgy; and Sir Gilbert Murray's translation of Aristotle's main example, *Œdipus Rex*, seeks especially the dramatic values. Very instructive comparisons may be made by reading all eight tragedies presenting the story of Orestes and his house, the "Oresteia": the *Agamemnon, Choephoræ,* and *Eumenides* of Æschylus, the only extant trilogy; the *Electra* of Sophocles; and the *Orestes, Electra, Iphigenia in Aulis,* and *Iphigenia in Tauris* of Euripides. Beside the *Œdipus Rex* of Sophocles most critics would place his *Antigone;* and beside the *Medea,* the most popular play of Euripides, his *Alcestis* and his *Trojan Women.* But it is no great task to read all extant Greek tragedies.

The general character of Greek dramaturgy and its historical place are outlined at once concisely and suggestively by Brander Matthews in his *Development of the Drama* (New York, 1903), chapter ii, to which may be added chapters iii, v, viii, ix, and xiii of his *Study of the Drama* (New York, 1910). T. D. Goodell's *Athenian Tragedy* (New Haven, 1920) is admirable. Gilbert Murray's *Euripides and His Age* (London and New York, 1913) discusses Greek dramaturgy generally in chapters iii, viii, and ix. More inclusive works for English readers are A. E. Haigh's *The Attic Theatre,* 3d edition revised by A. W. Pickard-Cambridge (Oxford, 1907), and R. C. Flickinger's *The Greek Theatre and Its Drama* (Chicago, 1918).

These few books are selected as specifically informing and suggestive for dramaturgy. A longer selective list will be found in L. VanHook's *Greek Life and Thought* (New York, 1923), pages 310–312. A comprehensive bibliography, so many are the historical significances of Greek tragedy, would fill a volume.

inence. It can no more be ignored than Gothic architecture. It is one of the great artistic achievements of the human spirit. But no such artistic achievement is ever finished in the sense of being relegated to a museum. Its eminence constitutes a presumption of vitality. Gothic architecture, though held in abeyance and even forgotten for centuries, is again operative. It compels attention to-day not only in reproductions, but in creation. Greek tragedy has profoundly influenced modern playwriting. Its increasing reappearance to-day in revivals, and the distinction of certain imitations such as *Samson Agonistes*, are less important than its influence on modern dramaturgy, as in Racine and again in Ibsen and finally in certain striking plays of our own time. This vitality implies that the Greek experience, in especially happy conditions of stage and audience, through a period of extraordinary artistic competition, was fruitful not merely in skilful adaptation to those conditions, but in dramatic principles.

(1). *Theater and Audience*

The emotions that are enhanced by representation before a crowd are typically such as are best felt by the crowd together, such as are communal.[2] Greek drama began, according to tradition, in the rites celebrated by the whole village to honor Dionysus, the god of fertility and enthusiasm. In the shouting, singing chorus there were at first no actors in the modern sense; but that was because in a broader sense all were actors. There was rude, impromptu mimic action. There was probably a good deal of improvised verse by individuals, and probably a good deal of recurring refrain by the whole crowd. Out of this com-

[2] This paragraph and the following are adapted from the author's *Writing and Speaking*, pages 412-415.

munal impersonation of the story of Dionysus grew very
naturally individual impersonations of the god and of his
more prominent mythical attendants, the crowd responding
with impromptu variations of the familiar refrain.   Every
crowd produces a leader.   The leader of the Greek chorus
became an actor in the modern sense of taking a fixed part.
In time other fixed parts were assigned to individuals, till
the mimic action had a definite dialogue; but the chorus
persisted as representative of the whole community.

Then, as always, came the individual genius to discern
the capacity of what had grown up among the people,
to reveal and enlarge that capacity, and to fix a great
form of art.   The shaping of drama by Æschylus and
its development by Sophocles and by Euripides expressed,
indeed, individual genius; but no less they expressed the
ideals of the Greek race and remained answerable to the
original popular impulse.   The Greek audience during
the great period of drama felt not only that the chorus
chanting in the orchestra was its representative, but that
it was itself as a body assisting at a communal celebration.
Always the enacting of legend or history known to every
spectator by heart, the drama was always judged sternly
not only by its poetic beauty, but by its faithfulness
to communal beliefs and feelings.   Its success was measured by the feeling of the community.

So the great open-air Greek theater was made for the
community.   It superseded the unfurnished hillside as
the community passed more and more from participants
to spectators; but it remained, to a degree rarely realized
in modern times, communal.   For Greek tragedy, even
at its height, never lost its reminiscences of ritual.   Every
representation being an act of religion, the theater crowd,
united by a common rite, was the more sensitive to common

sympathies.   That the theater is for the crowd, not for the
individual, has been realized by playwrights of every age;
but the first great age of drama opened this peculiar opportunity of dramaturgy widest because its crowd was unified.
The communal sense of tradition was focused by religion.

(2). *Diction*

Remembrance of this fact has led many modern readers
who have never seen a Greek play to conceive Greek
tragedy as formal and rigid.   This is much the same error
as supposes Greek architecture and statuary to have been
white.   It is an illusion of time.   Greek buildings and stat-
ues became white when no hands were left to restore their
colors.   Greek tragedies became formal and rigid when
they passed from the stage to the closet, when they lost
the rhythms of dance and of phrase.   With every revival
of them upon the modern stage the illusion is dispelled.
Indeed, it can be broken by merely reading them aloud.

Nevertheless, though they show to an exceptional degree that larger movement which Aristotle found to be
a dramatic essential, they were stately in gesture and
in lines.   Even without the associations of religion, the
very size of the theater would have precluded the facial
play that is a main reliance of modern acting, and induced
in the open air a delivery sometimes oratorical and always
large.   The tragic mask and cothurnus were adaptations
to a great open-air space.   To the same physical conditions were adapted the rendition and the lines themselves.[3]

The diction of Greek tragedy, though varying widely
of course from poet to poet, has certain recognizable

---

[3] " The words are so composed that their full effect can be appreciated
only through the clear and rhythmical enunciation of an actor who relies
mainly on his voice."   J. T. Sheppard, *The Œdipus Tyrannus of Sophocles*
translated and explained, Cambridge University Press, 1920, page ix.

constants. It is generally sonorous, sententious, and, to a degree never surpassed, direct. It realizes fully the emotional appeal of rhythm; for though its dialogue has less rhythmical variety than Shakspere's, it rarely lapses into monotony, and it is relieved by the abundant imagery and metrical variety of the chorus. Greek tragic dialogue is typically austere. It rarely amplifies, for it is poetry, not oratory; [4] but it makes every word count dramatically. The ideal of economy is felt even in the diction. Passages of narrative, such as those of messengers, are made dramatically effective not only by situation, but by variations of tone and tempo. Effects of style may seem to have preoccupied criticism too much unless we remember that the Athenian audience was habitually sensitive to rhythm, and that it was never distracted by novelty of story from attention to the dramatist's art. That the final touch of this art was the rhythmical finishing of the lines there can be no doubt.

Nor is dramatic verse a mere traditional convention.[5] Obviously it is appropriate to historical dignity; but beyond this we become aware, even from reading, much more from hearing, that the verse subtly and constantly enhances the emotion by enriching the connotation. It is not merely rhythm added to force, though how much rhythm, even in prose, is worth dramatically every good actor knows. It is not even poetry added to drama. It is an element permeating and integral. Good dramatic verse, to say nothing of the best, is not a lyrical addition, not a decoration, but as truly a dramatic means as the

---

[4] See pages 126, 127 above on the distinction made by pseudo-Longinus (xi–xii) between poetry and oratory.

[5] Parts of this paragraph and the following are taken from the author's *A Note on the History Play*, in *Shakesperian Studies*, Columbia University Press, 1916.

other means of characterization. That is why the tradition
of every great stage, such as the Comédie Française, lays
distinct stress on rhythmical rendition; and that is why
the dramatic rhythms of Greek tragedy are still inspiring.

Nor is even this the final value of verse in Greek tragedy.
Such verse enhances the characterization not only in
detail by widening the opportunity of the actor to convey
mood and emotion, but generally by enhancing the poetry.
The typical method of Greek tragic characterization is to
idealize. The mighty figures of the past, remote from the
urgencies of our confusing present, confirm our faith that
man may dominate and direct his world for good, or,
when they too fail, reveal with larger truth the tragic
flaws of humanity and the hope of its regeneration. Modern
history plays, as well as ancient, are poetic in diction
ultimately because they are poetic in conception, as
Greek drama was at once tradition and poetry. The
word audience, which in its etymological suggestions has
seemed inappropriate to a modern crowd gathered rather
for seeing than for hearing, is entirely appropriate to the
Greek theater.   The visual values of representation were,
indeed, realized in gesture and pose, though less in scenery
and spectacle; they were realized as never, perhaps, since
in group movements; but the auditory values, the sounding
line, the phrase harmony of the chant, always enhanced
representation by strong rhythmical suggestion.   A
Greek tragedy was in a real sense, though its music was
simply melodic, a symphony.

(3). *Chorus*

The symbol of the communal import of Greek tragedy
and of its characteristic form is the chorus. From being
almost the whole the chorus dwindled dramatically to a

subordinate part. The inference, however, that it was outgrown, that except for historical study it is negligible, is unwarranted. Even Euripides used the chorus dramatically; and Aristotle urges, not that it be abolished, but that it be made an integral part, one of the actors. Nor were the practise and the theory mere concession to Greek convention. The chorus was in fact dramatic.[6] Too readily conceiving it in terms of our meager modern experience, as in opera, critics often seem to have forgotten that the Greek chorus furnished not primarily tableau or grouping or even pageantry in a wider sense, but chanting and dancing. That dancing may be highly dramatic we have but recently rediscovered. Aristotle[7] knew dance as compassing the whole range of bodily expression. Far from being merely a lyric interlude, the chorus offered distinct dramatic possibilities.

To begin with, the combination of choral dance and chanting has a direct appeal to the simpler emotions that are communal; and in Greek drama it enhances the idealizing of communal fears and beliefs and aspirations. The idealism of Greek tragedy is conveyed largely by the chorus. Then the chorus is used to enhance the emotion of a preceding scene by iterating it sympathetically, or by recoiling in protest, or by reflecting on it *sub specie æternitatis*. Thus are achieved the relief of variety and also an intermediary effect, the effect of spectators of the action itself interpreting to the spectators of the play. The variety brought about by the choral throng was the more marked because the actors were few. In the chorus

---

[6] This has nowhere been better expounded than in the ninth chapter of Gilbert Murray's *Euripides and His Age*, London and New York (Home University Library), 1913.

[7] *Poetic*, 1447 a. See above, pages 140, 143.

were many opportunities for representation of the human world about these isolated individuals, and for dramatic symbolism through the group movements of the dance. The choral dance, always symbolic, had been developed from simple, primitive forms to a fine art. The preliminary to every dramatic production was the public granting of a chorus; and the training of this chorus by the dramatist himself was a main part of rehearsal. The chorus is associated in every one's thought of Greek tragedy inevitably and fitly. It is not merely an archaic convention; it is not merely a lyric accessory to drama; it has dramatic possibilities which may yet, if large open-air theaters win again a place in communal life, be revived.

(4). *Themes and Personæ*

The rhythmical effects of diction and of choral dance are hardly more characteristic of Greek tragedy than its unvarying use of legendary themes and persons. Euripides is thought to have chafed within these confines, to have been hampered by the conventional prescription of old bottles for his new wine. In any age the playwright who insists on ideas in advance of his crowd thereby sacrifices something of the communal appeal. But even Euripides kept outwardly the unwritten law, and Aristotle[8] accepted it as part of his theory. It is evident that such themes and such persons were a tragic convention; but the convention was still recognized in the middle ages;[9] it

[8] *Poetic,* 1453 a. See above, pages 135, 144, 155.

[9] For instance, Chaucer's Monk says in his prologue:

> Tragedie is to seyn a certeyn storie,
> As olde bokes maken us memorie,
> Of him that stood in greet prosperitee
> And is yfallen out of heigh degree
> Into miserie, and endeth wretchedly.
> *Canterbury Tales,* B. 3163.

was accepted by the Renaissance; it was formally adopted by the French seventeenth century; and its being a convention does not prove it any the less dramatic. Without disparaging the gain to modern tragedy from the widening of the tragic field we may take account of the typical values of the field of tradition.

The field of tradition is *ipso facto* the field of communal memories and aspirations and, even in modern times, of myth. Though the recreation of myth may be artificial and remote, that it need not be so, that it may on the contrary originally express both the poet and the conceptions of his audience, has been proved many times, and very convincingly in our own time by William Vaughn Moody's *Fire-bringer*. The fire of Prometheus is there seen, even after Æschylus, even after Shelley, to be undying. The modern science of anthropology, indeed, gives good ground for thinking both that myth is constantly human and that by its very persistence, as of a primitive trait, it opens opportunities for drama.

The modern study of folklore, by recovering some lost echoes in Greek tragedy, has enhanced its significance. Folk superstitions, though they retire from public gaze before more sophisticated conventions, are slow to die. Those which have become mere curious lore are of course dead dramatically; but those which express persistent human yearnings may be all the more vital dramatically because they are primitive. Such, for instance, is the folk-tale of the fairy mistress, the woman of unearthly beauty who has the magic to enrich the man she loves with joy and power. Widespread over western Europe in the middle ages, it has roots in remote antiquity. Euripides made it, not as the medieval writers the story of the delusion of the man, but the tragedy of the woman. In varying forms it has recurred again and again. In Walter Map's amazing tale of Gerbert[10] it concludes upon penance and renunciation. In Fouqué's *Undine* its native force is dissipated in sentiment. A dead superstition, on the other hand, has no dramatic appeal. Though we admire the steadfast piety that agonizes over the unburied body of a brother, we can no longer appreciate the situation of Antigone as fully tragic; for we have lost irrevocably the ancient superstition from which it springs. But Medea with her power to bless and ban her lover, and with her unearthly capacity for suffering, who will venture to say that she is dead? That she is primitive gives her only the more power to walk the stage to-morrow.

Mythical idealizing is readily symbolic. But in Greek tragedy direct symbolism, except in the chorus, is not common. Rather than as symbolical, the legendary figures appear as typical. It is as typical that the "illustrious persons" are recommended by Aristotle and represented by the dramatists that he expounds. Prometheus, Heracles, Agamemnon, Medea, are chosen as eminent not in rank, as some French dramatists are accused of thinking, but in typically human traits. They show grandly and conspicuously what obscurely is suffered by us all. "There you and I and all of us fell down." They are race heroes; we communally feel in them the race ghost. And the more mythical they are, the more we can feel the struggle of all human kind. For the very limitations on themes sets Greek tragedy in sharper relief against modern as exhibiting the dramatic vitality of legend.

Personages so fixed do, indeed, tend to preclude both

[10] *De Nugis Curialium*, IV. xi. Map's collection contains several other forms of the same story or of related stories.

novelty and subtlety of characterization. In this regard
Euripides, especially in his Medea, is sometimes exceptional. Generally the characterization of Greek tragedy
is broad and simple. The *personæ* are taken full-blown,
at some revealing crisis. But modern experience with
plays and with novels confirms the impression that broad
characterization is generally more effective before an
audience; subtle, minute, or cumulative, with an individual
reader. In this application, too, we may take Aristotle's
saying that plot is more important in drama, character
in epic. But lest we separate character from plot unduly,
we must remember that the movement of Greek tragedy
is not merely of events, but of human will. Will is the
exhibition of character in action. It is the mainspring of
every tragic crisis. At once the simplest and the strongest
expression of character, it animates Greek tragedy because it animates almost all tragedy.[11] Æschylus in
Prometheus Bound promises the victory of heroic fortitude.
Sophocles in *King Œdipus* conveys the agony of assertive
individuality at finding the struggle for self-fulfillment
vain, and brings even innocent willfulness to wreck.
Euripides sees the tragic conflict of the traditional blood-
wite with reverence to a mother as leading to madness.
Within the compass of the few dramas left to us from the
Greek stage the tragedies of human will in a few typical
personages are seen to be as various as they are convincing.
Even the rich variety of the great Elizabethan period
does not make them seem meager.

Rather they exhibit the dramatic richness of the typical.
By the very fact of being embodied in flesh and blood any

[11] Brunetière's point (*Annales du Théâtre*, 1893) is well interpreted by
Brander Matthews, *The Development of the Drama*, page 20, and again in
A Study of the Drama, chapter v.

"illustrious person" begins to be real. Even the allegorical figure of Everyman in the mediæval morality—and the Greek *dramatis personæ* were never allegorical—has held modern audiences because each spectator recognized himself with his secret foes and friends. That the persons of the Greek stage were few and familiar, then, was not of itself a disadvantage. The tragedies of a few famous families can strike pity and fear into all families who know the bitterness of hate. Moreover, the restriction to familiar themes, the exclusion of novelty from plot, focused attention upon conception and movement. Playwright and audience alike looked for originality not in subject, but in art. Comparison of play with play was readier and more specific; and the competition of the stage was almost purely artistic.

(5). *Plot*

Plot in Greek tragedy, the movement of the whole play, is discussed so extensively by Aristotle that little need be added. For his preoccupation with Sophocles hardly makes his exposition the less comprehensive. Later criticism has generally accepted Sophocles as historically midway between the occasional archaism of Æschylus and the occasional modernism of Euripides, as typical of Greek dramatic habits, and as the greatest Greek master of plot. Sophocles, as has been often pointed out, intensified drama by making his unit not the trilogy, but the single play, by developing a single theme with a clear conflict, and by making its interaction self-sufficient through the use of a third actor. Euripides, on the other hand, seems to care less for totality, though he achieves it in some plays, notably in the *Medea*. His use of a separable prologue instead of dramatic exposition within the

play has been condemned as impatient; [12] and the vividness of his lines, expecially in description, has been disparaged as distracting. In all this the art of Sophocles
is no more eminent than it is typical. He is the shining
example of Greek artistic economy.

This characteristic economy of Greek tragic art makes
it permanently inspiring to playwrights.   Modern audiences, being less conscious of art, may find the economy
sometimes too close; but playwrights discern in it both a
triumph of technic and an example. For the revolt against
even the "unities" of the French classic stage spent its
force long ago. Meantime the war of the romanticists
against the classicists should make clear, what the greatest
dramatists have always understood, that unity in drama is
valuable only as a means to coherence. Its only *raison
d'être* is to clear the way for steady movement and to lead
that movement to a convincing issue. Now in this compelling force of movement Greek drama, especially in the
hands of Sophocles, remains by common consent a model
of tragic art. That even audiences habituated to variety
and tolerant of looseness will still feel this force is suggested
by revivals of increasing frequency, by the eminence,
even in a period of very different dramatic habits, of such
plays as *Othello*, and by the deliberate preference of some
recent dramatists [13] for the Greek model. But whether
single, steady movement through a limited time be a
permanent dramatic principle or not, at least it is characteristically Greek. What one editor says of the *Antigone*
of Sophocles might be said of Greek tragedy generally:
"there is no halting in the march of the drama." [14]

[12] As to this see Gilbert Murray, *Euripides and His Age*, page 205.
[13] See above, page 163.
[14] E. S. Shuckburgh's edition of the *Antigone*, Cambridge University
Press, 1908, page xvii.

This effect is brought about technically by focusing on a single scene and a continuous critical period.[15] The whole tragedy, as has been quaintly said, is compressed within the fifth act; or, to speak in still more modern terms, the Greeks composed their tragedies as long one-act plays. Such a play differs from *Henry IV* or *A Winter's Tale* essentially; it differs from *Othello* only in removable accidents. The characteristic is not brevity, nor even unity, but continuity. That the habit of continuity was fostered by Greek stage conditions, the habit of discontinuity by Elizabethan, there can be no doubt; but neither can there be any doubt that the Greek stage conditions were modified more than once by a dramatist, or that the Elizabethan stage conditions did not determine the growth of Shakspere's art. In both great ages a dramatist took the stage as he found it, but built up his dramatic technic as he chose. The continuity of Greek tragedy is not merely a fact of archæology; it is an achievement of technic.

The limiting to a single place and time has been objected to as forcing off-stage some events that the audience would like to see, and as unnaturally crowding the action. In a word, the one-act form, for an action of some magnitude, has been called artificial. Any form may seem artificial if it is realized imperfectly; and the limits of this form impose merely a higher degree of the difficulty inherent in any dramatic form, the difficulty of focus. Even a five-act play imposes limits, prescribes selection, by the very conditions of the stage itself. The peculiar opportunity arising from the stage conditions of the Greek theater

---

[15] Not that there were never lapses of time or shifts of place (see Matthews, *A Study of the Drama*, Chapter xiii, and Goodell, page 82), but that Greek tragedies move habitually without time-break and in a single stage-setting.

was discerned to be emotional intensity. Intensity has even been urged as the characteristic opportunity of all drama. Whether this be granted or not, undoubtedly the Greeks conceived drama so, and developed their technic accordingly. They worked for intensity. Though they were not content with two actors, they were content with one stage set and with one period of time. Not only so, but the difficulties of their form stimulated their art. In these conditions playwrights heightened intensity by a technic of progressive continuity.

So much for the idea behind the objections. The particular charges seem hardly to hold. What is forced off the stage of Greek drama, or of any drama? Surely nothing that the dramatist wishes to have on-stage, or his art is imperfect. That the frequent murders are only heard, not seen, is due not to any exigencies of form, but to social convention and to the idea that dying is less tragic than death. For the rest, to put shifting human life on a fixed stage, even with liberty to represent more than one place and time, always involves foreshortening. Art cannot have the diffuseness of life. It works by selection. The Greek tragic artists chose to carry selection to the highest degree. That this event or that of the tragic story is reported by a messenger, not enacted before our eyes, is not a hindrance to the tragic march, not the makeshift conceded to an intractable form. Let the speech of a Greek messenger be read aloud, or better, let it be acted; and it will no longer be called undramatic.[16] Add its dramatic value in context, its relation to the scene that it enters; and no doubt will remain. The possibilities of narrative on the stage, though they seem to have been forgotten by many English playwrights, are clear.

[16] Murray, *op. cit.*, page 212.

But the Greek dramatist did make a virtue of necessity. He sometimes used a messenger, dramatically indeed, but perforce. What we hear from a messenger we could not see without change of scene. This was the dramatist's sacrifice, not to formalism, but to continuity. To that end he would have made even greater sacrifice.

The speeding of the action beyond the normal pace of life is not confined to this form. It is a condition of all drama. Nor does Greek drama seem either crowded or hurried. Though events may follow thick and fast, the Greek movement is typically unhurried. It has steadiness from careful preparation; it gains momentum as it advances; it culminates swiftly; it diminishes to a slow and quiet close.

That tragedy should have a full close, carrying the action through to a καταστροφή, or state of rest, must have been with the Greeks a principle; for it was an almost invariable habit. Though the tragedies of other and later nations do not always end so, they too have the full close often enough to suggest that audiences generally desire it.[17] Whether or not this is true of audiences, it seems true of playwrights in proportion as they work, as the Greeks worked, for singleness. In Greek tragedy the end crowns the work in the sense that the close completes the interpretation. The close of the action is the issue of the characterization. Characterization in Greek tragedy, more consistently than in any other, is motivation. In some Greek plays it offers hardly anything else. The characters are drawn for the play, not for themselves. The "part" is subordinated to the theme. When we see that this is true even for Medea, a "part" to be coveted by any modern actress, we realize that the significance of the whole play was habitually in the Greek conception

[17] See above, pages 147, 149, 150, 161.

the main object. This explains the full close as the goal
of a steady movement, and as the final stage of the idealization which habitually shaped both characters and plot.
And where a modern playwright has worked with the
same intention, we find again and again, as in *Othello*,
the same full close.

The ultimate technical question, then, is What is continuity worth? Euripides composed sometimes as if it
were worth less than salience. He has even been called
romantic; and the influence of Greek tragedy, since it
was overwhelmingly his among the Romans and in the
middle ages, may seem after all to be hardly the influence
of Sophoclean movement. But the great influence of Euripides is largely of his poetry apart from his dramaturgy.
It reigns through a time when tragedy was waning, and
through a later time when there was hardly any drama
at all. He is still the most interesting of Greek dramatists
to read. On the other hand, those of his plays which are
now most effective as stage performances have the typical
Greek continuity; nor does he often depart from the type
very far. That the type has a controlling idea of continuity is evident. To the Greek dramatists generally
continuity seemed to be worth much technical labor and
even much sacrifice. The crown of their technical skill was
to carry the theme, to develop it, to fulfill it at the last.

Behind this technic is an ideal of singleness. The
sacrifice to continuity springs from that *ascesis* which
has been remarked in other fields of Greek art. It has
aroused—it will always arouse—the protest of the roman-
tics. An art of singleness, lucidity, cogency, seems to
them, as perhaps it seemed already to Euripides, too far
removed from life. And not the romanticists only, but
after them the realists, have demanded a drama more like

life itself, freer, more various, less composed.   Perhaps
there is no ultimate reconciliation, or perhaps the two conceptions are complementary; but the Greek tragedians seem
to answer from their plays: art is not life; it is idealization.

B. SENECAN TRAGEDY [18]

How far the Latin tragedy of the actual stage followed
the great Greeks we can only speculate from a few fragments and from the references of critics.   That the lost
Medea of Ovid was Greek in more than name the habit
of composition seen in the *Heroides* leaves much doubt.
Certainly the tragedies of Seneca, while they revive the
great names of Agamemnon, Hippolytus, and Medea,
never enter the great art of Athens.   Indeed, their
relevance at this juncture is for contrast.   A Senecan
prologue is not only a separable prefix; it may be a summary of the whole plot, as the prologue of Latin comedy.
Separable the Senecan chorus is always in providing lyric
interludes.   It would thereby interrupt the action if the

[18] The plays ascribed to L. Annæus Seneca (distinguished as "the
younger" or "the philosopher," circ. 4 B. C.–65 A. D.) are *Œdipus,
Phœnissæ, Medea, Hercules Furens, Hippolytus* (or *Phædra*), *Hercules
Œtæus, Thyestes, Troades, Agamemnon.* Their authorship is discussed by
E. C. Chickering in *An introduction to Octavia Prætexta,* New York, 1910
(Columbia dissertation), which also contains a brief account of Roman
tragedy, reviews the question of the stage production of Seneca, and dis-
cusses his rank as tragedian. Ella I. Harris's *Two tragedies of Seneca,
Medea and the Daughters of Troy, rendered into English verse,* Boston, 1898
(all ten, New York, 1904), summarizes Senecan influence on English drama.
See further J. W. Cunliffe's *The influence of Seneca on Elizabethan tragedy,*
New York, 1893. All the Senecan tragedies are included in *The tragedies
of Seneca translated into English verse, to which have been appended comparative analyses of the corresponding Greek and Roman plays* . . by F. J.
Miller, introduced by an essay on the influence of the tragedies of Seneca
upon early English drama by J. M. Manly, Chicago, 1907. Miller's
translation is published also in the Loeb Classical Library.

tragedy had the Greek onward course; but instead Seneca's violent scenes are themselves separable, and his dialogue is sometimes a collection of speeches. Seneca wrote tragic scenes and spaced them with lyric pauses;[19] he did not gather momentum for a total impression. He made his *personæ* utter their feelings; he did not make them interact. The familiar names, the familiar stories, only heighten the contrast. Senecan tragedy is like Greek tragedy only in non-essentials. The essentials of Greek dramatic composition are not here.

What is here is not poetic, but rhetoric. That these pieces were written for recitation, not for acting, the external evidence is strong, though not conclusive,[20] but the internal evidence is abundant.[21] Most significant is the feebleness of plot. More obvious is the rhetorical method of characterization by typical traits,[22] the method of the character sketches (ἠθοποιίαι) in schools for boys as it was expanded in the schools for men under the masters of *declamatio*. A method essentially oratorical, it developed under the *declamatores* of the Empire not creative conception, but inventive ingenuity and a preoccupation rather with striking expression than with consistency. Most obvious of all, written large on every page, is the swelling rhetoric of the style. Not for nothing did this poet bear the name of Seneca.[23] To deny that such writing

[19] Chickering suggests (page 45) a resemblance to grand opera.

[20] It is reviewed by Chickering.

[21] "Ce sont des exercices de déclamation, des recueils factices de morceaux de bravoure écrits pour la lecture." G. Michaud, *Le génie latin*, Paris, 1900, page 116.

[22] See above, pages 71–2 and foot-note 8. "Quant aux caractères c'est du stoicisme découpé en personnages." E. Nageotte, *Histoire de la littérature latine*, page 469.

[23] Seneca "the elder," or the rhetorician, in his collection of *Controversiæ*, is the chief source of our knowledge of *declamatio*. See Chapter IV. II.

has a certain force is to forget what it might become in the mouth of a trained speaker and before an audience taught to admire its distinctive effects; to forget also how eagerly Seneca was appropriated fifteen centuries later; to forget finally that oratory in the theater has not yet lost all its appeal. But while we grant to rhetoric some share in the poetic art, we cannot put Senecan tragedy beside the tragedy of Athens without seeing unmistakably that such art as it has is not the distinctive art of drama.

C. Latin Comedy

The plays of Plautus and Terence keep the dramaturgy known as the New Comedy,[24] the comedy of Menander. Its figures, alike in Greek and in Latin, are types. Such individualizing as may be discerned, in the *Menæchmi*

[24] See Legrand, P. E., *Tableau de la comédie grecque pendant la péri-ode dite nouvelle—κωμῳδία νέα*; translated as *The New Greek Comedy* by James Loeb, with introduction by John Williams White, London and New York, 1917. An earlier study quoted below is Lallier, R., *La comédie nouvelle, introduction à l'étude du théâtre de Térence* (leçon d'ouver-ture), Toulouse, 1876.

Recent English translations of Plautus are: by Paul Nixon in the Loeb Classical Library (2 volumes issued); by E. H. Sugden of *Amphitruo, Asinaria, Aulularia, Bacchides, Captivi*, London, 1893; by H. O. Sibley and F. Smalley of *Trinummus*, Syracuse, N. Y., 1895; by B. H. Clark of *Menæchmi*, New York, 1915. W. H. D. Rouse has reprinted William Warner's Elizabethan translation of *Menæchmi* with the Latin text for the study of Shakspere's *Comedy of Errors*, London, 1912.

A second edition of F. Leo's *Plautinische Forschungen zur Kritik und Geschichte der Komödie* appeared in Berlin, 1912. More recent studies are: Brasse, M., *Quatenus in fabulis Plautinis et loci et temporis unitatibus spe-cies veritatis neglegatur . .* Greifswald, 1914 (Breslau thesis); Schild, Erich, *Die dramaturgische Rolle der Sklaven bei Plautus und Terenz*, Basel (thesis), 1917; Blancké, W. W., *The dramatic values in Plautus*, Geneva, N. Y., 1918 (Pennsylvania thesis); Cole, Mrs. H. E., *Deception in Plau-tus*, a study in the technique of Roman comedy, with bibliography, Boston, 1920 (Bryn Mawr thesis).

A complete translation of Terence was privately printed for the Roman

for instance, or the *Self-tormentor*, stands out as exceptional. Comedy, perhaps, tends more than tragedy to the typical. At any rate, Latin comedy has a set of *personæ* quite fixed: [25] two fathers, two sons in love and in debt, two daughters of romance or of pleasure, and two slaves to stir the intrigue. There might be a matron, a slave-trader, and a braggart soldier; and there would be pretty surely a parasite.

Stock figures involve conventionality also in plot. One of them may have a double,[26] and the plot may consist largely of mistaking one for the other; or the long-

---

Society, 1900, 2 volumes, with brief notes and partial bibliography. The most useful available translation is that of the *Phormio* by M. H. Morgan, Cambridge, Mass., 1894, with the Latin text and reproductions of the Vatican miniatures of costumes. This play has been translated also by Clark, B. H., New York, 1915; *The Self-tormentor*, by Shuckburgh, E. S., Cambridge, 1869, and by Ricord, F. W., New York, 1885. The Loeb Classical Library publishes the translation of John Sargeaunt in 2 volumes. See also Michaut, G., *Sur les tréteaux latins* (*histoire de la comédie romaine*), Paris, 1912; Knapp, C., *References in Plautus and Terence to plays, players and playwrights*, Classical Philology, xiv, number 1 (Jan., 1919); and a charming popular study by Lemaître, J., "Térence et Molière," in *Impressions de théâtre*, vi (1898) 15–27. The better to define ancient conceptions of comedy, Lane Cooper reconstitutes *An Aristotelian Theory of Comedy, with an adaptation of the Poetics and a translation of the ' Tractatus Coislinianus,'* New York, 1922.

[25] See the quotation from Apuleius on page 228. The *Onomasticon* of Julius Pollux enumerates 44 masks sufficient for all the rôles and all the situations of the New Comedy: 10 for old men, 10 for young men, 7 for slaves, 3 for old women, 14 for young women. There are even stock names, e. g., Davos and Chremes. *Miles gloriosus* was taken over by Latin comedy and again by French seventeenth-century comedy, though in fact neither society had this Athenian type. Over against him is the parasite, often the mover of the intrigue. The slave and he are the most active of the *personæ*. (This note is derived from Lallier.)

[26] The extreme case is the *Amphitruo* of Plautus with its two Amphitryos and two Sosias. In *Menæchmi* the servants are doubled; in *Bacchides*, the courtesans.

lost daughter, as in the *declamationes* and the Greek romances, may have been kidnapped by pirates. Typical is the plot of Terence's *Phormio:*

> One Chremes had a brother Demipho,
> who wishing for some cause abroad to go,
> had left his son young Antipho at home
> at Athens, while it pleased him thus to roam.
> This Chremes had a wife and daughter too
> in Lemnos domiciled, that no one knew;
> another one at Athens, and an heir
> that desperately loved a harper fair.
> From Lemnos came the mother with the maid
> to Athens, and there died. The daughter paid
> the last sad rites (now Chremes was away).
> And so it came about that on that day
> young Antipho the orphan child espied,
> fell deep in love and took her for his bride.
> ('twas through a parasite 'twas brought about).
> The brothers coming home with rage broke out,
> gave thirty minæ to the parasite
> to take her off and marry her outright.
> With this they buy the girl that Phædria prized;
> the other keeps his bride now recognized.[27]

In essentials this is the plot of any Latin comedy. That the Greek originals of the New Comedy were less crystallized is suggested by larger fragments recovered recently; and that Menander was a creator of plots may be inferred from the saying reported by Plutarch: "I have made my comedy; for the plan is arranged, and I have only to write verses for it." [28]   Even with so few situations as in Latin comedy there is room for variety of handling. Early commentators distinguish the *modus*

[27] Greenough's translation of the argument, prefacing Morgan's translation of the play.

[28] Plutarch, *Mor.*, De gloria Atheniensium, 347 F.

motorius,[29] the kinetic mode, from the *statarius*, or static, and find that Terence, except in the *Phormio*, tends to the latter. But even the movement of Plautus is rather bustle and go than onward progress. Dramatic movement will hardly be compelling where motivation is so much from circumstances and so little from character. *Modus motorius* seems to imply rather liveliness than sequence. To the large, miscellaneous, and turbulent Roman audience, it has been plausibly suggested, there would have been little appeal in cogency of plot.

A certain dulness in the audience is suggested by the fact that Terence was reproached for combining two Greek plots in one Latin play. He protests, naturally, that this is his right; and the *Phormio* shows his ability to weave an intrigue clearly and attractively. The dramatic lack mistakenly ascribed to his stories is rather of salience, especially of visibly significant action before our eyes. That this can vivify even conventional characters in a conventional plot is the chief dramatic message of Plautus. He trusts the intelligence of his audience so little as to make his prologue an oral program, a *catalogue raisonné*, explicit to the last degree.[30] With Terence he resorts to the aside, the soliloquy, and the convention of people on the stage together who do not see each other —all these when they could be obviated by a little dramatic ingenuity. Where Plautus spends his ingenuity is on

---

[29] Michaut (139) cites Evanthius *De Fabula* IV. 4 and Donatus. *Statarius* seems to be used, in the prologue to the *Adelphi* and in a passage cited by Michaut from Cicero's *Brutus* xxx. 116, of acting. Knapp cites the prologue to the *Self-tormentor*.

[30] "Qui sim, cur ad vos veniam paucis eloquar," prol. to *Bacchides*; and the play opens with both ladies together on the stage, so that there can be no mistake. Terence, who devotes his prologue usually to rebuttal of detraction, sometimes devotes his whole first act to exposition.

lively realism of detail, on abundance of stage "business."
He holds a scene, turning and returning a situation, until
he has used its whole value. Though this is sometimes
tiresome for reading, it shows good theatrical sense of the
actual audience. He may have learned it from acting.
Nothing is more instructive to playwrights than this
filling of a simple outline. The habit is almost the opposite of the compression of Greek tragedy, and the New
Comedy is doubtless inferior to tragedy in every point
of plot; but none the less it vindicates clearly the value
and the Plautine method of imaginative amplification.

II. NARRATIVE

A. THE *ÆNEID*

(1). *Epic*

Epic is now often divided into "primitive," "authentic," or "popular" epic, such as the *Iliad*, and "artistic,"
or "literary" epic, such as the *Æneid*. Of the former the
great example is Homer. The *Iliad* and the *Odyssey*
remain, for us as for the ancients, supreme. Meantime
the western European nations emerging in the early middle
age expressed themselves in epics of original native force:
the *Roland*, the *Beowulf*, the *Nibelungenlied*, and some
of the Norse sagas. To put these beside Homer is to
become aware of specific differences within a general
likeness. Homer is both more ample and more finished.
Primitive he certainly is not in any sense now recognized
by anthropology. Even the word popular has for us
implications quite inapplicable to the circulation of his
day. The classification of certain epics as primitive,
authentic, or popular is based on the idea that these are
characteristically communal, expressing more the emo-

tions of a whole homogeneous community, less those of the individual poet. It has even been held [1] that such epic began in aggregation of tribal lays, and that even the form in which it has come down to us is less the creation of any individual than the final artistic shaping of successive anonymous versions. The theory of communal composition, in this literal and extreme sense, has been sharply challenged. Without denying the use of traditional material and form, one may remain convinced that the *Iliad* or the *Odyssey* is the work of a single man, whom we may as well continue to call Homer, and that he was not merely the mouthpiece of a community, but a conscious and skilful artist. That his art was not wasted on his community, that this community was far from primitive, there is ample evidence in the remains of its other arts.

The same direction of study leads to a similar conclusion for the later epics of this class. The more we know of the middle ages, the less warrant we find for calling these epics primitive. True, they are less finished than the *Iliad;* true, they show clearer traces of old war-songs; but neither their art nor the society for which it was shaped can accurately be called primitive. Alike the literary conventions of the poems themselves and the social conventions of their times rule such a characterization out. The "Gothic night" fancied by supercilious eighteenth-century critics, the "dark ages" of imperfect historians, are found to have had considerable illumination.

[1] See F. B. Gummere's *Beginnings of Poetry*. The controversy which was spread by the Homeric studies of Wolf, has lately shifted to the popular ballad. See G. L. Kittredge's introduction to his one-volume selection of the *English and Scottish Popular Ballads* from the collection of Child, Boston, 1904, and the recent studies of Professor Louise Pound. J. A. Scott maintains *The Unity of Homer* in his University of California Lectures, 1921.

Nevertheless the twofold classification of epic, in spite of the inaccuracy of its terms, has some significance. Earlier epic, what we might call primary epic, is in fact more directly answerable to a homogeneous community. Its unknown poets evidently felt themselves to be spokesmen of communal emotions and achievements; and the world that they saw they expressed with less intervention. As if they were transmitters rather than creators, they expressed not themselves so much as their people. This people, too, was in that stage of civilization in which foray and warfare by small groups brought out individual heroes and kept life precarious and simple. Booty and food, a fine sword and a fine web, still had immediate appeal; and the physical sensations of battle-strain and sweat, of ceaseless surf and darkening deep, were still common experience. Thus primary epic, communal and objective, has the directness of immediacy. Arising from those simpler emotions which we all feel together, primitive perhaps in that sense, and expressing them in terms of familiar physical sensations, it has its own inimitable flavor.

Later, or secondary, epic is not the transmission of legends still active, but the re-creation of a past already remote. Still appealing to a communal sense of the heroic, it adapts the old epic mode to an audience more sophisticated not only in life, but in poetic art. The poet is thus at once more imitative and more original. He binds himself by traditions of subject-matter, of form, and of style; but within this recognized mode he composes with more individual freedom and to a more definite end. Relying less on scenes in a series, he selects and manipulates toward more artistic sequence. Since his descriptions must be less immediate, he develops the art of narra-

tive. Endeavoring to remain the spokesman of his people
—for otherwise he must forfeit the communal mainspring
of epic—he interprets their past by his own message for
their future. Thus he may be all the more a poet, or
maker. He cannot hope for the fresh immediacy of
primary epic; but in compensation he has greater opportunity to move his people by his own vision. Milton's conception, vast as is its scope, is essentially the
same. He interprets the Bible as the epic of mankind
in terms of a Puritan theocracy. Tasso re-creates a departed chivalry to animate a vision of devotion and re-
demption. Vergil, the great example of secondary epic,
makes of the Trojan story, of Roman legend, of myth
and cult and drama and history, of all that enriched the
Roman past, a progressive vision of Roman destiny.

Primary epic and secondary epic, though thus distinguishable, are both epic. They are complementary.
They reveal different capacities of a single artistic mode.
Epic is constant. It was; it was again; it is; for aught
that we can see, it will be. Extended poetic narrative
of great deeds for communal inspiration, though it has
never been common, has never been extinct. Primary
epic seems inevitable. The minstrel in the hall of Hrothgar
is poetically identical with the minstrel in the hall of
Alcinous.[2] Both hint to us of what epic was made, and
how; both show us its constancy. This primary form of
epic can never, of course, recur. It has been civilized
away. But meantime it has established a poetic art that
is permanent. The word epic still connotes a distinct
mode. To this Vergil deliberately conformed, and Milton. Secondary epic is still epic.

[2] C. S. Baldwin, *Introduction to English Medieval Literature*, New
York, 1914, pages 16–18.

What, then, are seen to be in ancient practise the essentials of epic? First, its inspiration and its appeal are communal. By contrast the modern novel, which is also extended narrative and also within Aristotle's definition of poetic, is seen to be individual; or, where in exceptional cases it is broader and simpler,[3] is often distinguished by criticism as having epic appeal. Then, epic is in style objective. It narrates habitually without interposition, by images visual, auditory, motor. Its scenery is merely the background of heroic activity. Its speeches are in primary epic for characterization, not for plot. There is no plot in the dramatic sense for the whole; and such as there is for component parts is only to bring out persons. The object of epic being persons, its commonest descriptive details are of personal activity: attitude, movement, speech, gesture. The method is to suggest that heroic life by its physical sensations, to make the characters, as Aristotle says,[4] reveal themselves. Epic gives few reflections. It does not comment even on Helen's coming to the Scæan gates, or on Hector's parting from Andromache; it merely describes. This objectivity is a main means of epic directness.

The characteristic form of epic [5] is for scope and variety. Drama is intensive; epic is extensive. It has time to give us a sense of the fulness of life; and its movement does not preclude excursions. We meet many people and see them in various aspects. We can linger over a scene for itself without being urged forward. Continuity may be but leisurely succession from scene to scene. A scene may within itself have dramatic progress; but the move-

---

[3] As I write, Knut Hamson's *The Growth of the Soil* has just been called epic.   [4] *Poetic*, xxiv.

[5] Aristotle, *Poetic*, xxiv. See page 158 above.

ment of the whole has not the dramatic causal compulsion. Drama has its characteristic force through unity. Unity in epic is neither compelling nor compulsory. In fact, to stretch the term unity over epic tends to deprive it of all force. No epic poet has ever composed more carefully than Vergil, or with keener awareness of the ways of drama. The *Æneid* was composed as a whole; its parts were carefully adjusted to a plan, and its plan was controlled by a single idea. Epic has never gone further toward unity; and Homer never dreamed of going so far. But even such dramatization of epic as Vergil's has time for the funeral games, and does not sacrifice to the story of Rome the story and the person of Dido. In poetic, unity means nothing unless it means unity of form. This epic cannot have as a whole. Nor does any one regret the lack, or think it a fault. The unity of drama is for intensity; the object of epic is the realization not of a crisis, but of great persons in a long and various course.

So the style of epic is typically sonorous and high. Height of style may be attained by simplicity, and epic is simple often, but not always. To speak of epic as characteristically simple is to belie much of Homer and most of Vergil and Milton. Epic is not characteristically, nor even usually, simple. It may be very elaborate. It begins by assuming a language recognized as on a higher plane than that of ordinary speech. The epithets of the *Iliad* or the *Beowulf* are a poetical convention; and the style of epic proceeds always by conscious art. Here is the poet who, daring to sing great deeds, means to sing them greatly. That the effort may end in frigidity or bombast means only that there is bad epic as well as good; it does not mean that epic should be simple. Epic poets have never thought so. The poets of primary epic, no less than Vergil or Milton, were occupied with style. For the term epic has always implied greatness. It is a word of praise. It means a story of greatness told greatly.

Homer was for the ancient Greek world, and Vergil became for the Roman world, a Bible of style. Both were conned in school not only for the examples of their great persons, but for the study of language. That their connotation was immeasurably enriched, their "sublimity" heightened, not only by rhythm, but by verse, no one will deny. It is even possible to feel in Milton's verse a beauty separable from that of his ideas, and greater, lifting his narrow and political theology to wider import. Aristotle [6] remarks upon the appropriateness to epic of the Greek dactylic hexameter. Dionysius [7] even finds control of rhythms to be Homer's main poetic means. We are more inclined to admit this view for Milton; but the ultimate truth is that we should not, except for analysis, separate verse from the other elements of style. That every great epic poet has been a masterly metrist means rather that for "the height of this great argument" he felt the need of all that verse can add of suggestiveness. Though prose epic, as Aristotle admits by implication, is quite conceivable, it has to move on a lower plane. The Norse sagas are more direct even than Homer, starker in narrative force as if stripped for action, equally express- ive of communal emotions, equally vivid in character- ization. They have all the epic means but one. That single lack does not, indeed, relegate them to a different class; but it shows by contrast that for its full realization epic demands verse.

[6] *Poetic*, xxiv.   [7] See above, page 106.

(2). *The Conception and Scope of the Æneid*

The whole poetic art of ancient epic is exhibited in the *Æneid*. Setting aside those interesting historical questions of epic origins, growth, and transmission which in the study of Homer can hardly be ignored, and on the other hand including the whole range of epic, secondary as well as primary, we can learn best from the great poet who devoted his mature years to conceiving, planning, and reshaping the epic of Rome. The artistic scope of the *Æneid*, as well as its artistic eminence, long secure beyond cavil, has been reaffirmed by recent criticism. Sainte-Beuve calls Vergil "le poète de la Latinité tout entière."[8] Mackail, whose studies have been primarily Greek, exalts the *Æneid* afresh.[9] Woodberry, whose criticism has been mainly of English literature, says: "The distinctive feature of the 'Æneid' is the arc of time it covers, the burden of time it supports," and again, "The 'Æneid' is, I think, the greatest single book written by man because of its inclusiveness of human life, of life long lived in the things of life."[10]

The idea of Roman destiny, animating the *Æneid* throughout, is something larger than the nationalism of other epics. It is imperialism, and of a spirit generous enough to win the sympathy of Dante. It has not the occasional character of such a nationalist story, for instance, as Geoffrey of Monmouth's *Historia Regum Britanniæ*. In a time of corrupt politics it is above political opportunism. Its Rome is not merely the throne of Augustus; it is the government of the world. Its Romanism is less political than religious. "Pius Æneas" is more

---

[8] Opening of the *Étude sur Virgile*.

[9] *Lectures on Poetry*, London, 1911.

[10] "Vergil," in *Great Writers*, New York, 1912.

typical than "much-enduring Odysseus" of the struggle
of man for an abode of justice and peace. This, more
than the personal glory that humanism centuries afterward read from the classics, is the conception of the
Æneid. The destiny of Rome reveals the hope of mankind; and the *Æneid* has the whole epic scope. Hardly
less than Milton, Vergil justifies the ways of God to man.

(3). *The Narrative Movement of the Æneid* [11]

That the *Æneid* has a controlling idea implies that it
is artistically shaped to stricter continuity than appears
in the Homeric model. The *Iliad* and the *Odyssey* are
everywhere freer. Homer writes a scene for itself; Vergil
also for its significance in a progress.[12] Salience is sought
by careful subordination. The Carthaginians, for instance, are not elaborated as are the Italian tribes.[13] The

[11] W. Y. Sellar in *The Roman Poets of the Augustan Age, Virgil,* Oxford
(3d edition), 1908, analyzes under convenient headings Vergil's position
in Latin literature. Henry Nettleship's discussions in *Lectures and Essays,* Oxford, 1875, 1885, have not been superseded, though they have
evidently been suggestive to more recent critics. Sainte-Beuve's *Étude
sur Virgile,* Paris, n. d., and T. R. Glover's *Virgil,* London, 1904 (4th edition, 1920), appeal more to the general reader. R. Y. Tyrrell's chapter in
his *Latin Poetry,* Boston, 1895, is unsympathetic with Vergil the artist.
Most of the innumerable editions of the *Æneid* have little to say of his
poetic art. This is specifically the subject of M. Marjorie Crump's *The
Growth of the Æneid,* Oxford, 1920, which, though little developed, is a
distinct contribution to technical study. But *the* book on Vergilian epic
is the exhaustive work of Richard Heinze, *Virgils epische Technik,*
Leipzig, 1902 (2d edition, 1908, 3d edition, 1915). References are to
pages of the third edition.

[12] Heinze, 319, compares in this aspect the Homeric duel of Paris and
Menelaus with *Æneid* xii. Typically, he points out, Vergil's "Handlung
fortschreitet," and the composition is "szenenhaft."

[13] Paul LeJay, *L'Énéide,* Paris, 1919, page lix. Heinze, 381, shows the
minuteness of this care in cases where two scenes are chronologically parallel. One of the two is always subordinated; and the first to be presented
is always carried to a state of rest before turning to the second.

slaughter of the last night of Troy is confined to a few vivid scenes. Using Hellenistic versions and evidently studious of their art, Vergil deliberately rejects their decorative detail and sentimental dilation. He reduces the mating of Æneas with Dido to a grave summary,[14] in order to give salience to those other emotions which for the *Æneid* as a whole were leading. Æneas does, indeed, in the fourth book yield his position as protagonist to the queen who among Vergil's *personæ* is the great individual; but even so strong an impulse of creative inspiration does not drive the poet from his main purpose. One of the few great love-stories, the fourth book is still held, as it were by force, to the larger story of mission.

The same art deals with the gods. They were for Vergil necessary to epic; they embodied at once the traditional sense of supernatural response in natural forces and Vergil's own sense of divine guidance. But they rarely interpose, and never interrupt. They work through men; and the course of events is always amply explained by human motive. The foundations of Troy were shaken by divine wrath; but we see them dislocated by human agency. The revengefulness of Juno, the protection of Venus, seem the more plausible because they operate through the passion of Dido. The one yields in the end, and the other prevails, because Æneas realizes his mission. Olympus, now ordered within itself under a calm and absolute ruler, expresses and animates, not interrupts, the progress of human order. Thus Vergil's gods are more then "epic machinery," and more than personification. The thoughts of men are not merely expressed conventionally in archaic personal shapes; they are seen

[14] Heinze, 361.

at once as determining each decisive action and as inspired by divine purpose. For not only has the *Æneid* a more consistent theology than the *Iliad;* it is also more religious.

The most frequent examples of Vergil's subordination are in his fine art of description. Picturesque with brilliant color, as well as with the Homeric light and motion,[15] and as precise as they are vivid, his descriptions are rarely separable. Not only are they contributory to the action; they are also inwoven.[16] Vergil's sensitiveness to the details of nature transpires in a sentence, even in single words,[17] which describe while they narrate. Here he discerned the artistic rightness by which Homer describes every thing movable as in motion,[18] and applied the principle with more careful attention to narrative continuity. He dispenses with Homer's superfluous mechanism of transition.[19] Memorable as are the descriptions—and nothing in the *Æneid* is better remembered— very few can be detached from the context for separate

[15] The exactness, brilliancy, and range of Vergil's color words are studied by T. R. Price, *The Color-System of Vergil*, American Journal of Philology, volume 4, number 13 (1882). See the more extensive work of Hugo Blümner, *Die Farbenbezeichnungen bei den römischen Dichtern*, Berliner Studien, volume 13 (1891).

[16] This is the technical secret of the distinction that Sainte-Beuve expresses as "sobriété . . . rien que le nécessaire," *Étude sur Virgile*, 93.

[17] Glover, 16, repeats Henry's praise of
Quale per incertam lunam sub luce maligna. VI. 270.
Surcharged precision intensifies
Lucet via longo
Ordine flammarum, et late discriminat agros. XI. 143.
But the same distinctinctness, at once precise and picturesque, may be found almost anywhere in the *Æneid;* it is Vergil's habit, and it is never obtrusive.

[18] Lessing, *Laökoon*, especially chapters xvi and xvii.

[19] Heinze, 406.

admiration.[20]   The detailing of architecture and decoration, though it unduly seized the fancy of the middle
ages, is hardly an exception.   The Carthaginian pictures
of Troy, the palace of Latinus, are there not for scene-
painting, but for historic suggestion.   They serve the
story.   Thus Vergil's descriptive art is at once less ample
than Homer's and more specifically subsidiary.   The Hellenistic tableau—ἔκφρασις is its ominous name—appears in
the glittering conventional pauses of Ovid.   Vergil had put
it aside.   This is the more remarkable because the ancients
seem generally to have regarded certain scenes—battle, for
instance, conflagration, storm, thwarted love—as rather description than narration.[21]   Vergil, while he works even
more than Homer to make us realize a scene by sharing in
it as actors,[22] works also to avoid interruption of the story.

Similar is the constant care to avoid interruption of
time or place.[23]   Vergil's unremitting prevision and revision have obviated any time-lapse that is insignificant
for the action.   The Homeric device of bringing in antecedent action by retrospective narrative is used more
artistically.   While it covers ground, extending the time-
lapse beyond the stage, the narrative of Æneas heightens
the love of Dido before our eyes.

> She loved me for the dangers I had passed;
> And I loved her that she did pity them.

It is a larger achievement, one of the greatest,[24] to

---

[20] The famous description of the harbor under the cliffs (Est in secessu
longo locus. I. 159) is really less characteristic than

> Adspirant auræ in noctem, nec candida cursus
> Luna negat; splendet tremulo sub lumine pontus.   VII. 8.

[21] Heinze, 396.   [22] Heinze, 374.
[23] Heinze cites the handling of Fama in IV, and of Allecto in VII.
[24] See above, page 199.

heighten epic by suggesting vast reaches of time, from
tribal wanderings through wars of conquest to the reign of
law. Here is the artistic significance of the visit in Book
VI to the world of the dead and the unborn, which, as
Mackail says, "slips in the keystone." To compare the
visit of Odysseus to the shades is to see Vergil's higher art
of composition. But the suggestion of the great loom of
time (*tot volvere casus*) is not confined to a single artistic
device; it is pervasive from the opening words through a
hundred careful allusions; and it makes the *Æneid* wider
than the *Iliad* or the *Odyssey* by making it constantly suggestive of the whole struggle of history. It reveals more
explicitly the struggles of heroic men as the struggle of man.

Thus the oft-repeated objection that the *Æneid* breaks
into halves is superficial. The break would not have been
thought of if Vergil had not been seen to be working for
a continuity stricter than Homer's. Stated baldly by
Tyrrell, the idea that the *Æneid* is an *Odyssey* plus an
Iliad presupposes a sort of imitation to which Vergil
shows himself everywhere superior. It would be as near
the truth to reply that the *Æneid* is neither an *Odyssey*
nor an *Iliad*. But prototypes aside, how and how far is
the *Æneid* held together? Surely by the most careful
articulation ever seen in epic, but surely not to the degree
of drama. Among the evidences of revision are indications that the plan for the wanderings of Æneas was first
achieved [25] when much of the poem was already written.
The adjustment of this part to the whole course, a technic
hardly explored by Homer, and the abbreviations of the

[25] Heinze, 94. Miss Crump analyzes the probable changes of revision.
Her theory that Book III survives from an earlier plan in which it stood
first, and that Vergil probably intended to revise it entirely, has grave
difficulties.

wanderings by careful selection, are of a piece with the consistent connection by repetition of the theme, from the opening lines,

> Trojæ qui primus ab oris
> Italiam, fato profugus,

throughout the whole poem. True, the seventh book invokes Erato for scenes of battle.

> Maior rerum mihi nascitur ordo;
> Maius opus moveo.

The following scenes are different, but not the theme. The art that deliberately avoided Homer's succession of battles by interposing such scenes as Evander's achieved more than variety. It suggests again and again what the battles were for. The close upon the tragic death of Turnus becomes more than the personal victory of the hero; it is the triumph, over *violentia*, over such individual prowess as Homer glorified, over personal ambition thwarting the state, of fortitude bringing in religion and law.

But to ask therefore that the whole movement of the *Æneid* should be unified is at once to recognize Vergil's art of continuity and to demand for epic the strictness of drama. That Vergil understood drama, that his art learned not only from Greek epic, but from Greek tragedy, was pointed out by Nettleship and is important to remember. But he is too great a master of his chosen form to sacrifice epic scope.

How, then, is the *Æneid* dramatic? In the composition of the whole only by such preparations and recurrences as add to the vividness of parts suggestions of their bearing. Having planned a progress of events, not merely a series, Vergil marks that progress by such articulation as had been used to this extent only in drama. In the composition of the parts singly his art is more dramatic. The *Æneid* as a whole is not dramatically unified, and could not be. What is unified is each book.[26] For purposes of recitation, epic had to be composed, whether as a whole or not, in distinct parts. Of this necessity Vergil made a virtue. He advanced the narrative art of situation by applying some of the technic of drama. This is conspicuous in his frequent use of peripety. Again, the memorable and well remembered Laokoön scene is interposed between the Sinon scenes. Each is made to heighten the other, and both to give first suspense and then compelling motive to the bringing in of the fatal horse. Again and again Vergil will be found thus to intensify his narrative by the technic of drama. The most obvious instance is the distinct group of scenes at Carthage. The entrance of Dido is in the dramatic sense and by dramatic methods prepared. First, Æneas hears of her from his goddess mother, and is kindled by her having achieved his own epic mission—*dux femina facti*. Follows his view of the city, big already in achievement, big also to every Roman listener with menace. Then the decorative pictures at once review the tragedy of Troy and reveal in this strong queen a propitious sympathy. Upon all this, as to a waiting stage and a waiting audience, *enter Dido.*[27] Moreover in the Dido scenes, instead of contenting himself with that mere strife of emotions which was familiar in Hellenistic poetry [28] and became a rhetorical commonplace

[26] Paul LeJay, *L'Énéide*, lxviii; Heinze, 263. For the detail of the composition of single books and groups see also Heinze, 180, 448, 453. For instances of peripety, see Heinze, 223, 323.

[27] Heinze, 120, is hardly extravagant in maintaining that this is beyond any other ancient achievement of the kind.

[28] Heinze, 133.

with Ovid, Vergil advances and heightens the leading emotion steadily, as in a play, up to its tragic close. The close is the inevitable result of something more than thwarted passion because Dido has been presented dramatically, without concession to the Hellenistic narrative dilation, by what she said and did. Vergil's Dido is a creation every way beyond the Medea of Apollonius. She must be placed beside the Medea of Euripides. In her consistent tragic nobility, in the higher morality of her appeal, perhaps she must be placed above. For the fourth book of the *Æneid*, as fully as the *Antigone*, is tragic in its purgation of pity and fear.

Thus to apply drama to narrative without sacrificing the typical epic opportunities of fulness and scope is among the greatest achievements of poetic. It is an art so far beyond any other ancient narrative as to remain solitary until Dante; and Dante's guide was Vergil. It guided also the creative hand of Milton. And not for epic only, but for all imaginative story, the art of the *Æneid* remains a test and a guide. In this sense he who became for medieval Latinists *the* poet, as Cicero was *the* orator, remains Master Vergil.

(4). *Characterization in the Æneid*

To turn from the narrative movement to the persons is to descend. At once we feel that the achievement is less and that the method is less fruitful for narrative art because it is less distinctively poetic. Vergil's narrative composition has universal validity; but his characterization, for the most part, is only Latin. It had none the less influence on the middle ages—perhaps all the more; but it had the less inspiration for later creations.

To estimate Vergil's characterization fairly, it is necessary first to remove certain misconceptions. He has been reproached for leaving in our minds few outstanding figures: Turnus, Evander, Mezentius, Pallas, Nisus and Euryalus. Some of these, like the Camilla whom Dante remembers, are only sketched; and most of them are secondary. Now though this is paucity beside the populous pages of Homer, we must remember that Vergil's whole roster of heroes is smaller deliberately because, much more than Homer's, they are *dramatis personæ*. He makes the dramatic innovation of focusing on a few and of subordinating the development even of these to the development of the theme.

A more frequent objection is that throughout the latter part of the poem the hero is no longer Æneas, but Turnus. This is to use the word hero in a sense that Vergil would hardly have understood. Seeing Turnus through centuries of romance, we are so occupied with his *bravoure* as readily to forget that Vergil's Æneas is not meant to have the interest or the significance of King Arthur. Nor, we should add, is he meant to have the interest of Achilles. His individual prowess is only incidental to his dominant fortitude. The achievement of personal glory is behind him. "He has outlived his personal life." [29] His work is to found the Roman people. The characterization of Æneas, moreover, shows a certain development.[30] He shows more growth than "much-enduring Odysseus." The battle frenzy of the return to the doomed city (*arma amens capio*), the vacillation at Carthage, are put forever behind. He becomes progressively more steadfast. Al-

[29] Woodberry, 132. See also J. R. Green, "'Æneas, a Virgilian Study" in *Stray Studies from England and Italy*, 227.

[30] Heinze, 271 seq.; W. Warde Fowler, *The Religious Experience of the Roman People*, lecture xviii.

ways *pius*, he enlarges his *pietas* into calm assurance of
mission. As for the story, so for the characterization of
the hero, the sixth book is the critical stage of a progress.

The creative power of Vergil is amply vindicated by
Dido. One may feel that she is too vivid for her function,
that she takes the stage, as actors say, away from Æneas,
that through her the nice planning of the whole is quite
warped. We shall doubtless never be able to judge this
as Romans. Perhaps even they were more absorbed
than Vergil intended in his tragic queen.[31] Perhaps
Vergil himself was swerved by his own creation. But
all this only reinforces the testimony to a compelling
characterization. There may be difference of opinion
as to Dido's part in the story; there can be none as to
Dido herself.

But our estimates thus duly corrected, we cannot but
feel that Dido stands out among the figures of the *Æneid*
because she is exceptional. We feel her to be drawn not
only better, but often differently. And this should lead
to scrutiny of Vergil's habitual method. To begin with,
it is everywhere apparent that he cares less than Homer
for individuality. A certain expansiveness in Homeric
dialogue often keeps the story waiting to give the individual his say. Vergil shifts the proportions. He rejects long
dialogues because he is more interested in narrative
economy than in personal expressiveness. Further, the
speeches are often more reasoned than Homer's, more
orderly, less like conversation and more like oratory.[32]
Sinon's are very naturally elaborate pieces of special
pleading, and the rhetoric of Drances against Turnus is

---

[31] Ovid (*Tristia*, II. 535) says that the fourth book was the most popular.

[32] Sellar, 395. For careful discussion of this whole aspect of Vergil's
diction, see Heinze, 410–427.

appropriate in a deliberative assembly; but the making of successive points, and the careful adaptation of style not only to the speaker, but to the hearer, are habitual, as even in the speech of Allecto to Turnus. In this reasoned order, rather than in any mere elaboration, Heinze finds Vergil to be rhetorical. Instead of following the pace of emotional utterance, abrupt and disjointed, he sometimes holds even violent emotion to a steady course. By thus composing emotional expression he sometimes sacrifices directness of characterization.[33]

Indeed, Vergil is generally less concerned than Homer with creating individuals, and more concerned with showing his persons as types. Whether the loss in individual distinctness is compensated by a gain in common consent opens a long debate. Modern taste inclines rather to Homer than to Vergil; but between stretch centuries of Latin habit, and that habit, best exemplified in Vergil, is to characterize typically. This method of idealization may in Vergil's case have Stoic preoccupations;[34] but more generally it is rhetorical. To characterize by age, sex, race, occupation, etc., is a prescription of rhetoric [35] fixed in recipes and school exercises. It was dilated into ingenious fictions by the *declamatores*. Ovid's characterization hardly rises above the schools. Vergil was too great to move

[33] That even Dido's desperate plea, as well as the calm reply of Æneas, proceeds from point to point, not all readers will agree with Heinze (425-6, on *Æneid* IV. 305). The variations of rhythm in this passage would surely be used by a sympathetic reciter to suggest agitation. But Vergil's general neglect of the familiar means of asyndeton and hyperbaton (see, for example, *De sublimitate*, xxi–xxii) to suggest emotional disorder shows a characteristic distrust of incoherence.

[34] Heinze, 279.

[35] How freely Latin authors transferred it to poetic may be seen in Horace's *Ars Poetica* (see below, Chapter viii). Compare Plutarch, *Quomodo adolesc.*, x, below, page 244.

on that level; but even he is preoccupied with that ideal
and generally content with that method. He carried
the method as far, perhaps, as it will go. That except in
subordinate sketches he departed from it only in one
surpassing instance is doubtless the fundamental reason
for our finding his characterization inferior to his composition.

(5). *Epic Diction*

Generations have felt in the *Æneid*, first of all, high
and constant beauty. No other great poem has seemed
more infallibly beautiful. The beauty has sometimes,
indeed, been acknowledged with a certain disparagement,
as if it implied the less strength; but so perverse an antithesis cannot delay attention except to the fact that
Vergil is beautiful even to his detractors. The worst that
has been said of his style is that it is sometimes inappro-
priately elaborate.[36]

> atque arida circum
> Nutrimenta dedit, rapuitque in fomite flammam.
> Tum Cererem corruptam undis Cerealiaque arma
> Expediunt fessi rerum; frugesque receptas
> Et torrere parant flammis et frangere saxo. I. 175.

This, it must be admitted, seems comparatively remote and unreal beside similar meals in Homer, and
absolutely too high a style for camp cookery. Nor is
it safe to urge that Vergil is holding his style to the
epic level; for that plea opens the way to such mere
etiquette as centuries later quite deviated the discussion
of epic from its main issues, and, besides, Vergil himself
does not thus describe Dares and Entellus. No, the

[36] Sellar, 101, quotes Comparetti: "an elaboration of language which
disdains or is unable to say a plain thing in a plain way."

plea must be rather of confession and avoidance. Such passages are not beautiful, and their style is not epic; but they are so few that to call them characteristic is quite unfair. Nor are they to be ascribed to preoccupation with rhetoric. Vergil is, indeed, sometimes more oratorical [37] than we wish; but he is not, in our modern sense rhetorical, and his rhetoric, no less than his poetic, must have found such passages inferior. Rather we may think that these few "rubs and botches in the work" were what led him to wish it burned; for after all his revision he was acutely conscious that it was unfinished. Unfinished in form it certainly is not. Unfinished in style it is here and there. But what a sense of beauty had the artist who could not bear even so few blemishes!

Not elaborateness, then, is characteristic of Vergil's style, but certainly elaboration. His tireless revision is testified by the tradition that he composed first in prose, and that he spent on the *Æneid* ten years.[38] No style is more highly charged. It is made to suggest at once vivid descriptive imagery and the sanctions of history and religion. Not only the story, but the diction, is full of Rome. His use of the language of Roman ritual [39] is characteristic of an expression piously preservative of cult. "By instinct and temper a ritualist," [40] he is continually suggesting the significance of traditional forms. The

[37] See above, page 210.

[38] "During all the years in which Virgil brooded over it and wrought upon it, he kept his material . . in fusion, not crystallized and hardened into final shape" (Mackail, 78); i. e., he continued to adjust.

[39] *Eximios tauros, farre pio,* etc., noted, among other critics, by E. Nageotte, *Histoire de la littérature latine,* 334. Apropos of Vergil's incomparable command of the resources of his language, Nageotte adds happily that a "tache de rouille antique a son effet prévu dans la gamme des couleurs environnantes" (324).

[40] Woodberry, 125.

Iliad and the *Odyssey* are in a special dialect. The *Faery Queene* has a language of its own. To achieve such suggestions in the *Æneid* with but the slightest resort to archaism is in itself a great achievement of language; but it is only part of a consistent allusiveness, an extraordinary connotation, ranging the whole gamut from sharp physical sensations to spiritual significance. A style eminently classic in precision and harmony is yet felt to be above all rich. No other poet seems more nearly infallible with the right word; no other so well to have charged classic restraint with romantic exuberance by the energy of his expressiveness. The influence of Vergil, immediate, wide, and long, is indubitably the influence of his style. Later ages, unappreciative of the poetic art of his composition, felt the spell of his imagery and rhythm almost as an incantation. "Virgil is that poet whose verse has had most power in the world." [41]

(6). *Originality in Imitation*

The notion that imitation must be subversive of originality betrays a crude conception of both. Yet it lingers in such criticism as thinks the *Æneid* to be a Latin *Iliad* and *Odyssey*. To measure it so is to miss not only the art of a single great poem, but much of all poetic art. For since all art works in forms received and recognized, less by invention than by transformation, it is of cardinal significance to distinguish, in a poem conspicuously imitative and conspicuously original, just what artistic imitation is. Therefore what has been implied in the preceding sections may here be drawn together in summary.

Imitation is always of movement or style; it has nothing to do with material. To preface this should be superfluous;

[41] Woodberry, 111.

but many quests for "sources" have left some confusion. Vergil took much of the Trojan story from Homer. To be sure, he used other sources too. Nothing is more remarkable in the *Æneid* than the wealth and variety of its material. Its sources are beyond the dreams of Homer. But even if Vergil's material were all Homeric, he would not on that account be the more imitative. Ancient literature, and mediæval too, generally make freer with preceding stories than modern. The material is not thought to be any one's property. In this respect Vergil is singularly independent. He uses more sources; he is more selective; and what he adopts is often a composite. He works in the modern way rather than in the ancient; but he is not on that account either more or less imitative. Some of Shakspere's plays derive their plots from single sources; some are in plot composite; but all are alike original. A modern French tragedy took the plot not only of an ancient story, but of the best known of all ancient plays. It is none the less original; and its imitation, as all artistic imitation, is of the ancient technic.

Imitation in art, then, means following certain artistic ways. To begin with, Vergil evidently set out to write an epic, and undoubtedly looked to Homeric epic as a type. This is important not only in his case, but throughout literary history. Though its importance may be exaggerated in Brunetière's *évolution des genres*, evidently epic meant something controlling to Vergil because of Homer, and has meant something wider ever since because of Vergil. To any poet, to Tasso and Milton as to Vergil, epic necessarily implies a pattern. It directs and limits *personæ* and diction; but it does not hamper artistic progress, for it does not limit interpretation. Vergil remade not only the epic material, but the epic form, to a new end. His Sinon [42] is a typical instance of artistic rehandling. Drawn doubtless from several ancient sources, he has become through his new function and motivation creatively original. Battles there must be in epic, even battles of the Homeric sort; but Vergil does not rely on the general *mêlée;* he modifies it subtly in the direction of the more organized Roman fighting, and he changes the Homeric series into a progress. In short, even where he is perforce most dependent on Homer, his imitation is never repetition. Imitation is creative when it adapts the art of the past to the interpretation of the present. The *Æneid* is not a Latin *Iliad;* it is a Roman epic.

Vergil's adaptation of the epic movement involves a departure from Homer in the direction of drama.[43] How, and how far, imitation of drama can serve extended narrative we learn fully from him because he imitates selectively. He does not try to make his story a play, or merely a series of plays; he finds how far epic can be conducted dramatically without sacrificing its epic appeal. No less selectively he rejects the Hellenistic technic of Apollonius.[44] Epic diction, he discerns, in order to have the old communal appeal, must sound traditional; but echo of Homeric style would make it sound merely conventional. He gives it traditional connotation by means of his own. His diction, therefore, is far less imitative than his composition. In fact, it is rarely imitative at all. In the limits, no less than in the method, of his imitation his art runs true. Through that obedience which great artists yield to the art that they inherit he shows the way to imaginative freedom.

[42] See above, page 206.
[43] See above, page 205.
[44] See above, page 203.

B. The Narrative Poetry of Ovid

Among the Latin poets Vergil has the siege perilous. He achieved that high poetic emprise beside which others must seem less. In comparison no one suffers more than Ovid.[45] Yet he who presented the gods without seeing their divinity, and retold the myths instead of recreating them, has literary qualities not only striking, but at once typical of his time and very widely influential. Vergil has been revered; but Ovid has been imitated and absorbed. Without attempting to measure his brilliancy, it is necessary to distinguish the characteristic habits of a poetic whose influence spread over western Europe.

That poetic is seen at once to be unfailingly expert in every artistic detail. Its metrical facility, proverbial [46] from the first and instructive of the verse of many centuries and many lands, is only the most obvious skill of a man who loved style. Though he does not make a habit of the elegiac tendency to rime, he plays variously upon alliteration and other consonance;[47] and his use of refrain suggests those stanza patterns set centuries later by

---

[45] Ovid has a large place in every comprehensive history of Latin literature (e. g., in W. Y. Sellar's volume on *Horace and the Elegiac Poets* in his *Roman Poets of the Augustan Age*, Oxford, 1892), and is discussed at least briefly in the compends (e. g., C. T. Cruttwell's *History of Roman Literature*, American edition, New York, 1890). The last edition of the Encyclopedia Britannica has an extensive appreciation by S. G. Owen, whose critical edition of *Tristia* provides a bibliography of Ovidiana. Of English translations the most accessible are those in the Loeb Classical Library: of *Heroides* and *Amores* by Grant Showerman, of *Metamorphoses* by F. J. Miller, both with introductions and bibliographical notes.

[46] Sponte sua carmen numeros veniebat ad aptos,

Et quod tentabam dicere versus erat. *Tristia,* IV. x. 25

is almost as familiar as "lisped in numbers, for the numbers came."

[47] Morsque minus pœnæ quam mora mortis habet. *Heroides,* x. 82.

French courtly makers in rondel [48] and ballade.[49]   For
though he knows the subtlest spells of sound, Ovid is
never neglectful of such notes as must catch the ear.   His
verse is more than popular; but it is popular, and many
a Spaniard, Gaul, and Briton has been grateful to feel
its music running in his head.

Equally obvious is Ovid's decorative description.   Its
bent is not toward epic suggestion of character by attitude,
gesture, and action, but toward picturesqueness.   Bright
imagery garnishes the familiar.   Groves and streams and
their tutelary nymphs, men, women, and gods, are not
individualized; they are merely realized.   But what exuberance of suggestion!   To open dull eyes and spur
jaded feelings, to vivify a legendary scene, to dilate a
conventional mood, to redecorate an old landscape, Ovid
had an inexhaustible fund.

For he elevated poetic convention to a fine art.   A
storm at sea [50] lacks none of the properties; a fainting hero-
ine or hero,[51] no appropriate gesture.   The pallor of love
can move once more,[52] and the golden age [53] make the
over-civilized pensive.   "Mortal art thou, or divine?" was
said by Odysseus to Nausikaa when gods walked with
men; but Ovid had the art to repeat it [54] when the gods
were dead.   Repeat?   He himself became the pattern of

[48] Ilia, pone metus; tibi regia nostra patebit,
      Teque colent amnes.   Ilia, pone metus.
   Tu centum plures inter dominabere nymphas;
      Nam centum aut plures flumina nostra tenent.   *Amores*, iii. 6, 61.

Rime in Latin elegiac poetry is well summarized by K. P. Harrington
in his volume of edited selections, *The Roman Elegiac Poets*, New York,
1914, page 61.

[49] E. g., at the close of *Heroides*, ix, Impia quid dubitas Deianira mori?
in line 146 is repeated in lines 152, 158, 164, i. e., in every sixth line.

[50] E. g., *Metam.* xi. 494.   [51] *Metam.* vii. 826.   [52] *Ars Amat.* i. 729.

[53] *Metam.* i. 89, *Amores*, iii. 8, 35.   [54] *Metam.* iv. 320.

these things for centuries. Not only is he forever the poet of "Gather ye roses while ye may," but "Stay, dawn; why must thou haste?" [55] echoed across Europe,[56] was heard in the cry of Chaucer's Troilus [57] and Shakspere's Juliet,[58] and still reverberates.

The Alexandrian [59] dilation of such description [60] appears also in the long-drawn emotions of soliloquy.[61] The fixing of this as a literary type must have been promoted by the prevalence of the schools of *declamatio*,[62] where Ovid had studied. Practised in elementary form even by Roman schoolboys, developed by *declamatores* in exhibitions of virtuosity, the fiction of what so-and-so must have said on such-and-such an occasion is still a rhetorical exercise. As an exercise it has some value in promoting poetic appreciation; but it seems hardly the way toward poetic creation. Ovid, at any rate, hardly creates persons. The address of Sol, for instance, to Phaëthon,[63] is only a more extended and more professional school theme; and the mixture of allegorical personification with myth [64] shows

[55] *Amores*, i. 13. 3.

[56] See, for example, Rudolph Schevill, *Ovid and the Renascence in Spain*, University of California Publications in Modern Philology, vol. 4, number 1 (November, 1913), pages 24 and 95.

[57] *Troilus and Criseyde*, iii. 1415–1470.   [58] *Romeo and Juliet*, III. v.

[59] Owen in Encyclopedia Britannica speaks of Ovid as "the most brilliant representative of Roman Alexandrinism."

[60] A typical ἔκφρασις is "dira lues" in *Metam*. vii. 523.

[61] E. g., Byblis in *Metam*. ix. 474, Myrrha in *Metam*. x. 320.

[62] Discussed above in Chapter IV. II. Cruttwell says of the *Heroides*: "They are erotic suasoriæ, based on the declamations of the schools." *History of Roman Litterature*, 306; and Heinze, "die Gattung der poetischen *declamatio* inaugurierte." *Virgils epische Technik*, 434. Cf. Sellar, 331, 356; Carl Brück, *De Ovidio scholasticarum declamationum imitatore*, Munich, 1909.   [63] *Metam*. ii. 33.

[64] Iris, Tisiphone, Luctus, Pavor, Terror. *Metam*. iv. 480. The method seen more largely in Invidia (*Metam*. ii. 760), essentially a school exercise, passed through the *Roman de la Rose* into medieval habit.

him rather as a rhetorician[65] than as a poet. That he is not a myth-maker, only a myth-teller, may be seen by putting any of his demigods beside the Prometheus of Æschylus—or even the Prometheus of Shelley. For re-creation Ovid lacked what the Great Unknown[66] thought to be the primary source of expression, intellectual vigor of conception. Thus his mythical persons, though always appropriate and sometimes vivid, are not alive.

More has been claimed for his story-telling. Cruttwell[67] says of the *Metamorphoses:* "The skill with which different legends are woven into the fabric of the composition is as marvellous as the frivolous dilletantism which could treat a long heroic poem in such a way." The skill of the weaving is indisputable; but is it more than an art of transition? To call the *Metamorphoses* a long heroic poem suggests a cruel comparison with the *Æneid*, and partly begs the question. What Ovid seems to have intended, and what he achieved, is a deftly articulated collection. It is not a single poem in the sense of having emotional progress or totality, nor is any other of Ovid's collections. His distinctively narrative art, therefore, is to be sought not in the connection between stories, but in the composition of each one. It is even probable that this art was the more popular because it offered, not a long sustained narrative, but many separable short tales.

The "vivid inventiveness" and "unflagging animation" urged by Owen[68] as characteristic of Ovidian narrative may be accepted without discussion, and should not be

---

[65] Heinze discusses more generally the rhetorical habit of Ovid in *Virgils epische technik*, 434.   [66] See above, page 126.
[67] *History of Roman Literature*, 309.   [68] Encyclopedia Britannica.

undervalued. Inventiveness was overvalued, indeed, in the melodramatic fictions of *declamatio*, and implies an art rather facile than creative; but it is none the less sure of popularity. As for animation, whatever else a story may be, it may not be dull. Here Ovid often wins by his very levity. He makes no demands. No one can be followed more easily; for he moves on the surface. Where he skates on thin ice, he does so quite simply for excitement. There is none of the modern pretense of exploration. His problems are purely artistic, problems not of motive, but of interesting mood and attitude, of appropriate and various utterance. His animation, partly rhythmical, partly descriptive, is more largely unflagging expressiveness. Always expressive, his people can always be understood without effort. He holds attention without provoking thought.

The "rapid movement" claimed by Owen is often mere succinctness, rarely the speed gained by modern narrative use of dramatic technic. For that he usually has too much separable description, too much soliloquy, too little motivation. He seeks intensity less often than expansiveness. Nevertheless, though he pauses deliberately for description or *tirade*, he does not lag. There is no clumsy prosing or deviation. He has the art, more valued in ancient and medieval times than in modern, of lucid, fluent narrative, the art of the tale. That he does not follow it oftener is due to his readers' fondness, and his own, for dilation. The onward movement of poetic is thus sacrificed to rhetoric. The parts become more important than the whole. For Ovid was a rhetorician, not only bred in the schools, but habitually thinking of poetry less as composed movement than as lucid and brilliant, as ample and harmonious style.

C. The Metamorphoses of Apuleius

Sighting from the *Metamorphoses* of Ovid through the *Metamorphoses* of Apuleius,[69] one clearly discerns the coming of the Greek Romances. So runs the Alexandrian narrative line from decorative description and expansive emotion, through exciting incident and uncontrolled variety,[70] to sheer violence. Ovid's stories are sometimes like dreams; the Greek Romances are nightmares. Apuleius, between the two, already seeks the violent and the bizarre. His metamorphoses are no longer mythical, nor in the least allegorical; they are mere sorcery. The appetite of his time for horrors and other excitement had been both fed and whetted by *declamatio*.[71] Ovid, too, knew *declamatio*; but Apuleius, himself a rhetor,

---

[69] Apuleius, born about 125 A. D., and probably educated at Carthage, where he passed much of his life, became a rhetor at Rome about 150, and soon thereafter published the *Metamorphoses*. *Florida* is the title given to a collection of excerpts from what we should call his lectures (see Chapter VIII, 230). Nettleship (in an essay on Nonius Marcellus, *Lectures and Essays*, 282) calls him "a very striking representative of his age." Though his work is largely translation or compilation, he has caught the fancy of several English *literati*, and was made by Pater one of the *personæ* in the twentieth chapter of *Marius the Epicurean*. Adlington's translation (1566) of the *Metamorphoses* has been reprinted with an introduction by Seccombe, and revised for the Loeb Classical Library by Gaselee. The separable Cupid and Psyche chapters (Books IV–VI), often translated, appear in the fifth chapter of Pater's *Marius*, and have been again translated by Purser (London, 1910), with a suggestive introduction on Apuleius as a rhetor. Butler has translated also the *Florida*.

[70] "L'art de composition faiblit, comme il arrive toujours quand la sincérité du sentiment diminue; car c'est la préoccupation sincère d'une idée dominante qui maintient d'un bout à l'autre l'unité de ton et l'harmonie; quand le bel esprit l'emporte, il s'amuse aux détails, il s'attache au ' morceau,' et n'a plus la force de lier l'ensemble." Croiset, *Histoire de la littérature grecque*, vol. V (*Période Alexandrine*), page 158.

[71] See Chapter IV. II.

was less restrained by earlier literary standards from giving rein to the sensational.

Though the bulk of his extant work is narrative, Apuleius devotes no attention to onward narrative movement. Superficially continuous, his *Metamorphoses* are nevertheless often quite separable, as is evident in the most famous of them, Cupid and Psyche. Such course of plot as there is eddies in harangues, *tirades* and decorative descriptions. The abundant dialogue is uncontrolled by dramatic concision. Everywhere Apuleius is orally expansive. A rhetor telling stories, he goes little beyond the poetic of the platform: work for excitement, relying on lust and witchcraft; expand what is showy, emphasizing each part without regard to sequence; use dialogue for variety, letting *prosopopœia* suffice for characterization; and if nevertheless the tale lags or becomes confused, make a fresh start by bringing on brigands. This habit of mind, and not the incidental satire, explains the narrative looseness. Apuleius is no Rabelais; he is only a facile second-century rhetor carrying the rhetorical fiction of his time to greater length. In style, though habitually diffuse, he is sometimes charming and often lively; but in composition he merely extends a meretricious convention.

During his lifetime Iamblichus wrote the *Babylonica*, or Rhodanes and Sinonis (166–180); and, soon after, Chariton of Aphrodisias the *Chœreas and Calirrhoe* (before 200).[72] Thus was established the mode followed later by Heliodorus and Achilles Tatius, the perverted narrative

---

[72] These dates are taken from Wolff's admirable summary of the Greek Romances as an Alexandrian derivative in the opening chapter of his *Greek Romances in Elizabethan Fiction* (New York, 1912, Columbia University Press).

known as the Greek Romances. Any one who has the
patience for these phantasmagoria of passion, horror, and
adventure will see their likeness to the *Metamorphoses* of
Apuleius, and will probably reproach him the more for
ignoring that onward causal movement without which the
art of narrative seems to lapse.

CHAPTER VIII

RHETORIC IN ANCIENT CRITICISM OF POETIC

A. The Pervasiveness of Rhetoric

The Aristotelian distinction of poetic from rhetoric has been sometimes blurred, sometimes ignored, by criticism. Such confusion as thus arises became more common in ancient criticism with the waning of ancient art; it was widespread in the middle age; it has reappeared many times since the Renaissance.[1] For consistent development of poetic as a technic distinct from rhetoric is beyond the occasion of most criticism, whether ancient or modern. At an ebb tide of creation especially, the average critic is likely to confine his observations to style; and there the two technics have much common ground. Even in criticism of composition we have seen often in our own time such familiar terms as unity, emphasis, and coherence restricted to their rhetorical definitions, and yet imposed in these senses on composition whose actual control was quite different. The unity of the *Ancient Mariner*, for instance, has been interpreted as the logical control of the proposition "He prayeth best who loveth best," though surely that composition was unified quite otherwise. Or the term coherence is permitted to suggest that the progress of Burke's speech on *Conciliation* from paragraph to para-

[1] See D. L. Clark, *Rhetoric and Poetry in the Renaissance*, New York, 1922 (Columbia University Studies in English and Comparative Literature).

graph is like the progress of *Othello* from scene to scene, though the two technics have little resemblance. Such warping of poetic has sometimes been even urged by ancient or modern schoolmasters and text-books. It has seemed thrifty to make Molière, for instance, exhibit those principles of composition which pupils must use in writing essays upon him. But even without such pedagogical perversion it is easy to think of poetic in terms of rhetoric; for rhetoric is in everybody's head.

It was so much more a preoccupation of ancient thought that the conception of poetic as a distinct movement seems to have become less and less active. Though a few critics, even under the Empire, held the Aristotelian distinction, generally ancient poetic was more and more warped toward rhetoric. With rhetoric determining education, with even Cicero and Tacitus discussing poetic as contributory, with the later *declamatores* habitually blending the two, with even poets yielding to the common tendency, poetic could hardly be conceived often as a distinct movement of composition. While Vergil's art revealed a critical conception unknown to Seneca and Lucan, Horace could repeat Aristotle without following his distinctive idea. Cicero and Tacitus, best of Latin critics, naturally contemplate in poetic rather its imagery than its movement;[2] and Quintilian,[3] even more naturally, explores only its treasures available for orators. That ancient criticism never lost the Aristotelian distinction altogether appears in the anonymous and undated *De sublimitate*[4] and in a few of the many words of Dio Chrysostom;[5] but Plutarch's poetic is indistinguishable from rhetoric.

---

[2] So, e. g., does Petronius, *Satyricon*, 118.
[3] See above, page 80.　　　　　　　　[4] See above, Chapter V. B.
[5] Section C. 1, below.

B. Criticism from Grammarians

The overwhelming preponderance of rhetoric in ancient critical thought followed naturally from the dominance of rhetoric in education.[6]   Formal schooling in poetic, what we now call primary instruction in literature, began with *grammaticus*,[7] and he was committed in advance to preparing his boys for their studies in rhetoric.   With his task of inculcating correctness in reading, speaking, and writing were associated his lectures (*prælectiones*) on the poets. Though these may often, given the highly selected group of students, have done much for appreciation of literature, they can hardly have ranged far in poetic.   *Grammaticus* probably confined himself in most cases to what is known in French schools as *explication des textes*.   Within its limits this is admirable; but given the age of the pupils and their specific object, it cannot often have gone beyond words and sentences into the poetic composition of the whole.   Criticism *ad hoc*, the detailed study of a particular poem passage by passage, is a method not only necessary for schooling, but valuable more widely.   By sheer prevalence it must always be influential; illumination must in fact have come oftener from such interpretation than from a systematic treatise on poetry.   None the less it needs more correction and extension from other forms of criticism than was usually possible in the ancient world.   By itself it tends toward a pedestrian analysis of diction and toward em-

---

[6] To what has already appeared from the preceding chapters may be added the opinion of George Converse Fiske: "from the Hellenistic period on, and throughout the Roman world of letters, the study of rhetoric was a prerequisite for literary composition in every field."   *The Plain Style in the Scipionic Circle*, page 62 (University of Wisconsin Studies in Language and Literature, number 3, 1919).

[7] See above, page 68.

phasis on those aspects of poetic which are available for rhetoric.

Criticism by labels, the classifying of authors by accepted adjectives, is not, unfortunately, confined either to antiquity or to grammarians. A certain amount of criticism, apparently, must always be devoted to telling people what they ought to say. But the classifying habit seems to have been especially prevalent in ancient criticism. At any rate, the labels affixed by grammarians were widely repeated. Even so discerning a critic as Quintilian thus makes his tenth book a convenient "survey." The satisfaction of an audience in neat and recognizable characterization is given by Apuleius.

> "Any speech composed by Avitus will be found everywhere so consistently perfect that Cato would not miss in it his dignity, nor Laelius his smoothness, nor Gracchus his vehemence, nor Caesar his warmth, nor Hortensius his clear plan, nor Calvus his subtleties, nor Sallust his conciseness, nor Cicero his richness." Apuleius, *Apologia.*

Each orator has the right label, as in a cram-book; and the same classifying neatness disposes of the poetic of Philemon.

> "You who are sufficiently acquainted with his talent, hear briefly of his end. Or will you hear somewhat also of his talent? This Philemon was a poet, a writer of the Middle Comedy. He wrote pieces for the stage in the time of Menander, and in competition with him, perhaps not as an equal, but certainly as a rival. In these contests, I am sorry to say, he was often the winner. At any rate, you will find in him much that is piquant, plots neatly woven, recognitions clearly unfolded, characters adequate to the action, thoughts approved by experience, humor not too low for comedy, seriousness not involving tragedy. Seductions in his plays are rare; even legitimate loves are treated as aberrations. None the less he shows the

perjured pimp, the passionate lover, the shrewd slave, the de-
ceiving mistress, the interfering wife, the indulgent mother,
the scolding uncle, the conniving crony, the bellicose soldier,
not to mention greedy parasites, stingy fathers, and voluble
harlots." Apuleius, *Florida*, XVI.

Nor was the habit confined to rhetors. It was widespread in the "three styles" [8] of oratory, in the ten ca-
nonical Attic orators, in "Asianism" versus "Atticism,"
in the bias of even Dionysius of Halicarnassus [9] toward
classification. True, it appears generally in criticism of
rhetoric, and is common enough in modern times; but in
ancient criticism it amounts to a preoccupation, [10] and is
more readily carried over into poetic.

Grammar in those wider reaches now comprehended in
the term philology has much to contribute to the criticism
of older poets. Theon, for instance, whose manual of
school exercises ($\pi\rho o\gamma\upsilon\mu\nu\acute{a}\sigma\mu\alpha\tau\alpha$ [11]) has come down to
us from the time of Augustus, annotated with *scholia* the
tragic and the comic poets. The tradition of the Alexandrian grammarians included, besides syntax and exegesis,
textual criticism. But such criticism depends for much of
its value on science little explored by the ancients; and
typically it makes little contribution to poetic. [12] By no
good fortune, then, "philology and poetry went hand in
hand in the ancient and classical literature of Italy." [13]

[8] See above, pages 56, 57.

[9] See above, page 102. What Alfred Croiset says of him seems true
rather of the habit of his time: "questions arrêtées d'avance et toujours
les mêmes; c'est dresser son signalement suivant un formulaire, qu'il
s'agit simplement de remplir." *Hist. de la litt. grecque*, V. 368.

[10] Nettleship, *Literary Criticism in Latin Antiquity* (Lectures and Essays, Second Series).

[11] See above, page 63.

[12] See the scornful comment of Croiset, V. 358.

[13] Nettleship, *Lectures and Essays*, I. 176 (on Horace's *Ars Poetica*).

The result of this companionship was not, indeed, always nor necessarily so arid and confined as the criticism of the second-century lexicographer Aulus Gellius; [14] but at most it had little range.

C. Criticism from Professional Public Speakers

Not only did the prevalence of rhetoric make poetic generally subsidiary, but the prevalence of *declamatio* [15] in later teaching and practise tended actually to confuse the two. This rhetoric was itself largely poetic, largely an art of appeal by description. Sometimes carrying descriptive dialogue into a sort of oral fiction, it had no occasion for poetic movement. The pattern of a speech sufficed as well as another where the opportunity was less of the whole than of the parts.[16] Immediate popular oral effects were then, as now, gained rather by stinging epigrams and dramatic realizations than by any onward course. The poetic that shall win a crowd on the spot is more likely than the poetic that shall be savored by individual readers to be sensational. Sensational in fact it was commonly, to judge by examples ranging all the way from Seneca's *Controversiæ* well into the Christian centuries.

Even those rhetors who were not sensational in their own practise were little more likely, in a time of such preoccupations, to conceive poetic distinctively; and rhetors purveyed, among other things, literary criticism. Besides teaching and exhibiting at home, the more popular rhetors traveled as occasional orators and lecturers. Though their speeches were oftenest, of course, occasional, and, when

[14] See Nettleship, op. cit., 248. Saintsbury, *Loci Critici*, 74, quotes his *Noctes Atticæ* xvii. 10, on Vergil's *Æneid*, III. 570.

[15] See pages 68–73, 94–97.

[16] See foot-note 50 to Chapter IV, foot-note 70 to Chapter VII.

they were rather lectures, were commonly in the fields of philosophy and ethics, still professional public speakers must have purveyed, at home and on their journeys, a good deal of the current literary criticism.   Where this was incidental, it need not be taken too seriously.   No device of public speaking is more persistent than the flattering of an audience by literary allusions and accepted adjectives of admiration.[17]   Such passages, in ancient speeches or in modern, show merely what is regarded as the right thing to say, and are almost always limited to style.   But where a rhetor develops a literary topic, even for a paragraph or two, he may be as significant as any other literary critic.

The particular rhetor might be a teacher of rhetoric primarily, or secondarily, or hardly at all.   Though he hardly ranked as a philosopher,[18] yet he was an active purveyor of philosophy.   An expert in public address, he professed a variety of considerable range.   Occasional oratory of itself invites ranging in both emotion and thought. Conventional as he appears when considered merely as one of a numerous class, he might nevertheless be an outstanding individual; and even as a type he was at least accomplished and influential.

Apuleius, lively and daring enough in his narrative,[19]

[17] See the quotations from Apuleius in the preceding section.

[18] For the varying relations of the "second sophistic" to rhetoric on the one hand and to philosophy on the other see the introduction to H. von Arnim's *Leben und Werke des Dio von Prusa, mit einer Einleitung, Sophistik, Rhetorik, Philosophie in ihrem Kampf um die Jugendbildung*, Berlin, 1898; and, for later periods, A. Boulanger, *Ælius Aristide et la sophistique . . . au IIe siècle*, Paris, 1923; W. C. Wright, *Philostratus and Eunapius, the Lives of the Sophists*, London and New York (Loeb Library), 1922, introduction; L. Méridier, *L'influence de la seconde sophistique sur l'œuvre de Grégoire de Nysse*, Paris, 1906, chapter i.

Philostratus, *Vit. Soph.* ii (Wright, p. 34), says that Hippias of Elis discoursed (διελέγετο) on painting and sculpture.

[19] See page 221.

seems in the excerpts preserved from his oratory quite conventional.   The *Florida* show certain typical *encomia*, two
passages of critical labels, three long pieces on philosophy,
and several of those *exordia* which traveling lecturers prepared, and still prepare, for extempore adaptation.   If the
Great Unknown's *De sublimitate* [20] was a public address—
and its suggestiveness is strongly oral—its author rose
quite above the type without losing the typical opportunity
of oral criticism.   One may fancy the close of that noble
appeal echoing long in the ears of a rapt audience.   But
without any flight of fancy one may read the possibilities
of ancient oral criticism in certain of the orations of Dio
of Prusa, often called Dio Chrysostom.[21]

(1). *Dio of Prusa*

Dio's speech known as the Olympic, and having for sub-
title The Primary Conception of God, opens with a proem
characteristic of the form, an introduction separable, adjustable, ostensibly impromptu, but none the less following a type.   A fable of the owl—occasional oratory seems
inevitably to begin with a story—leads to other proverbs,
to historical allusions, to the speaker's profession of mod-
esty, sincerity, and homeliness.   "I am just come from
the Getæ.   Shall I tell you about this interesting people? "
A rhetor's offering the choice of theme to the audience
might be merely conventional; for Dio effectively recalls

[20] See Chapter V. B.
[21] The definitive discussion of Dio is that of H. von Arnim cited above
in foot-note 18.   The latest complete edition is that of J. de Arnim, Berlin, 1893.   A translation by W. E. Waters is announced for the Loeb Classical Library.   Meantime Professor Waters's translation of Oratio XII
(discussed below) is printed in Volume XIV (1919–1922) of the *Colonnade*,
published by the Andiron Club of New York University, 1922, pages 183–
201.   The translation below of Oratio LII is my own.

it by adding: "Here at Olympia, beside your wondrous
statue of the Olympian, shall I not rather speak of Zeus
himself? "

So is approached a discourse upon embodiments of deity
in poetry and in sculpture, a lecture carefully conducted
from point to point, and delivered doubtless in these words,
certainly by this plan, in more than one welcoming city.
Such a prepared address needed only the adjustment of
the proem to the place and the occasion.[22] The lecture
itself remained substantially the same. This one makes
first the following points.

> The knowledge of Zeus comes through nature; men become
> aware of him as the nourisher of them all.   To such realiza-
> tion is added that of poetry, of cult, and finally of the arts of
> painting and sculpture, not to mention the theories of the phi-
> losophers.   Limiting ourselves to poetry and sculpture, let us
> begin (49) with Phidias, whose marvelous statue here compels
> our admiration.   Does this statue embody deity truly?

That question was answered to the Athenians of the
same generation quite differently, by a speaker less different than his conclusion, a Roman Jew of Tarsus, one
Paul. Dio goes on, after an encomium of Phidias:

> Phidias might well reply that it is true to tradition as that
> is conceived and defined by the poets (55–57), that since we
> yearn for a personal divine, the human body is its best expres-
> sion, and that Homer too (62) made his gods human.

There follows a comparison of sculpture with poetry (70).
Though this stresses unduly, perhaps, the mere range of
verbal suggestion, it make none the less clearly a fundamental distinction.

[22] H. von Arnim (op. cit. 171) finds manuscript evidence of several such
adjustable preludes.   Compare those preserved in the *Florida* of Apuleius,
e. g. page 227, above.

"Again, besides this, the very conditions of working out a conception in sculpture impose one form for each statue, a form immovable and permanent, [yet] such as to comprehend in itself the god's whole nature and power; but poets may easily include in their poetic many forms and all sorts of shapes, for they add such movements or repose as they think appropriate to each moment, actions too, words, and finally, I think, the illusion of time."

So (Phidias is supposed to go on) my Zeus, embodying in a single representation the typical Greek conception (74) of the ruler of an ordered world, shows him as gentle, grave, serene, as giver, father, savior, protector, and yet does not exclude his other aspects (75). How could I represent him (78) continually hurling the thunderbolt, sending rain or stretching the rainbow, renewing battle-lust? Our art is adjusted to the immediate and clear test of actual seeing (79).

An encomium of Phidias, a *discours de circonstance*, has been made to involve two large principles of artistic theory. The first is ethical, expressing a fundamental relation of art to human life. Art, and especially poetry, is a revelation to us of what we vaguely feel to be divine; it interprets communal experience as communal vision. The second is æsthetic, deriving a difference of technic from the fundamental difference between stimulating mental images by successive verbal suggestions, visual, auditory, motor, and actually representing to the eye alone all together and all at once. While poetry ranges through successive suggestions, sculpture focuses statically by typical representation. Though it is easy to read into these principles from modern criticism more than Dio intended, they can hardly be regarded as less than penetrative and fundamental. The first, often reaffirmed in modern times and sometimes apparently rediscovered, is often implied in ancient criticism. Dio's contribution is to formulate it explicitly, and to express it with unusual warmth. The second is clear, though less explicit, in Aristotle's *Poetic*. It is ignored by both Horace and Plutarch.[23] As Dio's words went down the ancient wind, so Lessing's almost identical distinction [24] has not precluded much bland modern confusion of the arts.

More and more a moralist as his life advanced, turning from rhetor into preacher, Dio nevertheless maintains a variety reminding us that this form of oratory had great range. The prelude of his *Euboica*, extensively descriptive of simple frontier life, is almost a short story. Quite different from the conventional expatiation, which Dio elsewhere does not despise, it shows him expert not only in the theory of narrative, but also in its practise. Some of his discourses are less speeches than what we should call essays. The one on Practise in Speaking [25] is in topics, plan, and style quite conventional. The remarkable one on Greek drama is as it stands an essay in literary criticism. By the insertion of recited passages it could easily and effectively have been expanded into a lecture; but even without these it is both sustained and suggestive.

DIO CHRYSOSTOM, ORATIO LII

ÆSCHYLUS, SOPHOCLES, AND EURIPIDES, OR THE BOW OF PHILOCTETES

1. [I rose early, walked, meditated, prayed, exercised, bathed, breakfasted.] 2. I chanced upon certain tragedies

---

[23] See the following sections.

[24] For the significance of the well-known passage in the *Laokoön*, and of the psychological formulation of Lemaître, see my *College Composition*, page 183. For further discussion of this oration, see Ehemann, *Die XII Rede von Dio Chrysostom*, Kaiserlautern, 1895. See also W. A. Montgomery, *Dio Chrysostom as a Homeric Critic*, Baltimore, 1901 (Johns Hopkins dissertation).

[25] Περὶ λόγου ἀσκήσεως, Oratio XVIII, de Arnim, II, page 250.

of the masters, Æschylus, Sophocles, and Euripides, all upon the same theme. It is that of the theft of the bow and arrows of Philoctetes—perhaps one should say the seizure. At any rate, Philoctetes was deprived of his arms by Odysseus, and himself brought to Troy, largely of his own free will, partly also by the persuasion of necessity, since he was bereft of the arms which provided at once his living on the island, his courage in such disease, and his glory. 3. Well, I feasted on the spectacle, and I reflected that even if I had been at Athens in their time, I could not have seen all three great men in competition. Some, indeed, did see the competition of the young Sophocles with the old Æschylus, and of the older Sophocles with the younger Euripides; but Euripides was quite outside of the generation of Æschylus, and competed with him seldom, if ever, in the same drama. My having all three to read together seemed a revel, and a fresh consolation for my inability [to see them].

4. Well, I imagined myself putting the plays on quite splendidly, and tried to fix my attention as a judge of the first tragic choruses. But though I had taken my oath, I could not have given a decision; nor, for all me, would any of those masters have been held inferior. The greatness of mind in Æschylus and his sense of tradition, as well as his austerity of thought and expression, seemed appropriate to tragedy and to the ancient heroic ethics—nothing contrived or glib or low. 5. Even Odysseus he introduced as shrewd and crafty in the way of that time, [a way] so far removed from the baseness of to-day that what is really traditional [in Æschylus] seems beyond those who now try to be simple and high-minded.

When Athena transforms him, nothing more is needed to keep Philoctetes in ignorance of who he is. So Homer made the story, and after him Euripides. Therefore, if some unfriendly critic should accuse Æschylus of taking no care as to how Odysseus shall be convincing without being recognized by Philoctetes, (6) his defense, I think, would be as follows. While the time was not, perhaps, so great that the character could not be sustained (i. e., through ten years), yet the disease of Philoctetes, his misery, and his having passed the interim in a desert are sufficient to make plausible his not recognizing Odysseus. For many have experienced the same lapse, some from weakness, some from misfortune. No, the chorus had no need, as in Euripides, to excuse themselves to him. 7. Both [poets] represented the chorus as composed of Lemnians. Euripides has made them at once apologize for their former neglect because for so many years they had not come to Philoctetes or helped him at all. Æschylus simply brought on the chorus—a method far more tragic as well as simpler, whereas that of Euripides is more oratorical and precise. If [dramatists] could escape all absurdities in their tragedies, perhaps there would be reason for not neglecting this; but actually they make their heralds accomplish in one day several days' journey. 8. Now the case was not quite that none of the Lemnians came to him or gave him any care. Probably he would not have passed ten years without finding any help at all. Probably he did find it, though rarely and of no great account; and no one chose to take him in and tend him because of the loathsomeness of his disease. Euripides, forsooth, out of his own head introduces Actor, one of the Lemnians, as an acquaintance who went out to Philoctetes and often helped him.

9. Neither does it seem to me that any one can justly find fault with making [Philoctetes] narrate to the chorus, as if they did not know it, his abandonment by the Achæans and everything else that happened to him; for an unfortunate is wont to recount his mishaps often, even to those who know them in detail, and wearies those who have no need to hear his woes by telling them over and over again. Moreover the deceit of Odysseus toward Philoctetes, and the arguments by which he induces him, are not only more in character, such as befit a hero and unlike the pleas of Eurybatus or Patæcion, but also, I think, more convincing. 10. For what need was there of manifold art and device with a sick man, and a bowman at that, whose strength became useless so soon as one but stood near? And the announcing of the mishaps of the Achæans, that Agamemnon was dead, that Odysseus was to blame most disgracefully, that the army had perished utterly—all this is not only useful for putting Philoctetes in a good humor and disposing him to accept the speech of Odysseus, but is not in any wise improbable, considering the length of the campaign and what had happened not long before through the wrath of

Achilles, when Hector almost went to burn the beached ships.

11. The intelligence of Euripides, that unfailing care which neither leaves anything unconvincing or unprovided nor simply uses actions but [uses them] with all force in the expression, is as it were the converse of the habit of Æschylus, being most oratorical, most rhetorical, most available for the use of debaters. At the very beginning, for instance, Odysseus has been represented in the prologue as revolving in his mind political enthymemes and at first doubtful of himself, lest while he seems to the crowd to be wise and distinguished in intelligence, he may be the opposite. 12. It is open to him to live unfretted and inactive; but his wish is to be always in deeds and dangers. The cause of this, he says, is his emulation of men goodly and noble. For these who are bent on good report and universal fame willingly undertake the greatest and most difficult toils. "Nothing is born so proud as man." Then sapiently and precisely he discloses the plot of the drama and why he has come to Lemnos. 13. He says he has been transformed by Athena so that when he meets Philoctetes he shall not be recognized. (Euripides imitates Homer in this; for Homer had Odysseus transformed by Athena when he met not only others, but even Eumæus and Penelope.) He says an embassy is about to come from the Trojans to Philoctetes, to ask that he offer them himself and his arms in return for the kingship of Troy. [Thus Euripides] makes the action more various and invents occasions for the arguments by which, when he turns them the other way around, Odysseus seems most resourceful and most sufficient for anything.

14. He has represented Odysseus as arriving not alone, but with Diomed (Homeric this, too). All in all, as I said, through all the drama, he displays the greatest intelligence and plausibility in action, extraordinary and marvellous force in the speeches, dialogue at once sapient and natural and oratorical, and lyrics that not only please, but also strongly move to virtue.

15. Sophocles seems to be between the two, having neither the austerity and singleness of Æschylus nor the precision and sharpness and oratorical cast of Euripides, but a grave and magnificent poetic embracing all that is most tragic and most eloquent, uniting the greatest charm with sublimity and grav-

ity. For his action he has used the best and most convincing plan, representing Odysseus as arriving with Neoptolemus, since it was fated that Troy should be taken by Neoptolemus and by Philoctetes using the bow of Hercules. [He has] Odysseus concealed, but Neoptolemus sending to Philoctetes and advising him what to do. He has made the chorus not, as Æschylus and Euripides, Lemnians, but shipmates of Odysseus and Neoptolemus.

16. The characters are marvellously grave and free. That of Odysseus is much gentler and more single than Euripides has made it; that of Neoptolemus, surpassingly single and high-bred, first when he wishes to get the better of Philoctetes not by craft and deceit, but by force and in the open, then when at the instance of Odysseus he has deceived him and got possession of the weapons. When Philoctetes becomes aware and urges a cheated man's reproaches, Neoptolemus is so moved that he is about to give them back; and even when Odysseus intervenes, still at last he gives them, and as he gives them tries by argument to make Philoctetes go to Troy of his own free will. 17. When Philoctetes will in no wise yield nor be persuaded, but begs Neoptolemus to keep his promise of taking him back to Greece, he undertakes that and is ready to do it, till the intervention of Hercules wins the consent of Philoctetes to embark for Troy.

17. The lyrics have not so much of the sententious and hortatory as those of Euripides, but a marvellous charm and magnificence. Not at random Aristophanes said of him: "The mouth of Sophocles is anointed with honey, as if he had licked the box."

Conventional as this is in making the usual contrast between Æschylus and Euripides, with Sophocles as a golden mean, it defines these distinctions afresh with suggestive precision. Moreover, the essay is free from the usual preoccupation with diction. What is said on that point, though not original, is tersely subordinated. If the manuscript is complete, therefore, the close upon the quotation from Aristophanes gives a false emphasis;

for the criticism as a whole is quite different from the usual comparison of style with style.

Plot, indeed, is not developed extensively as a separate item; but it is clearly implied in the treatment of characterization. The constant theme is motivation, the bringing out of character through the movement of the plot, the dramatic management of persons through interaction. Thus Dio has made his criticism singularly consistent. Instead of merely appreciating one dramatist after the other, he has made his comparison progressive. The oral criticism uttered by Greek and Roman rhetors of the Empire, we may guess from what has survived in manuscript, was not often either so sustained or so free from the bias of rhetoric. Perhaps Dio's unusual grasp came from his missionary sense of the tradition of Hellenism.

D. PLUTARCH's *HOW YOUTH SHOULD READ POETRY* [26]

Literary criticism has often taken direction from philosophy. In ancient criticism such a slant was habitual. Most ancient critics show definite preoccupation with some school of philosophy.[27] For example, there was a Stoic theory of style; and "the æsthetic theories of Panætius are reproduced in the first book of Cicero's *De officiis*." [28] Such cases are typical even to the in-

[26] *Quomodo adolescens poetas audire debeat,* in the collection generally entitled *Moralia.* For English translations of the *Morals* see the preface to F. M. Padelford's modern translation of this particular essay, *Essays on the Study and Use of Poetry by Plutarch and Basil the Great,* New York, 1902 (Yale Studies in English, XV). Padelford has added a concise and suggestive introduction on Plutarch's theory of poetry.

[27] This bald statement may be confirmed by the more comprehensive histories of Latin literature.

[28] G. C. Fiske, *The Plain Style in the Scipionic Circle,* University of Wisconsin Studies in Language and Literature, 3, page 62.

volving of æsthetics with ethics; for ancient literary criticism, more generally and avowedly than modern, is ethical. Aristotle is almost alone in proposing for poetic principles frankly æsthetic. The general tendency of ancient criticism is to give poetic a moral color. This ethical direction of critical thought confirmed the tendency to conceive poetic in terms of rhetoric. Not only are the implications of rhetoric inevitably moral, but the theories of rhetoric associated with ancient theories of morals were often extended to include even poetic expression. Ancient poetic was thus rhetoricated partly by being moralized.

An extreme instance of this ancient habit is Plutarch's Greek treatise of the first century, *How Youth Should Read Poetry*. Here the familiar idea that poetry is a means of ethical education is so expounded as to reveal the limits of Plutarch's conception. He is not merely, as *grammaticus* commenting Homer in school, offering poetry as a propædeutic to philosophy; he is repeating a narrow and commonplace æsthetic. His treatment of imitation, ignoring Aristotle's use of that term,[29] has in mind faithfulness to fact. Ignoring also the Aristotelian idea of poetic movement, he repeats the commonplace and misleading analogy from painting [30] with a barren literalness.

> "We shall still more thoroughly ground the young man, if, on introducing him to poetry, we explain to him that it is an imitative art and agent, analogous to painting. Not only must he be made acquainted with the common saying that

[29] See above, page 141.

[30] See Nettleship, *Lectures and Essays*, Second Series, page 49 (on Dionysius of Halicarnassus). For the pictorial habit of much ancient description see above, page 217, on Ovid, and compare Croiset, *Hist. de la litt. grecque*, V. pages 771 and following.

poetry is vocal painting, and painting silent poetry, but we must also teach him that when we see a painting of a lizard, an ape, or the face of Thersites, our pleasure and surprise are occasioned, not by the beauty of the object, but by the likeness of the painting to it. . . . In such instances it is especially important that the young man come to understand that we do not praise the action imitated, but the art, provided the subject is treated accurately." [31]

Poetry is pictorial in this sense not to authors whose creative bent is distinctively dramatic or narrative, but to the describers and expatiators, not to Vergil, but to Ovid.

For this narrow conception of poetic truth Plutarch's recurring terms [32] are not merely narrow; they are distinctly rhetorical. They are the very ones commonly used by rhetoricians to describe success in *prosopopœia*, [33] or characterization according to type. That Plutarch means them so is clear in section x on characterization in Homer.

"It is worth while, in this connection, to notice the conduct of Agamemnon; for he passes Sthenelus by without noticing him, yet he does not neglect Odysseus, but answers him, 'seeing how he was wroth, and took back his saying.' Had he apologized to all, he would have appeared undignified and servile, and had he disdained all, arrogant and unreasonable. . . . It is also a good idea to take notice of the difference between the ways in which a discreet man and a pompous soothsayer addresses a crowd. Thus Calchas . . . One should notice as well the differences in racial characteristics. For example, the Trojans rush ferociously to battle with savage cries, but the Greeks 'in silence feared their

[31] III, in Padelford's translation, which is followed in this and the other quotations.

[32] ὅμοιον, εἰκός, πρέπον, πιθανῶς. Padelford, page 24, points out their narrowness.

[33] See above, pages 71–73, and also pages 99, 218.

captains'; for to fear officers in the presence of the enemy is
the mark of heroism and obedience. . . . Hence foresight
is Grecian and civil; rashness, barbaric and rude; the one to
be emulated, the other to be avoided."

In a word, Plutarch's moralizing of poetic is definitely
rhetorical. For the schools of philosophy generally poetic
was incidental to the consideration of diction; for him
it was indistinguishable in method.

E. HORACE's *ARS POETICA*

That the unsystematic epistolary reflections of a Latin
poet on poetry should for centuries have influenced criticism of poetic more than the searching analysis and
consecutive synthesis of the greatest Greek philosopher
has seemed strange to the point of irony. Not only was
Horace quoted while Aristotle was forgotten, but even
after the recovery of the *Poetic* he was quoted still. He
is quotable. He abounds in *sententiæ;* and they have a
long life. Though he would have been himself the first
to smile at the putting of his epistle to the Pisos beside
Aristotle's *Poetic,* he knew none the less the sort of criticism that people like. We have been often reminded that
Ars Poetica is neither Horace's title nor accurately descriptive. But it is a title naturally given by grammarians who hardly conceived poetic as a distinct technic,
and naturally accepted by readers who found Horace's
epigrams no less suggestive because they were detached.
Certainly the epistle is not an *ars;* but certainly its criticism has enough shrewdness, lucidity, brilliancy, adapt-
ability to the short flights of ordinary thinking on the
subject, to explain all its popularity. One need not be
cynical to think that the poetic of a Horace will usually
be more popular than the poetic of an Aristotle.

At the risk of wronging Horace, his editors and other critics have tried to brief this epistle. Wickham,[34] for instance, finds three parts: (1) 1–118, "the original principles of poetry, unity of conception, choice of words, style of diction; " (2) 119–284, characterization in drama, the Greek practise of drama; (3) 285–end, "the two aims of poetry, the necessity of excellence." But this is not a division at all. Wilkins,[35] admitting difficulties of sequence, even digressions and repetitions, nevertheless finds "three main sections ": (1) 1–72, unity of style and conception; (2) 73–288, application of "these general principles . . to the various kinds of poetry, and especially to the drama"; (3) 189–476, requisites for cultivating poetry, and difficulties. None of these coincides with any of Wickham's. Plessis [36] more cautiously says: "His principal counsels are three: the importance of composition and of the harmony of the parts, the supremacy of taste, perfection of craftsmanship." Three again, and again not the same three. Could there be clearer proof that the epistle is not logical, nor even consecutive?

Since it is in fact one of the least consecutive of Horace's epistles, so expert a composer must have meant it to be taken, as it has been taken, not as a logical progress, but as a collection of *sententiæ*. These, whatever their particular source or sources,[37] may safely be taken as generally current in Græco-Roman literary circles.

[34] *The Works of Horace,* Oxford, 1891, Volume II, page 384.

[35] *The Epistles of Horace,* London, 1889, page 334.

[36] *La poésie latine,* Paris, 1909, page 320.

[37] Nettleship's hypothesis, that Horace, "writing with a Greek treatise before him, was using it for practical application to the particular circumstances of his own time," and that the Greek treatise was probably by Neoptolemus of Parium (*Lectures and Essays,* I. 168), is rejected by Wickham (page 385).

Thus they have the more significance; for Horace's originality is hardly in conception. His contribution to
criticism, like Cicero's, is in finality of phrase. The maxims that have echoed so often down the corridors of
criticism have the carrying power of simplicity.

> Denique sit quodvis, simplex dumtaxat et unum (23).
> Lucidus ordo (41).
> Non satis est pulchra esse poemata; dulcia sunto (99).
>   Si vis me flere, dolendum est
> Primum ipsi tibi (102).
> Qualis ab incepto processerit, et sibi constet (127).
> Difficile est proprie communia dicere (128).
> Parturient montes, nascetur ridiculus mus (139).
> Semper ad eventum festinat et in medias res
> Non secus ac notas auditorem rapit (148).
> Aut prodesse volunt aut delectare poetæ,
> Aut simul et iucunda et idonea dicere vitæ (333).
> Omne tulit punctum qui miscuit utile dulci (343).
> Ut pictura poesis (361).
>   Mediocribus esse poetis
> Non homines, non di, non concessere columnæ (372).

Commonplaces some of these must have been even in
Horace's time; but they have persisted in criticism because he stamped them.

The one that is most clearly a distinctive principle of
poetic is the familiar "*Semper ad eventum festinat*," etc.
(148). The idea of so adjusting the time of the plot as to
insure a significant beginning and a continuous and ac-
celerated movement up to an issue is central in Greek
drama. That Horace applies it to epic evinces no sharp
discrimination of technic. *Ut pictura poesis* (361) is not,
as in Plutarch,[38] a comparison of the technic of poetry
with that of painting; it merely insists that a poem,
as a picture, be judged according to its kind, accord-

[38] See above, section D.

ing to its specific object. Horace may, indeed, imply a vindication of his own poems beside those of longer reach and more sustained power; or he may be merely repeating his dominant idea of appropriateness; but in either case he is not formulating a principle of poetic. The rule of five acts (189), wherever he got it, is not vital.   Though he spends more time on drama than on any other mode, though he uses Aristotle, he does not carry out the principle of dramatic movement.

The conception of characterization is clearly rhetorical,

"It will matter much whether a god speak or a hero, ripe age or the ardor of budding youth, a matron of authority or an anxious nurse, a traveling merchant or a farmer bound to his field, a Colchian or an Assyrian, a Theban or an Argive. Follow tradition, or invent what fits each character. If perchance your poem revives time-honored Achilles, let the active, touchy, stubborn, fierce hero think that laws were not made for him, and rest his claim on arms. Let Medea be cruel and unconquered, Ino tearful, Ixion faithless, Orestes gloomy." (114–124.)

"Each time of life demands your study of its habits. As natures and years move on, you must assign to each what is appropriate. The boy who is old enough to answer when he is spoken to, and steps off firmly, yearns to play with his mates, takes offense as quickly as he lays it by, and changes from hour to hour. The beardless youth . . ." (156–178.)

and so on through Horace's seven ages of man. Thus stripped of their style, these counsels might have come from any classical rhetoric. Nothing was more firmly fixed in the tradition of the schools than characterization according to age, sex, race, occupation. Such characterization by type suffices for *prosopopœia* in school, for the fathers and sons and pirates of *declamatio*, for even the spendthrifts and slaves and parasites of Latin comedy; it does not suffice for Œdipus or Neoptolemus, for

Medea or Dido. Nor is the difference merely in degree;
it is in the distinctively poetic habit of creating. Poetic
movement, if Horace indeed glimpses it as distinct from
that of rhetoric, he does not fully define; poetic characterization he seems not to regard as distinct at all.

Indeed, most of the *Ars Poetica* applies equally to *ars
rhetorica*.

> Aut prodesse volunt aut delectare poetæ,
> Aut simil et iucunda et idonea dicere vitæ (333–4).

If *oratores* be substituted for *poetæ* we have the familiar
docere, delectare of rhetoric, as we have it in the summary
miscuit utile dulci (343); and with Horace the *movere* that
remains hardly suggests a different technic. *Si vis me
flere, dolendum est* (102) will be found in Cicero and Quintilian. The counsel of congruity with which he begins,
and to which he reverts again and again, is a preoccupation of ancient rhetoric. No better phrase has been found
for the progress of a speech than *lucidus ordo* (41); and
the *iunctura* (47) to which it is immediately applied is a
term of *compositio*. In the thought of Horace's circle the
distinction between rhetoric and poetic as two movements,
two ways of composing, seems to have been inactive.
Rather Horace seems to think of composition as generally
constant throughout various forms, and as involving
mainly the control of conception by congruity and plan,
of expression by adaptation and finish. That such ideas
were salutary when *declamatio* had begun to threaten both
rhetoric and poetic, and that they are salutary still, no
one should deny; but they make no contribution to the
distinctive development of poetic.

Grammarians, rhetors, philosophers, men of letters
seem thus to converge under the Empire toward a poetic

strongly tinged with rhetoric, no longer distinct as a movement having its own technic. The inference, though not conclusive, is suggestive as an hypothesis. Less conclusive, but still suggestive, is the further inference that this habit of critical thought was intensified in the specifically Latin tradition. In sustained emotional movement the *Æneid* is solitary; and even while it was revered, its poetic seems less influential than that of Ovid. Vergil had turned for his poetic from the newer Greek ways adopted by his countrymen to the tradition interpreted by Aristotle. That older tradition is no longer active in the poetic descending from the Roman Empire through the Holy Roman Empire.

The ancient experience with rhetoric and with poetic is seen in retrospect as typical. The theory of rhetoric as the energizing of knowledge and the humanizing of truth is explicitly the philosophy of Aristotle and implicitly that of Cicero, Tacitus, Quintilian. What the later ancient professors of rhetoric had rather in mind is the training of immediate personal effectiveness; and this theory of rhetoric as the art of the speaker is at once as old as the other and as permanent. Its name is sophistic. Aristotle deprecated it in his first chapter; St. Augustine turned his back on it at the end of the ancient world; but meantime it had been for centuries, and it has been again and again, a popular pedagogy. Further discussion of these traditions, and of such details as the persistence of classical metric after the beat of more popular stress rhythms had become insistent, is properly historical. Historical interpretation of the ancient lore of composition and of its influence in the middle ages is relegated to another volume. The expository task of this one concludes naturally with the completion of the ancient experience.

TABULAR INDEX OF LATIN AND GREEK RHETORICAL TERMS

The references are to pages. The terms are also included alphabetically in the General Index, and may be explored in the indexes of the Cope and Sandys Aristotle, the Wilkins Cicero, the Rhys Roberts Dionysius, and the other editions cited in the bibliographical notes at the head of each section.

The plan is generally that of Quintilian (see pages 63–66).

The Greek terms of drama and epic may be found in the General Index and, through the tabular view of Aristotle's *Poetic* on pages 135–139, in the Greek index of Bywater's edition.

I. προγυμνάσματα, 63, 68, 228
   A. grammatica, 66, 68, 73, 102, 226–229, 240
      1. prælectio, 63, 64, 66, 226
      2. μῦθος, chria, χρεία, κατασκευή, etc., 63, 68, 72
      3. pronuntiatio (see VII below)
   B. rhetorica, 64, 68, 71, 73, 88, 90, 94 (see sub-headings)
      1. fabula, argumentum, historia, 64
      2. laudatio, ἐγκώμιον; comparatio, σύγκρισις, 64, (234–238)
      3. materia, 66, 69, 73, 78, 88
      4. amplificatio, exaggeratio, αὔξησις, 25, 44, 55, 64, 98, 124, 127
      5. ethopœia, ἠθοποιία, 68, 71, 187; prosopopœia, προσωποποιία, 71, 72, 73, 99, 218, 222, 241, 245
      6. declamatio, μελέτη, 46, 48, 68–74, 87, 88, 89, 90, 94–97, 100, 101, 187, 190, 210, 218, 220, 221, 225, 229, 245, 246
         (a) suasoriæ, 64, 70, 72, 73, 88, 90, 91, 218
         (b) controversiæ, 62, 64, 70, 72, 73, 87, 88, 89, 90, 91–96

GENERAL INDEX

[The references are to pages. A parenthesis indicates that the Latin or Greek term occurs in the original of the translation or summary on that page.]

253